An Introduction to News Product Management

T0272015

Drawing on innovations in the business of journalism, this book offers a comprehensive guide to using the human-centered design methods of product management to serve readers and bolster digital success in news organizations.

An Introduction to News Product Management sets out how "product thinking" should be used in news organizations and practiced in accordance with journalistic ethics and customs. Beginning by looking at the history and theory behind the profession, this book builds a foundational understanding of what product management is and why news is a unique product. In the second unit, the author discusses how the human-centered design philosophy of product management aligns with the mission and ethics of journalism, and how that influences the view of audiences and frames strategies. The third unit of the book focuses on the daily use of product management in news organizations, providing students with a guide to its use in researching, prioritizing, and building sustainable projects that deliver news to readers and viewers. Written in an accessible style, this book features input from industry experts and draws on global examples to provide practical guidance.

This is an ideal text for advanced undergraduates and graduates studying entrepreneurial journalism, media innovation, and digital media economics, as well as media professionals keen to learn more about product management and human-centered design methods.

Damon Kiesow is Knight Chair in Journalism Innovation at the Missouri School of Journalism, USA.

Damon Kiesow has written a book that, for the first time, fully, clearly, and eloquently outlines the ideas behind news product thinking, why it matters, and how to do it. No one knows the topic better, his prose is wonderfully clear, and the book's organization is inspired.

Tom Rosenstiel, *Co-author of* The Elements of Journalism

Through critical analysis and real-world examples, Damon Kiesow demonstrates how news product management can drive sustainable innovation and ensure that what media organizations do leads to better service for communities.

Feli Carrique, *Executive Director, News Product Alliance*

No one better than Damon Kiesow—an innovator and leader in news product—to explain the importance of this first new job description in news in a century. This book will teach journalism's next leaders how to build the future of news, one focused as much on serving publics as making products.

Jeff Jarvis, *Newmark School of Journalism at CUNY, author of* The Gutenberg Parenthesis

This book is a must read for anyone interested in the digital transformation of news. Like all good news product managers, Damon Kiesow brings together business strategy, design thinking, technology frameworks, and journalism's mission to create a blueprint for how practitioners can ensure the needs of their audiences are the driving force behind their work.

Julia Beizer, *Chief Digital Officer, Bloomberg Media*

An Introduction to News Product Management

Innovation for Newsrooms and Readers

Damon Kiesow

Routledge
Taylor & Francis Group

NEW YORK AND LONDON

Designed cover image: © tampatra/iStock via Getty Images
and Damon Kiesow

First published 2024
by Routledge
605 Third Avenue, New York, NY 10158

and by Routledge
4 Park Square, Milton Park, Abingdon, Oxon, OX14 4RN

Routledge is an imprint of the Taylor & Francis Group, an informa business

© 2024 Damon Kiesow

The right of Damon Kiesow to be identified as author of this work has been asserted in accordance with sections 77 and 78 of the Copyright, Designs and Patents Act 1988.

All rights reserved. No part of this book may be reprinted or reproduced or utilised in any form or by any electronic, mechanical, or other means, now known or hereafter invented, including photocopying and recording, or in any information storage or retrieval system, without permission in writing from the publishers.

Trademark notice: Product or corporate names may be trademarks or registered trademarks, and are used only for identification and explanation without intent to infringe.

Library of Congress Cataloging-in-Publication Data
Names: Kiesow, Damon, author.
Title: An introduction to news product management : innovation for newsrooms and readers / Damon Kiesow.
Description: New York, NY : Routledge, 2024. | Includes bibliographical references and index.
Identifiers: LCCN 2023025830 (print) | LCCN 2023025831 (ebook) | ISBN 9780367724344 (hardback) | ISBN 9780367724337 (paperback) | ISBN 9781003154785 (ebook)
Subjects: LCSH: Press--Economic aspects--United States. | Newspaper publishing--Economic aspects--United States. | Online journalism--Economic aspects--United States. | Product management--United States.
Classification: LCC PN4734 .K48 2024 (print) | LCC PN4734 (ebook) | DDC 070.5/7220973--dc23/eng/20230918
LC record available at https://lccn.loc.gov/2023025830
LC ebook record available at https://lccn.loc.gov/2023025831

ISBN: 978-0-367-72434-4 (hbk)
ISBN: 978-0-367-72433-7 (pbk)
ISBN: 978-1-003-15478-5 (ebk)

DOI: 10.4324/9781003154785

Typeset in Galliard
by KnowledgeWorks Global Ltd.

Contents

Acknowledgments

I am grateful to Annette and Josh, who were probably as surprised as I was that this took three years to write.

Special thanks to the founding steering committee of the News Product Alliance for doing good and providing endless support:

Becca Aaronson-Davis, Shannan Bowen, Brian Boyer, Luciana Cardoso, Emma Carew-Grovum, Kim Fox, Tony Elkins, Aron Pilhofer, Marco Túlio Pires, Cindy Royal, Ryan Nakashima, Eric Ulken, and Anita Zielina.

And to the many educators, professionals, and students who have been sounding boards and a source of inspiration:

Tia Alphonse, CW Anderson, Aaron Babel, Valerie Belair-Gagnon, Mark Briggs, Carrie Brown, Feli Carrique, J. Scott Christianson, Aly Colón, Srijita Datta, Jill Geisler, Jessica Gilbert, Jeremy Gilbert, Richelle Gordon, Jonathan Groves, Nasr ul Hadi, Derrick Ho, Avery Holton, Brant Houston, Aske Kammer, Asma Khanom, Melody Joy Kramer, Sam Manas, Mindy McAdams, Rebekah Monson, Jessica Morrison, Andre Natta, Roberta Pickerell, Trân Nguyễn, Elizabeth Osder, Randy Picht, Mark Poepsel, Damian Radcliffe, Tom Rosenstiel, Randall Smith, Ryan Thomas, Nikki Usher, and Shuhua Zhou.

There are other product leaders quoted throughout the book. A thank you to them for sharing their time and expertise. And, of course, thanks to everyone on the NPA Slack and Twitter (more recently Mastodon, Bluesky and Threads) for the free research and feedback along the way, even if you weren't aware.

Introduction

The day I agreed to write this book, September 23, 2020, a group of journalists launched the international training and advocacy organization, the News Product Alliance. The headline on the NPA's website that day:

The future of news is product.

That is a bold statement. And to elaborate: The future of news is understanding our communities and organizations to better support both.

News product is rooted in journalism's values, ethics, and mission. Serving the community, earning trust, and building sustainable organizations is our job. The product of news is understanding—though practically speaking, the various channels used to deliver the news are the practical focus of our daily work.

We bring some core beliefs to bear:

- News is a public good and must be sustained in some practical form.
- News product management is journalism and upholds its highest standards.
- The goal of news is to help communities understand themselves.
- News organizations must look like their communities.
- News products are built with and for readers.
- News product is data-informed, not data-driven.
- Anyone in a news organization can be a news product thinker.

As human beings, we go through our days constantly asking questions and making guesses. Is today Wednesday? What time is the news meeting? Will I be late because of traffic? Is it going to rain during lunch? Each question has a different urgency, process of inquiry, and level of potential uncertainty.

If you doubt the day of the week, it can be verified instantly. And the ordering of days follows a predictable pattern.

Your schedule for the day is important to you and others on the team and can hopefully be found on your smartphone or paper calendar. But there is always a risk that the calendar entry is wrong or the schedule has changed.

DOI: 10.4324/9781003154785-1

The weather forecast is never certain. A forecast for rain always includes a "probability of precipitation" that estimates the chances of it raining at a specific time—like noon. But regardless of the 8 a.m. forecast, the closer you get to lunch, the more information is available to refine the estimate—including a look outside the window at 11:45 a.m. But what is the risk—assuming you remembered to bring an umbrella?

Traffic is unpredictable and chaotic. The risk is managed by leaving early and depends on how early your first class or meeting is today. If you make this commute frequently, you are probably familiar with the typical day and are confident in your timing estimates. But, for additional comfort, you can check traffic cams or use a smartphone app to provide live updates of the data.

Those four routine information-seeking behaviors mirror the challenge of making business decisions:

- Some answers can be precisely known and are fixed or change only in highly predictable ways.
- Some answers can be known but may change unpredictably.
- Some answers are forecasts but operate within a rules-based though dynamic system.
- Some answers are forecasts that may change chaotically.

This is a book about making educated guesses and then making smart investments of time and resources. For product managers, asking, researching, and supporting good decision-making is the job. And it takes a point of view about how to do that in the service of producing and subsidizing quality journalism.

Threaded throughout is a discussion not just about product management but the integration of those skills into the professional culture of journalism, which is known for its skepticism and suspicion of change.

Early in my career, I received helpful advice about newsrooms: *The first person with a plan wins.*

Journalists are not blindly resistant to change-for-the-better; they are just busy and appropriately cynical about easy answers, trendy solutions, and corporate jargon that often arrives in a box called "innovation."

News product management is designed to avoid that trap. It resists easy answers and demands rigor in understanding audiences, being honest about our organizational capabilities, and being pragmatic about where to place our bets. At the end of the day, decisions must be made. The goal is not to demand perfect data, insights, and deliberation but to demand we do our best at every step. An educated guess, informed by the best research and analysis we can develop, is better than no plan.

The three units in the book roughly parallel three questions:

1 What is product management?
2 What is the role of product management in a news organization?
3 How do new products and services get prioritized and built?

In the book's first unit, we look at the history of product management and some of the theories behind the practice. Understanding those basics is vital to understanding the broader profession and what makes News Product unique.

This is a book not only about product management but also about journalism. In the second unit, we discuss how the **human-centered design** (**HCD**) framework of product management aligns with the mission and ethics of journalism and how that influences our view of audiences and guides our strategies. And more importantly, it speaks to how product management can be used to improve both journalism and the communities we serve.

Product managers take on many different roles, depending on the organization. No one book can cover it all. We won't be writing business plans, studying profit and loss statements, or developing a pitch deck to get venture capital funding. Though in some roles, those entrepreneurial activities are aligned with and performed by product managers. Instead, we will focus more on intrapreneurial skills—supporting and innovating on the products, features, and services typically offered by local and national news media companies.

Product thinking is on the rise in news because the skills are useful across job titles and departments. It is used in projects from web design, advertising, and reader engagement to content management, audience analytics, and data warehouses. Whenever we consider a new feature or service, product thinking techniques can help reveal the who, what, where, when, and why of the need. Those insights, as we will discuss, are the foundation of success.

The third and final unit is dedicated to the methods we use to build and deliver products to the public. News product is thoughtfully reflective, but we also must ship the goods. As journalist and journalism professor Matt Waite wrote in 2009, "Ideas are cheap and plentiful. Execution is hard."[1] Or, as he put it more succinctly, "demos, not memos," meaning the time comes to stop talking about the things we want to do and just get started. Especially as the real learning comes from building and then observing.

Like many news product managers, my career has taken the scenic route. I attended the University of Maine to be a reporter and left as a photojournalist. After almost a decade working at newspapers in the Northeastern U.S., and six years as a photo editor and manager at AOL in Northern Virginia, I returned to New Hampshire in 2005 as the digital editor for *The Nashua Telegraph*.

My title in Nashua was "Managing Editor/Online," the first digital-focused title the paper had hired. With a staff of several, we redesigned the website, installed a new content management system, launched one of the first news accounts on Twitter,[2] built a video studio, and produced a series of live streaming events, including interviews with every major candidate in the 2008 New Hampshire presidential primary. That, it turns out, was my first job in product management.

I joined the Poynter Institute in 2010. As a Digital Media Fellow, I spent a year studying, teaching, learning, and writing about digital trends and wondering how journalism could keep up with technology.

As a Senior Product Manager at *The Boston Globe,* I focused on mobile app strategies, including the *Globe*'s replica edition—the print newspaper in PDF form. It was surprisingly popular among readers.

At the time, that popularity confused me. Who would prefer a clunky PDF with day-old news over a streamlined and constantly-updated website? There was no simple answer, and to even understand the question, I had to shift my focus from technology to people.

While in Boston, I got an M.A. in Human Factors in Information Design at Bentley University, receiving formal training in audience research and HCD methods.

HCD underpins product management, which aims to bring the voice of the customer into every phase of the innovation and development process. Previous approaches to product development might have tested the replica edition for usability: Can users open the app, navigate the pages, and read a story? It might have asked what users like about the replica and if they are satisfied with it. These are fair questions and concerns but are designed to understand functionality, not value.

HCD concerns itself with understanding not just a product but also the goals of the user. As producers of journalism, we want to understand how the news fits into a person's life, both to support known needs and to identify new business opportunities. So HCD methods would ask not just "is the replica usable" but "when is it used, how, and why?"

The process is designed to generate insights, not just answers. Perhaps people who are occasional replica readers find the product intensely valuable when traveling for work or vacation. That fact would not show up in the analytics, but it might inform the development of a new product or service based on an otherwise unnoticed need.

After moving to McClatchy in 2014, I discovered that building the right product requires more than understanding consumer needs. Even the best ideas must clear organizational hurdles to become finished products. Expected costs, revenues, and resources all shape the path. Meanwhile, interpersonal politics, company culture, and a lack of shared vision often lead to imperfect decisions. One flavor of HCD, Design Thinking, boils the tensions between audience needs, technical feasibility, and business viability into a Venn diagram (Figure 0.1) we will refer to frequently.

After becoming Director of Product, I found the simple clarity of the Venn diagram useful in thinking about how to maintain our focus as we rapidly grew the department. My experiences on product teams at McClatchy and *The Boston Globe* are the first of four pillars for the book.

After transitioning into academia as the Knight Chair in Journalism at the University of Missouri, that Venn diagram has been core to my teaching of product management. I have spent the past five years doing news product thinking in a variety of journalism courses at Mizzou, including in a senior capstone where students work with external media clients to research, analyze, and propose product solutions. We have worked with clients that include the

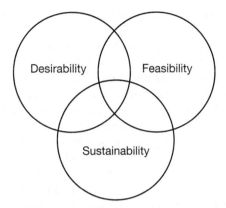

Figure 0.1 The three pillars of human-centered design for business represent audience needs, organizational capabilities, and business or strategic viability.

Associated Press, BuzzFeed, *The Wall Street Journal*, WBUR, Outlier Media, and The CITY. The lessons I continue to learn in those classes are the second pillar.

Beginning in 2018, I was part of a group of product thinkers who coalesced around the idea of news product management as a distinct practice that was increasingly important to newsrooms but was not yet clearly defined within the industry. After two years of work, small conferences, listening, and planning, we launched the News Product Alliance in the fall of 2020. The thoughts and values of that group of collaborators are the third pillar.

The fourth and final pillar: The process of writing this book has played a key role in writing this book. You don't know what you don't know until you write it down. I have learned a lot.

Errata

In each chapter, some words are in **bold type**. These are keywords defined in the text or the glossary at the end of the book.

A bit on the terminology used in the book. What exactly do we call a business (commercial or non-profit) designed around a journalistic function to deliver news and information to a community?

- Newspaper.
- News Organization.
- News Publisher.
- The Press.
- Media Company.

There is no perfect choice. And the above list snubs TV and radio broadcasters, not to mention the growing cadre of digital-only publishers. I mainly worked in newspapers, but news product thinking is used in and is critical to all news media.

In casual conversation, I often say "news organization," which is inclusive but unwieldy. To keep the discussion centered on the core function of journalism, I default to "newsroom" in this book with the understanding it represents the entire business. (Also, **synecdoche** is a great vocabulary word.) If "newsroom" turns out to be needlessly ambiguous in places, I will clarify with more specific terms to describe the broader business-specific relevant departments.

Next, what do we generically call the people who consume the news and information a newsroom publishes? Are they readers, listeners, viewers, visitors, users, community, or audiences? Each has merits, though the habit of calling web visitors "users" is on the wane. I have settled on "readers" in most cases. A primary focus of news product is the text-based world wide web. Reading is what we most often do on websites, apps, email newsletters on Twitter and Facebook, and so on. The other labels will pop up from time to time as more specific descriptions of specific media consumption or when talking about a broader audience or community.

Damon Kiesow
Columbia, Missouri
June 2023

Notes

1 Matt Waite. (2009, April 27). The Key Lesson I Learned Building PolitiFact: Demos, Not Memos. MattWaite.com. http://www.mattwaite.com/posts/2009/apr/27/key-lesson-i-learned-building-politifact-demos-not/
2 Jones, M. L. F. (2007, December). Twittering Away. *Presstime*, 19(12), 22.

Unit I

What is product management?

1 The news product manager

In this chapter

- The early origins of product management in newspapers.
- The (un)typical career path of a news product manager.
- What makes a good product manager?
- Why empathy is important.
- Why news product management is unique.

You may have heard this before: A product manager is "the CEO of the product."

It is a catchy phrase, but it misleads.

Most importantly, a chief executive officer is responsible for the success of the entire business. In doing so, she has the authority to decide strategy, hire or fire, write job descriptions, set goals, create incentives, and specify tasks. These duties are carried out directly or delegated to subordinates.

By comparison, a product manager is given responsibility for a specific product or service, has a voice in strategic decisions, coordinates across teams to develop a plan and set goals—and has no authority over many (if any) of the other people and departments involved.

Due to that lack of formal authority, product management is inherently collaborative. We prefer to **devolve** power rather than accumulate it. Our **North Star** is finding unmet community needs, not indulging organizational whims. And we aim if not for consensus in decisions, then at least a productive alignment between goals and actions. Product managers practice **servant leadership**. We work humbly and act in partnership to improve the team and the product.

So, product managers are less the CEO and more the researcher, teacher, accountant, cat herder, and coach all in one. This is especially true in the news media, where product management is still a relatively new arrival and often lacks a robust organizational structure, influence, and well-defined mandate.

DOI: 10.4324/9781003154785-3

In Chapter 2, we will review the history of product management, how it developed in the consumer packaged goods industry, and how it is now foundational at high-tech companies like Microsoft, Apple, and Google.

We often think of product as something developed and practiced primarily in Silicon Valley. But news organizations have followed a similar path for our transition to digital. So, even traditional newspaper companies like *The Times of India*, *The Washington Post*, *The Straits Times* of Singapore, and *The Wall Street Journal* now have large and active product management teams, as was rarely the case 15 years ago.

Product management at *The New York Times*

Unsurprisingly, *The New York Times* was an early adopter in the United States. Martin Nisenholtz joined the paper in 1995 as president of The New York Times Electronic Media Company. As the founding leader of the paper's digital efforts, it is not a coincidence that he was also the first to report jointly to the Executive Editor and the CEO. As we will learn, breaking down organizational **silos** is a hallmark of digital product thinking.

In 1995, Nisenholtz's team was located a five-minute walk away from *The New York Times* headquarters in Time Square. The digital staff of 20 included designers, producers, digital ad sales specialists, and a small engineering group. It did not have product managers.

Nisenholtz recalls he wanted to add value to the site beyond simply publishing journalism destined for the print newspaper.[1] Those early efforts included a CyberTimes news desk covering Silicon Valley and hyperlinking *Times* book reviews to Barnes & Noble sales listings.

Getting approval to staff new projects then, as now, was not an easy sell with executives. "It was hard to convince people that we need to be innovative in ways that involved engineering, not just journalism."[2]

As a digital innovator, the *Times* faced unique challenges in developing its online offerings. How best to understand what readers expect of journalism on the web? How to differentiate print and digital products? How to find a sustainable revenue strategy? And how to hire and organize the new teams required to develop and execute those strategies?

Rob Larson, one of the first digital staff to assume a product role at the *Times*, studied film as an undergrad and then earned an M.A. in instructional technology. He was hired initially with hopes to build an educational site to "connect current events to the classroom."[3] But Larson's first title at the *Times* was "producer" and, along with a small team, was responsible for migrating stories, photos, and headlines from print to digital on the late shift.

Nisenholtz and staff looked to the early product successes and job roles at Yahoo! to inform the digital structure at the *Times*. Yahoo! had evolved from a simple directory of websites to a full-service portal with sub-sites, including finance, movies, TV, and news. The digital upstart typically built out these vertical offerings with a mix of news, commentary, online events, community, and tools, including stock and showtime look-ups. Larson put that model into action in the *Times'* online movie section, launching the first capsule reviews and critics' picks on the site, selling movie tickets, and digitizing the archive of *Times* reviews.

News product at Knight Ridder

Shannon Kinney pursued a similar path on the other coast at Knight Ridder in San Jose, California.[4] An advertising major in college, Kinney developed early expertise in digital ad sales and technology. She moved to Chicago in 1998 to lead the dealership-focused half of the Cars.com product development and launch. The project was owned by Classified Ventures, a consortium of news publishers, including Tribune Co., *The Washington Post*, Gannett, McClatchy, and Knight Ridder.

Kinney then moved west to lead online classified ad efforts at Knight Ridder a year after the company had relocated its headquarters from Miami to Silicon Valley. Knight Ridder had no formal product management roles then, so when growing the team, Kinney looked to nearby start-ups Lycos, Excite, and Inktomi for inspiration. Three years later, as the director of classifieds and product management, her group included 350 product managers, software engineers, user researchers, and project managers.

Still early days

The *Times*, Knight Ridder, and other digital pioneers had a head start, and there are lessons to be learned from their examples. Despite the quarter of a century since the NewYorkTimes.com launched on the web, the industry at large has yet to unequivocally resolve any of the fundamental challenges of managing digital media products.

Product management is still a relatively new role in many newsrooms. Current practitioners often say they came to the job by accident or by necessity without knowing what "product" is.

Becca Aaronson, the founding executive director of the News Product Alliance, majored in cultural theory with a focus on linguistics in college before joining *The Texas Tribune* as a data reporter and realizing the solutions she wanted to build in the newsroom required a new approach.

"I was doing the work of helping my organization make more strategic decisions that aligned audience, editorial, and technology." Still, she was struggling to find a theory of the case to explain the work. After discovering product management as an emerging practice in other newsrooms, she realized, "This is the framework. These are the tools that I need to do this work better."[5]

Julia Beizer, the chief product officer and global head of digital at Bloomberg Media, began her career at a trade magazine for museum professionals before joining *The Washington Post* as a lifestyle reporter for the website.

Beizer soon found herself in meetings with editors and engineers, translating project needs between the two groups. After landing on an article page redesign project, she realized how vital cross-team insights were in software development work.

"What I found was these engineers really needed **subject matter experts** who knew the CMS—and I knew the CMS," she says. "I knew how to hack it to get it to do what I wanted." That knowledge helped developers align technical solutions with editorial workflows and reader-focused storytelling needs.[6]

Very commonly, nascent news product managers have a vision for a better way to report or tell a story, improve the publishing process, or measure the impact of coverage in the community. And to do that, they need to collaborate with other people in other departments with expertise in technology or design or audience research.

Building these collaborations and solving problems often becomes part of their job. Of course, many arrive with years of experience in journalism but no formal knowledge or training in product management. This can leave those who jump from the product thinker to product manager unsure how to define their job responsibilities.

What news product managers do

In Unit Two (Chapters 5–7), we will dig more deeply into the qualities that differentiate news product management from industries like big tech. But, before we go any further, you might ask:

Q: What is a news product manager?

Thanks for asking. A partial list of things news product cares about, in alphabetical order:

- A/B tests
- Agile processes
- Analytics
- Annual revenue per user
- AP Style
- Audience needs
- Audience research
- Advertising revenues
- Ad Tech
- Budgets
- Business analysis
- Civic health
- Click-thru rates
- Collaboration
- Community engagement

- Community impact
- Content management systems
- Content delivery networks
- Conversion funnels
- Customer acquisition
- Customer care
- Customer relationship management systems
- Customer retention
- Democracy
- Design reviews
- Design thinking
- Diversity, Inclusion, Equity
- E-commerce
- Editorial workflows
- Email service providers
- Event planning
- Forecasting
- Goal setting
- Human-centered design
- Innovation
- Journalism
- Key performance indicators
- Laws and regulations
- Loyalty metrics
- Mobile applications
- Newsroom mission
- Maintenance
- Marketing
- Market research
- Membership
- Newsgathering
- Organizational governance
- Open rates
- Pivot Tables
- Prioritization
- Privacy policy
- Product requirements
- Product lifecycle
- Product performance
- Project management
- Resource allocation
- Rhetoric
- Roadmaps
- Search engine optimization
- Secure Sockets Layer (SSL)

- Short messaging services
- Social media
- Software engineering
- Spreadsheets
- Storytelling
- Strategy
- Subscription revenues
- Sustainability
- Technical debt
- Testable hypotheses
- Training and development
- User interface design
- Usability
- User experience
- Visual design
- Video hosting
- Web Hosting
- Web page performance
- Web publishing

Product managers are the jack of all trades and masters of some. We are **"T-shaped"** in the parlance of job descriptions—possessing a depth of skill and experience in one or two relevant fields (the vertical stem of the "T") but credibly informed and experienced enough to work effectively with other departments and disciplines (the horizontal stroke of the "T").

The ever-changing variety of projects and challenges in the typical news organization requires individual expertise and the ability to work with other experts. There are always new things to learn and new people and teams to work with to complete a project effectively.

Product, program, or project management—or product owner?

Q: I see job listings for many different titles. How are the four "PM" roles different?

There are many similarities, and each is ultimately involved in managing the details of a project, prioritization of work, and guiding teams to success. Sometimes, the different roles and titles may overlap broadly or merge entirely.

- **Project manager** is often a role held by a certified "Project Management Professional" responsible for daily operations and tracking of an initiative's scope, schedule, finance, risk, quality, and resources.
- **Program manager** is more of a "big picture" project manager, focused on architecting, planning, assigning resources, and guiding the implementation of multiple projects within a company.

- **Product owner** is a formal role within Agile Scrum responsible for reviewing user stories, maintaining the development backlog, tracking the release schedule, and representing the voice of the consumer to the development team. It shares many overlapping responsibilities with product managers or may serve both roles in smaller organizations.
- **Product manager** is responsible for integrating audience and market research into a business case for roadmap prioritization. They might be the subject matter expert on a specific product or bring a holistic understanding of the business, audience, and competitive environment. In the absence of a product owner, they might adapt some or all of those responsibilities as well.

Qualities that define product managers

Q: OK, that is a good list, but those are primarily practical skills and processes. What are the intangibles?

- **Agile** in our ability to adapt to changing demands and priorities. Ask most product managers what they do in a typical day, and you might get a blank stare. It is a difficult question because "typical" is constantly changing, driven by the emerging needs of the features or product being developed this month. There is always research to be done, meetings to attend, and decisions to be made. Product managers need to be flexible enough to move between readers, executives, developers, and designers, from discussions of long-term strategy to reviewing the fine print in the terms of service.
- **Curious** in wanting to know how things work: People, processes, the business. This need to know is not selfless; it is rooted in recognizing that understanding these systems' complexities helps us solve important problems. It is having a sincere interest in customer needs, in a co-worker's goals, the challenges facing other teams, and in the social and technical structures we operate within.
- **Empathetic** because the job demands the ability to put yourself in someone else's shoes and understand how their life experience influences their beliefs and actions. Having empathy does not mean we abandon our perspectives or beliefs, but it requires that we can at least recognize and accept the motivations of others as legitimate and rational.
- **Collaborative** in our work with readers and breaking down internal silos that often prohibit communication and support between teams within the business. This concept is at the core of human-centered design—that we do not have all the answers and that a business in service to a community needs to listen to and represent the needs of a diverse group of stakeholders.
- **Intentional** by being consciously aware of our thoughts, feelings, and motivations and how those influence our assumptions and actions. And by questioning our implicit assumptions when working with others. It means

questioning every decision, demanding rigor in our processes, and learning from our successes and failures.

- **Optimistic** in our approach to working with people and dealing with challenges. We believe that problems can be solved that benefit our organization and our readers. We reject cynicism and short-term thinking that follows a zero-sum game approach. We don't expect easy answers, but we trust that a process focused on audience needs is the best path to success.
- **Resilient** as defined by the ability to learn and adapt in the face of adversity. Product management is a relatively new role in the news media, and as it encounters new challenges, it is inevitable not every discussion will be won. To avoid cynicism requires understanding long-term and short-term goals and gains. Not every setback is a defeat, and the need for that informed perspective is one reason resilience is a skill you build over time.
- **Holistic** in looking at the big picture and understanding that no reader need or solution exists in a vacuum. We must study and understand the social and economic structures influencing and impacting our audience. But we also understand our business as part of complexly interrelated organizations, processes, and technologies.
- **Constructivist** is a fancy word that means we believe every element of the human-designed world, including organizations, processes, and technology, is shaped by the culture that created them—each is constructed by society. This means our work is entangled with economic, technological, and societal complications that create implicit and explicit feedback loops influencing the pace and direction of our innovations.
- **Pragmatic** because we care about outcomes and will adopt whatever tool or process supports a positive result. This means believing in frameworks and methods but not dogmatically. We also recognize that product management ultimately works within a business that must achieve sustainability, a significant constraint. We work to find solutions that honor and respect the community and support the organizational mission through the sustainability of that mission.

Hard and soft skills

Q: So, that list was really ... intangible. Why are "soft skills" so necessary in product management?

That is another excellent question. Let's discuss the distinction between "hard" and "soft" skills because it is both a false dichotomy and a decent framework to understand product management—a mix of science and art.

Hard skills can be taught—but more importantly—measured quantitatively. AP Style, the Python programming language, or creating a pivot table in Excel are skills that can be trained, tested, and ranked for proficiency. In the workplace, these skills are listed in a job description and are practical requirements to complete expected daily tasks.

Soft skills can also be learned, practiced, and improved. But they are more challenging to teach and directly evaluate. Creativity, empathy, and teamwork can be observed but are most often described, not ranked. "Being a good teammate" is a critical job skill, but not one you can get a degree or certificate in.

There is an inherent bias in how we value qualities we can measure vs. those we cannot. As author and consultant Peter Drucker never actually said, in business, "If you can't measure it, you can't improve it."[7]

The lack of easy metrics to assess creative and social skills often means those capabilities are under-valued. But these traits make us better listeners, learners, collaborators, and problem-solvers. They make us better product managers.

Most business tasks require both hard and soft skills. Negotiating a contract, writing a product strategy, documenting requirements, and building partnerships all involve at least two human beings constantly weighing cost and effort as well as trust and confidence in each other and the plan. Scratch the surface of any spreadsheet or financial statement, and you will find that business can only be understood through the lens of subjective and very human decision-making.

The balancing act of product managers is to know the numbers, understand the audience, and influence the organization. The argument is not about "hard" and "soft" skills but recognizing the portfolio of talents needed for data-informed, human-focused decision-making.

Understanding empathy

Q: Got it. So, which of those "intangibles" is most important?

Let's talk more about empathy—a foundational **prosocial** skill for product managers. As commonly defined, it is the ability to recognize the feelings of others. As human beings, we want to be empathetic because it is a **moral good**. But in business, empathy is both more and less than that. For product managers, it is a method and instrument to understand audience needs and inform organizational actions.

We must use a formal method to develop an understanding of readers because **implicit bias** is an example of the gaps that occur when we don't recognize the values or needs of a person or community we intend to serve. No business decision or product is ever perfect, but we must at least avoid ignorance of community needs or infliction of harm through a lack of due consideration.

The benefits of empathy in product development are difficult to measure quantitatively but are easy to recognize when missing from the process.

In 2020, a Twitter user noticed the service commonly centered the faces of white subjects in tweeted images—but black faces were often auto-cropped out-of-frame. Colin Madland, then a Ph.D. student in British Columbia,

Canada, performed a series of live experiments to test his discovery, leading Twitter to acknowledge and eventually fix the algorithmic flaw.[8]

But automated bias against images of non-white subjects is not a new problem. In 2015, Google faced criticism when it sometimes categorized black human faces as gorillas in search results. The company apologized but initially "fixed" the problem by simply halting the automatic tagging of all gorilla photos.

This bias extends to the physical world as well. Some automated soap dispensers, which rely on infrared sensors, fail to recognize dark-skinned hands. The problem made it into public awareness in 2017 after a Facebook employee in Nigeria posted a video of a device in the company restroom not working.

Bias extends to gender differences as well. On average, a woman involved in a car accident is 73% more likely to be seriously injured and 17% more likely to be killed than a male occupant of similar age. Experts argue this results from industry safety tests that have historically utilized a 171-pound "standard male" crash test dummy that is 5-foot-9 inches tall.[9]

When Apple launched its Health app in 2015, iPhone owners could record and monitor a vast constellation of personal metrics, including height, weight, daily steps, and sodium intake. But, as 50% of the population pointed out, the app did not allow tracking of menstrual cycles. Critics questioned whether any women were on the team that developed that product, and the feature was added in 2016.

The lack of empathy extends to missed opportunities as well. As Katrine Marçal documents in the first chapter of her book, *Mother of Invention,* attaching wheels to luggage may have been first contemplated in 1940s England. But Bernard Sadow's 1972 patent for a suitcase with built-in wheels did not find commercial appeal until the 1980s. Marçal notes the product's success coincided with an increase in female airline passengers traveling alone.[10] Before that, it was assumed "a real man carries his own bag," as well as his wife's.[11]

In the U.S., the Americans with Disabilities Act of 1990 required equal physical access to public and commercial facilities. But that formal enforcement has not typically been extended to the virtual expanse of the web.

Providing equal access to digital resources continues to be a low priority for most publishers and platforms, as evidenced by the state of accessibility on the web. Users that rely on screen readers face sites with confusing HTML layouts and header structures, missing link text and alt text, and sites that overly rely on JavaScript rendering—making the content difficult to navigate, much less read. Users with vision impairments and color blindness struggle with web pages that feature low text contrast or difficult color combinations.

Journalism is also clearly implicated in a lack of empathy for segments of our communities. Our action or inaction can lead directly to a toxic environment that discourages engagement and encourages direct harassment against vulnerable community members. If your newsroom allows reader comments below articles—are real names required? Is the conversation closely moderated to maintain civility?

More critically, local newsrooms have a long history of pernicious coverage of poor and minority populations—a problem inventoried by The Kerner Commission Report in 1968. But in the 50 years since the commission recommended the diversification of American newsrooms, the industry has remained primarily white.

Some newsrooms have taken steps at least to admit to past failures. The *Los Angeles Times*, *The Kansas City Star*, and the *Montgomery Advertiser*, among others, have offered documentation and lengthy apologies for the past damage done by their often explicitly racist news coverage. But the industry has also overlooked stories important to many readers, perpetuated stereotypes in crime coverage and poverty, and continued digital practices such as online mug shot galleries.

We can broadly label these mistakes as lacking "empathy." For product managers, it describes a failure to recognize our community's full diversity, understand their needs, and provide products and services that optimize value and minimize harm. And there are a range of underlying causes:

1 A misconception of your audience that includes only those most likely to pay for journalism.
2 A blind spot for the full array of community needs.
3 A lack of attention to needs that may be recognized but are not considered urgent or valuable.
4 An unearned trust in new technologies. (In several of the above examples, algorithms were developed using collections of images with an unbalanced representation of the population.)
5 A decision-making process that fails to recognize decisions are always subjective and prone to unrecognized bias.

Avoiding these common errors requires only that we listen to the experts.

Journalists no more inherently understand the individual and collective needs of an entire community than readers can about the available or potential solutions to fill gaps in their information-seeking routines. News product thinkers are experts in the production and distribution of news. Readers are experts in their own habits, needs, and frustrations. A productive understanding and set of solutions can be developed only by combining forces.

The job of research is to understand the context of audience needs and match them with our available skills and resources to develop products and services within the realm of practical reality for the organization.

As product managers who are also human, we tend to interpret audience needs through the lens of our own experiences and the context of our personal or business goals. It is impossible to escape that frame entirely, but we can work to mitigate the effect.

The first step is to accept that we are not perfectly objective witnesses or entirely rational evaluators of facts. We are fickle about the information we select and interpret when making decisions, and we are eternally faced with incomplete or absent data in our quest for certainty. So, when making choices, our intuition fills the gaps. We "feel" our decisions are correct but can't always clearly explain why.

At the same time, product management is a business function, and our search for unmet audience needs is constrained by an often very pragmatic definition of the business we are in. Journalism plays a vital role in monitoring public health in a community. Still, it can't abandon its newsgathering and reporting mission to build a hospital or run a water treatment plant instead.

The **bounded rationality** of our audience poses another challenge. Given a new service or product, we can never know precisely how readers will perceive its value or how it might fit into their daily habits. And even for a current product, measuring the "what" captured by metrics is easier than the "why" reflecting a reader's needs and motivations.

So, when the data we have available for evaluation is imperfect, our understanding of the audience is incomplete, the time we have available to research and deliberate is limited, and our personal and organizational biases influence our decisions, designing and developing the perfect product or service is impossible.

Every activity a product manager undertakes is designed to turn empathy into a currency that can be understood and utilized in a business context. In the process, a flattening of reality will inevitably occur, and some details of the "humanity" of your readers will be lost in translation. So, product management is responsible for instilling an understanding of our audiences deeply and broadly enough for an informed and sincere respect and empathy to be reflected in every decision. Listening to and deeply understanding our audience is an antidote to the fragility of purely quantitative or implicitly biased decision-making.

News is (somewhat) unique

Q: How is News Product different from Product Management in other industries?

As Josh Benton at *Nieman Journalism Lab* says, "Local newspapers are basically little machines that spit out healthier democracies."[12]

But journalism is not just a product. It may also be a service and a process. Newsrooms are not factories in any traditional sense, and most journalists don't consider technology at the core of their craft. Historically journalists have been kept at an arms-length from the business and technology functions of the company. Though the three have always been intertwined.

What has changed over the past few decades is that the business of news (especially traditional newspapers) and the audience for news have been disrupted by digital technologies in several important ways. First, the print advertising business model was decimated by a transition to digital advertising that concentrated profits at Google and Facebook, a consolidation of national retailers, and the growth of Amazon, causing advertising inserts and display ads to evaporate. Second, the rise of the **attention economy** has meant a proliferation of options for readers to be entertained and informed on their computers, TVs, and mobile devices. This new competition for local readers comes in the form of large national or international businesses—from Netflix to Facebook—who lack interest or investment in the information needs of individual communities but come to town chasing **eyeballs** and extracting profits.

Unlike a technology-centric business, building products that value profit over public service, news organizations are not suited to **pivot** their mission in pursuit of wildly divergent business opportunities or audiences. Big media conglomerates might run educational services (*The Washington Post*), subscription crossword puzzles (*The New York Times*), or even quirky internet communities (Advance Publications owns Reddit). Smaller newsrooms might offer live events, host yard sales, or operate bookstores. But those efforts are intended to subsidize, not supplant, the core journalistic mission.

Conversely, Twitter was originally developed in 2006 as an internal messaging tool for the podcasting app Odeo,[13] and YouTube was originally conceived as a video dating site.[14] But leadership at *The Guardian* in London will not come into the office one day and suggest journalists churn out toaster ovens instead of news stories—regardless of the relative profit margins.

This constraint drives news product managers to chase not raw innovation and growth but community value, process improvement, and optimized revenue initiatives.

As Becca Aaronson says, we are not trying to recreate product management; we are trying to improve it in the service of journalism and community.[15]

Q: How do I get a job in news product?

According to research by Dr. Cindy Royal in partnership with the News Product Alliance, news product managers often start their careers in a newsroom.[16] But the paths are so unique as to defy broad generalization.

Durga Raghunath, the former head of digital at *The Times of India,* started in book publishing and founded several digital businesses between digital roles at *The Wall Street Journal, Mint,* and *The Indian Express.*

Brian Boyer spent eight years in software engineering before getting an M.A. at Medill, leading to a second career that included time at *ProPublica,* the *Chicago Tribune,* and NPR in editorial, product, and people leadership roles.

Jessica Gilbert began her career as a print newspaper designer in Florida, joined McClatchy as digital creative director in 2016, and then led the company's product, experience, and customer service groups before joining *The Washington Post* as Head of Product in 2022.

Marga Deona, at *Rappler* in Manila, says that one thing news product thinkers have in common is, "You'll never know you're doing product until a few years later."[17]

Deona has worked on video production, operations, and innovation at *Rappler* since 2012 but has done product thinking for over a dozen years. Deona considers herself a "non-journalist," and her undergraduate degree in creative writing led to digital and social marketing jobs before joining *Rappler*. She dates her adoption of product thinking to a radio show and podcast she developed in 2007 that served runners-in-training with music and coaching tips. But only recently has she formalized that recognition and added the title "Lead for Digital and Product Management" to her resume.

The structure of product

Q: How are product teams organized?

It depends. Product managers enjoy searching out and understanding complex topics. So, "how is product organized in your company?" is a frequent point of discussion anywhere two or more of us meet.

It is a big question and demands details such as:

- How large is the team?
- Which departments report up through Product?
- What internal groups do you work most closely with?
- What tools and methods do you use?
- Who is the top "Product" person in the company?
- Is that person at a director, VP, or c-suite level?
- What is Product responsible for?
- What is Product accountable for?

These are fun discussions that end without definitive answers. There is no "best way" to organize product management. Every team is built differently because the needs of every organization are unique.

Consider the structure and operation of a business as a jigsaw puzzle. Similarities between different puzzles abound—lighthouses, landscapes, and space scenes are popular options. But in our metaphor, the exact image, shape, and number of pieces are always unique. Each of our puzzles is incomplete, with different pieces either unsolved or missing. And our picture changes over time. Sometimes the change is slow, but it can be abrupt and chaotic during economic and technological disruption.

Product management is designed to help the business complete its puzzle. But to do so, we must be flexible, finding and placing available pieces and adapting our teams to fit the remaining gaps. And often, as we do that, we are also helping the business change the picture. As the joke goes, "Product management is the process of redesigning the organization to add a new field in the CMS."

That was a lot

Q: Can you summarize all that?

How about a few broad themes woven throughout the book:

- Crossing boundaries.
- Identifying needs.
- Managing uncertainty.
- Developing collaborations.
- Working with intent.
- Acting ethically.
- Serving communities.

For discussion

1 Is it inaccurate to call a product manager the "CEO of the Product"?
2 What is a typical career path for a news product manager?
3 How is news different than other businesses?
4 Is journalism a product or a service?
5 What is the most important skill for a product manager?

Learn more

- News Product Alliance – https://newsproduct.org
- Product Management for Dummies (2017). John Wiley & Sons.
- *Product Management in Practice* – Matt LeMay (2017). O'Reilly.
- Invisible Women: Data Bias in a World Designed for Men – Caroline Criado Perez (2019). Abrams Press.
- Range: Why Generalists Triumph in a Specialized World – David Epstein (2019). Riverhead Books.
- Mother of Invention: How Good Ideas get Ignored in an Economy Built for Men – Katerine Marçal (2021). Abrams Press.
- *Rules: A Short History of What We Live By* – Lorraine Daston (2022). Princeton University Press.

Notes

1 Conversation with Martin Nisenholtz. (2022, January 7).
2 Ibid.
3 Conversation with Robert Larson. (2022, January 19).
4 Conversation with Shannon Kinney, S. (2022, January 25).
5 Conversation with Becca Aaronson. (2020, October 25).
6 Conversation with Julia Beizer. (2020, October 25).

7 Zak, P. (2013, July 4). *Measurement Myopia*. Drucker Institute. https://www.drucker.institute/thedx/measurement-myopia/

8 Dickey, M. R. (2020, September 21). Twitter and Zoom's algorithmic bias issues. *TechCrunch*. https://techcrunch.com/2020/09/21/twitter-and-zoom-algorithmic-bias-issues/

9 Barry, K. (2019). A Crash Test Bias Puts Female Drivers at Risk. *Consumer Reports*. https://www.consumerreports.org/car-safety/crash-test-bias-how-male-focused-testing-puts-female-drivers-at-risk/

10 Marçal, K. (2021). *Mother of Invention: How Good Ideas Get Ignored in an Economy Built for Men*. Abrams Press.

11 Ibid., 19

12 Benton, J. (2019, April 9). When Local Newspapers Shrink, Fewer People Bother to Run for Mayor. *Nieman Lab*. https://www.niemanlab.org/2019/04/when-local-newspapers-shrink-fewer-people-bother-to-run-for-mayor/

13 MacArthur, A. (2020, November 25). The History of Twitter You Didn't Know. *Lifewire*. https://www.lifewire.com/history-of-twitter-3288854

14 Dredge, S. (2016). YouTube was Meant to be a Video-Dating Website. *The Guardian*. https://www.theguardian.com/technology/2016/mar/16/youtube-past-video-dating-website

15 Conversation with Becca Aaronson. (2020, October 25).

16 Royal, C. L. (2020). State of the News Product Community 2020. https://gato-docs.its.txst.edu/jcr:9ebf309f-73b9-4567-985e-380f7440ac6a/State%20of%20the%20News%20Product%20Community%202020.pdf?pdf=News-Product-Report2

17 Conversation with Marga Deona. (2022, February 5).

2 A brief history of product management

In this chapter

- How business management and administration have evolved.
- The growth of marketing and Brand Management.
- The origins of product management at Procter & Gamble.
- The need for bridge builders.
- Product management goes digital.

Product management as a human activity has been around since the first stone tool was crafted 3 million years ago in present-day Kenya. When some early Australopithecine found a conveniently shaped stone to carve up dinner, she set about making it sharper and better. The innovation succeeded because it fit a need, required only a small research and development budget, and benefitted from a persuasive word-of-mouth marketing campaign.

Product management as a profession dates back to 1931, and a three-page request to hire two new Procter & Gamble employees. Written by Neil McElroy, it led to a customer-focused reorganization of the company.

Responding to customer needs seems an unremarkable suggestion now. Still, Hewlett–Packard co-founder David Packard remembers being "laughed out of the room" when he expressed similar customer-first sentiments at a 1942 conference at Stanford University.[1]

The journey from Stone Age tools to the world wide web is long. And since news product management is a child of the digital age, it may be surprising we begin this chapter in the development of **business administration** in the 19th century and the emergence of **brand management** in the early 20th century. The story of product management is the underlying narrative of those movements: How the business-consumer relationship changed as new industries grew and diversified over the last 150 years.

DOI: 10.4324/9781003154785-4

The early origins of business administration

Before the mid-1800s, the leading forms of commercial enterprise in the U.S. were agriculture and manufacturing. In Alfred D. Chandler's history of business, he notes these industries, though capital- and labor-intensive, were typically local operations where the entire operation of a "group of mills could be viewed within half an hour" by a manager.[2] The railroads' rapid growth and geographic spread in the second half of the 19th century drove a need to develop new management structures.

Daniel McCallum, an engineer and general superintendent of the New York and Erie Railroad Company, wrote that a single manager could travel and directly oversee 50 miles of track but not 500. McCallum, at the time, oversaw more than 600 miles and is credited with developing the first organizational chart of a U.S. business in 1855.[3,4]

As rail networks expanded through construction and acquisition, increasingly sophisticated systems were required to manage information and coordinate work. These systems developed gradually to meet chronic needs and sometimes rapidly in the face of acute failure.

The Western Railroad, which connected Worcester, Massachusetts, and Albany, New York, at only 150 miles in length, created significant management issues. The line was constructed in three sections, and each division had its own managers but little coordination. The line ran three trains round trip daily—creating a dozen potential points of conflict on the rails—any of which could cause unnecessary delays or accidents.[5]

> *Since they ran on a single track, without the benefit of telegraphic signals, through mountainous terrain, such scheduling threatened tragedy. It came quickly. Even before the road had reached the Hudson River, the Western suffered a series of serious accidents, culminating in a head-on collision of passenger trains on October 5, 1841, killing a conductor and a passenger and injuring seventeen others. The resulting outcry helped bring into being the first modern, carefully defined, internal organizational structure used by an American business enterprise.[6]*

Chandler argues that reorganizations at DuPont, General Motors, and others starting in the 1920s were due to changes in economic demand: A drop during the Great Depression, growth after World War II, and a diversification of product lines. These administrative reorganizations were partly an effort to increase control by better forecasting supply and demand. But he also notes the changes were designed "to improve products, alter their design, or develop new ones in the face of changing market tastes and needs..."[7]

Organizational design is also driven by a desire to recreate in a large and sprawling business the **entrepreneurial** spirit and efficiency that existed in the original smaller enterprise.

It is that thread we are most interested in. As industries mature and competition increases, focusing on market expansion and operational efficiencies provides diminishing returns on investment. It is natural that product improvements, including design and marketing, become priorities. Both strategies require the business to better understand and respond to consumer needs.

Divisional structure at DuPont and General Motors

The company that was DuPont (until a 2017 merger with Dow Chemical) was formed in 1902 by the integration of several smaller businesses already owned by the du Pont family, some dating back to the early 1800s.

Each of the smaller operations produced explosives for military and civilian uses.[8] So, the newly merged company produced three products: Black powder, high explosives, and smokeless explosives. The similarities in manufacturing and sales expertise required were sufficient to allow DuPont to operate with a centralized **unitary form** of corporate structure.[9] Two general managers responsible for manufacturing and marketing originally shared responsibility for DuPont's portfolio, with other functions also headed by company executives.[10]

But following World War I, DuPont faced a surplus of raw materials as military demand for arms declined. The company searched for alternative uses for nitrocellulose, a key ingredient in TNT. This diversification effort led the company to begin the development of paints, plastics, and artificial fabrics.

These products required different materials and manufacturing processes and served different consumer markets. This change required an increased specialization in each of the teams involved in the research, the sourcing of raw materials, the development of manufacturing processes, and the marketing and sale of the finished materials.

Pierre du Pont led the company in a reorganization to allow that specialization, instituting the first **multi-divisional** corporate structure in the U.S. Instead of a dozen different products sharing engineering and sales teams, each would have a dedicated staff with the needed time and expertise to run the business. But the head of each product division would report to the CEO.

At General Motors, Alfred P. Sloan faced a similar challenge. Built upon a series of acquisitions, GM had a weakly organized structure, with its component brands operating semi-autonomously.[11] Sloan joined GM when his roller bearing company was acquired in 1916 and became president of the corporation in 1923.

He led a reorganization of the company that centralized financial controls and decentralized product-level decisions to individual brand leadership. This multi-divisional structure allowed strategies such as tiered pricing across GM's different makes: Chevrolet, Pontiac, Oldsmobile, Buick, and Cadillac. Sloan described the strategy as "a car for every purse and purpose."[12] This type of product and market differentiation creates tension between centralized and decentralized control. Decisions made in response to consumer preferences must be informed by customer insights. But to deliver those insights to market also requires a level of independence from corporate-directed resources and priorities. That was Neil McElroy's dilemma at Procter & Gamble.

McElroy's memo

In 1931, Neil McElroy was a junior advertising manager for Camay. He believed his soap received less than its fair share of corporate support than the flagship Ivory brand. The two products shared a single corporate advertising department at Procter & Gamble, and competition for resources was a **zero-sum game**.[13]

The immediate goal of McElroy's now anachronistically named "Brand Men Memo" was a common one for middle managers: Convince the boss to hire additional staff. But he also proposed a formal team structure to help the business keep up with rapidly changing markets. And though he neither created nor mentioned the title "product manager," he was the first to describe the duties that should evolve into the modern conception of that role.

It's no coincidence McElroy developed this innovation at Procter & Gamble. In the two decades before his arrival, the Cincinnati, Ohio-based company had started an employee profit-sharing plan, reorganized itself to bypass intermediary wholesalers, and invested aggressively in consumer marketing.[14]

The company was also an early advocate of consumer-focused product development, founding a research lab in 1890 and a market research department in 1925 that included "door-to-door" interviews to study marketing strategies. The shape of a bar of Camay soap was the first use of this market research process in product design.[15,16]

By the mid-1920s, Procter & Gamble's annual sales were approaching $2.5 billion in 2020 dollars. It had a growing collection of brands and its first overseas subsidiary in Newcastle-on-Tyne, England. The company culture, while sometimes "stodgy and tradition-bound"[17] was also open to experimentation in support of profit and displayed an ongoing willingness to rethink how it operated. Likely in response to the increasing diversity of its product portfolio, the company hired its first brand manager in 1928 for Lava Soap[18] which it had acquired a year earlier.

In this context, while McElroy's memo was a watershed event for Procter & Gamble, it succeeded only after decades of prior work by the company and because it arrived at a time executives were facing questions his strategy promised to answer. This is often the way of successful innovations. What looks like a flash of insight is more commonly the result of a sustained effort aligning with a previously unmet need at the right time and place.

McElroy needed a more focused, informed promotional effort to support his soap brand. He proposed two new marketing staffers and a dedicated team led by a brand manager who would be directly responsible for the product's overall success. The team and its manager would:

1 Understand all current and prior advertising and promotional activities for the brand.
2 Work directly with wholesalers, retailers, and consumers to understand past sales trends.
3 Study internal and external marketing activities to identify best practices.
4 Develop sales and marketing strategies utilizing the assembled research.
5 Support operational planning for marketing campaigns, including review of all printed materials.
6 Take responsibility for all advertising campaign expenditures.
7 Coordinate efforts with other relevant departments in the company.

This framework, which came to be known as the Brand Management System, was adopted first by Procter & Gamble and, over time, spread broadly across the consumer products industry.[19]

As with DuPont and GM, often when a company pursues new business strategies in response to competitive threats or new opportunities, its operating structure also changes. And for Procter & Gamble, McElroy's concept of a brand team was a precursor to the divisional structure the company would eventually adopt in 1954.[20]

Organizational structure

When McElroy wrote his memo, Procter & Gamble had a functional organizational structure—one of the four basic models:

1 **Flat**—More typically seen in smaller companies, there are few or no management layers between line employees and executive decision-makers.
2 **Functional**—Employees are organized by specialty or function, so a single department (e.g., Accounting, Human Resources, Development, Design) works with colleagues in other departments across the entire company.
3 **Divisional**—The company is split into multiple smaller businesses aligned with a specific product or geographic territory. Each division replicates most functions needed to support local operations.
4 **Matrix**—A mix of Functional and Divisional structures, employees are hired into a specific department (e.g., Design) but are assigned to work on a cross-functional team supporting a particular product or project.

What each model has in common is an attempt to efficiently align external needs (brands, products, or territories) with internal resources (coordination of activities, information management, and decision-making.) Each has strengths and weaknesses, and companies typically implement a mix of approaches.

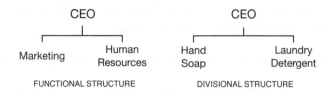

Figure 2.1 A functional organizational structure (left) is arranged by department, while a divisional structure (right) is divided by industry, product, or geographic location, with each unit hosting the needed functions locally.

The progression through models: From flat to matrix could be seen as the natural result of maturation and growth. As a company expands, as Procter & Gamble did in the 1920 and 1930s, it might well outgrow its existing organizational structure. Where once the founder could oversee and direct every activity, layers of managers and specialists are quickly needed as the scale of the operation increases (Figure 2.1). But reorganizations are not driven by product diversification or staff growth per se but rather by the level of information complexity and decision-making uncertainty related to that growth.

Decentralization vs. coordination

McElroy's Brand Team was an attempt to manage the ubiquitous organizational tension between management control and employee creativity.

Put another way, when decisions are centralized among a few executives or a single founder, the input and expertise of staff will always be under-utilized. This malady struck Ford Motors in the 1920s as Henry Ford's autocratic style stifled the company's response to external competition and changing consumer tastes.[21]

However, when decision-making is too decentralized, individual departments or staff may pursue strategies that are inefficient, contradictory, or harmful to broader corporate goals.

In practice, businesses often adopt a hybrid approach, centralizing some functions but not others.

Researchers argue that each point along the centralization-decentralization axis incurs different costs and benefits. For instance, divisions operating in other countries should be allowed decentralized independence to facilitate response to local conditions. But functions like Finance that must support stable and replicable processes are more amenable to centralization.[22]

Monitoring and rebalancing these tensions is an ongoing process. But as it is tied to organizational structure, adjustment can be slow and bureaucratic. A more flexible approach is seen in **boundary-crossing** behavior, where employees collaborate across **organizational silos** to seek information and reduce decision-making uncertainty.

Boundary crossing and uncertainty

No organizational structure is perfect. As a business adapts to customer needs, communication and collaboration gaps develop between internal teams. These gaps result in missed insights about customer preferences, the behavior of competitors, or the activities and goals of other teams within the business. And a too-rigid, too-centralized structure may discourage employee initiative and result in the organization asking the wrong questions or simply searching in the wrong place for answers.

In response to these concerns, employees will often look across organizational boundaries—the formal structure of a team, department, or business— and seek new sources of information to help develop insights and guide decisions. This can be as simple as water cooler talk between co-workers in different departments or a more intentional effort among external partners and customers. And the greater the perceived uncertainty within the organization, the more boundary crossing is likely.[23] By listening to a more diverse group of **stakeholders**, these information-seeking behaviors allow a business to respond more quickly to new threats and opportunities. Where a sales department might have traditionally worked only with wholesalers, employees who turn their attention to retail customer behavior might identify a new opportunity to sell directly to local stores and revolutionize the business as Procter & Gamble did in the 1920s.

Much of Neil McElroy's plan at P&G was to formalize these listening patterns and embed boundary crossing within the structure of his new team. And he proposed that decisions should be informed by or made by those employees closest to the customer. In this way, the insights gained by boundary crossers would not be lost in the bureaucratic process but would help guide strategy.

Organizational uncertainty

Information is the most valuable asset in a business, given that "all human productivity is knowledge dependent."[24] Every business decision depends on timely and relevant information when weighing benefits and risks. To reduce uncertainty in decision-making, managers strive to understand the details of consumer and market needs, the products or services delivered by the firm, and the internal processes involved.

Classical economic theory rests on the premise that decision-makers are perfectly informed, fully understand the potential outcomes of every possible option, and are entirely motivated to optimize benefit (what economists call **utility**.) The theory can be applied to any decision a person might make in a day, from selecting a breakfast cereal to hiring a new employee.

In practice, actual humans, including product managers, act according to theories of **bounded rationality**[25] which argue that imperfect knowledge and individual goals, ethics, and values lead to decisions that may appear imperfectly rational to an outside observer. This is partially a problem of **knowledge**

management, the acquisition, and use of information for organizational decision-making. As a business adds more customers, employees, and products, the amount of information to be acquired and weighed grows exponentially.

The risks incurred by poorly managing critical information in a dynamic business environment include:

1 Not everyone in the decision-making process is aware of all pertinent information.
2 Decisions are made with incomplete or outdated information.
3 Managers disagree on what sources of information to trust.
4 Decisions are made without thoroughly evaluating every option.
5 Subjective criteria override rational utility optimization.

Many of those challenges are exacerbated by built-in imperfections in the human mind. We tend to prefer immediate over longer-term payoffs; we inordinately trust our instincts even if we have been wrong in the past, and we favor data we have seen more recently or most frequently. These are all varieties of **cognitive bias**.

Since information management is difficult and business-critical, many business activities are designed to improve the process. A primary role of management is the effective alignment of resources to optimize measurement, information processing, and decision-making. When organizational structure hinders the collection or transformation of information into useful knowledge, a company will reorganize itself to reduce organizational uncertainty.[26] Instituting a discipline of product management is one common result.

Brand management and marketing

News product managers don't always think of our role as closely connected to **marketing**, which we often misunderstand to be limited to advertising and promotion. This fails to appreciate how product management and marketing have evolved and overlapped for the past 100 years.

Think of marketing as listening to consumer needs and creating, delivering, and promoting products and services that provide value.

The American Marketing Association provides a more formal definition:

> *Marketing is the activity, set of institutions, and processes for creating, communicating, delivering, and exchanging offerings that have value for customers, clients, partners, and society at large.*[27]

The four Ps of marketing

Product is the first of the "four Ps" of the traditional marketing mix:

- Product.
- Price.

- Promotion.
- Place.

The concept of the **marketing mix** was developed in the 1950s by Neil Borden at the Harvard Business School. But its more popular form was described by P. Jerome McCarthy in 1960.[28,29]

Scholars and practitioners have adopted and adapted the framework, with some suggesting as many as seven or eight "P" be included. But McCarthy's version suggests that marketing asks and answers:

- What is the **P**roduct or service being provided?
- What is the **P**rice and perceived value?
- On what platform or **P**lace will the consumer gain access?
- What **P**romotional tools will be used to communicate with consumers?

With not even a few minor edits, that also describes product management.

The eras of marketing

Textbooks commonly describe the history of marketing as comprising four eras:

1 Production-focused.
2 Sales-focused.
3 Marketing-focused.
4 Relationship-focused.

This taxonomy was first described by Robert Keith.[30] At the time, he was the Executive Vice President of consumer products for the Pillsbury Company, and his view was informed by the evolution of marketing strategies there.

As commonly defined, the four periods above align with the shifting balance between supply and demand in an economic market. When production and distribution are constrained, demand outpaces supply, and manufacturers may succeed simply by delivering a product to store shelves. The era of production-focused marketing is represented by Henry Ford in 1909, "Any customer can have a car painted any colour that he wants so long as it is black."[31] Like other manufacturers of the era, Ford wanted his factories to reduce **unit costs** and increase output. Offering a single "Model T" in a single color helped reduce the complexity of the assembly line allowing more cars to be built at a lower average cost.

However, when a product becomes commoditized, consumers will evaluate multiple brands and products and make purchasing decisions based on features, quality, and price—not simply availability. When consumers gain that ability, marketing strategies must adapt. So, the eras represent an ongoing readjustment of market power between producers and consumers. As that power shifts, marketers attempt to gain a competitive advantage by better understanding and building consumer relationships.

This historical interpretation, while popular, is also disputed as a vast oversimplification of a complex topic.[32] However, it is a useful **mental model** and sheds light on the evolution of both marketing and product management, so we will accept it as a useful, if imperfect, explanation.

The Hewlett–Packard way

Bill Hewlett and David Packard built the original Silicon Valley startup. The pair famously launched Hewlett–Packard from a garage in Palo Alto, California, in 1939, after completing degrees next door at Stanford University.

From the start, Hewlett and Packard were intent on building a business that was profitable and a good corporate citizen. "Management has a responsibility to its employees, it has a responsibility to its customers, it has a responsibility to the community at large," a 29-year-old Packard told a room of dubious businessmen in 1942.[33]

The founders hoped to build a work culture that valued respect, learning, flexibility, achievement, integrity, and innovation—a philosophy they came to call the "HP Way."

These aspirations were embodied by HP's early use of salary bonuses, open floor office plans, profit-sharing, **management by objective** (MBO) goal setting, and Packard's efforts to understand the growing operation by his practice of **management by walking around** (MBWA).[34]

Those last two concepts are related, with the MBO process delegating corporate goals to staff working in a decentralized organizational structure close to customers. The MBWA approach supports the need for leadership to then be both visible and accessible to staff and to understand the work being done "on the factory floor."

The practice of good citizenship extended to the company's relationship with consumers. In the foreword to Packard's autobiography, HP alumni Jim Collins summarized the company's guiding principle as, "Do our products offer something unique – be it a technical contribution, a level of quality, a problem solved – to our customers?"[35] The company's organizational structure and job descriptions were rooted in that question.

HP initially built specialized electronic equipment and expanded into personal computing devices, starting with scientific calculators in the 1960s. To manage this diversity of offerings and a growing staff, HP restructured itself into product groups in 1968.[36] Each group was led by a general manager and marketing manager and populated by teams supporting a distinct family of products.[37]

To maintain agility and a culture of informal collaboration, HP limited the size of these divisions to fewer than 1,000 employees. "Most people can keep track of about five hundred names on a first-name basis," believed Hewlett. "Past that, you have to use last names."[38]

This process of reorganization is a challenge many companies face, and it is not without complications. Natural divisions may be found by geographic location, strategic focus, raw materials, or manufacturing processes. HP's engineering leadership favored division by technology: Digital vs. analog teams or microwave vs. non-microwave radio products. Packard rejected those options, preferring a structure that prioritized consumer needs. "We're not going to organize by the technology," he said. "It's by the customers we are trying to please, that's the way we're going to organize it."[39]

As a result, in the early days of HP, lead engineers were effectively "product managers." Before receiving a project approval, the engineer would do market research, develop prototypes, and provide sales volume and cost estimates. After development and testing, they were responsible for end-user documentation and copywriting for the sales catalog. In practice, these roles acted as business leads for a specific product in HP's decentralized business structure. Eventually, those tasks were shared across a team as the number and complexity of projects grew.[40]

Making cars better at Toyota

Inside Toyota's automotive factories, you will find a "community of scientists" who design experiments to reduce waste and optimize manufacturing quality.[41]

Those "scientists" are line workers and supervisors who work collaboratively to take ownership of key aspects of the process of building cars. To do this, workers ask practical questions about the production line: What is the most efficient method to attach a car seat, when should we order parts from a supplier, or how can we reduce errors and waste on the assembly line?

In a **learning organization**, employees are empowered to implement changes in process and product informed by the new knowledge and insight gained from the answers.

The **Toyota Production System** (TPS) formalizes this work by setting exacting quality and process standards and handing authority over to employees. The standards are a hypothesis: "A car seat can be attached in seven steps over 55 seconds." When the theory fails, line workers study the problem and conduct experiments to test potential solutions. As a result, training procedures might be modified, a workspace reconfigured for efficiency, or the standard changed.[42]

Development of the TPS, also referred to as **lean manufacturing**, was influenced by American engineer W. Edwards Deming in the years following World War II. Deming applied statistical methods to quality control efforts in factory production and helped popularize the use of the **scientific method** in that effort.

Demming and Toyota's approach contrasts with the **command-and-control** management structures that might treat workers as automatons instead of experts in operations and problem-solving. Critics note the more collegial approach, while commendable, may still be abused by managers who impose unrealistic expectations.[43]

Toyota's system is built on a dozen pillars, including:

- **Genchi Genbutsu** means "go and see for yourself," reflecting the need to go back to the source of facts to inform decision-making. For Toyota, that means the factory floor and line workers.
- **Kaizen** is the practice of continuous improvement reflected in the setting of standards and the need for gradual improvement and innovation.
- **Kanban** means "signboard" and is a key project management tool that has been adopted by knowledge workers.

The method:

- Provides transparency through a visual representation of work posted on physical or virtual Kanban boards with cards representing tasks and progress.
- Limits **work-in-progress** to levels achievable with the given staff capacity.
- Manages the movement of work between stages by monitoring for bottle-necks and defined handoffs between teams.

Demming popularized the Shewhart Cycle for Continuous Learning and Improvement.[44] Variously described as the **Plan-Do-Check-Act** (PDCA) or Plan-Do-Study-Act (PDSA) cycle, it consists of:

1 **Plan** (develop a hypothesis).
2 **Do** (run an experiment).
3 **Study**/Check (evaluate the results).
4 **Act** (refine the experiment; then start a new cycle).

That same scientific approach to business experimentation was later reconfigured by Eric Reis as the Build-Measure-Learn loop[45] in his book *The Lean Startup*—and adopted across much of Silicon Valley.

Product management goes digital

The principles of customer focus, scientific method, and continuous learning have spread from the factory floor into other industries as each has needed to solve similar challenges.

The manufacturing of soap, calculators, or cars is not very different from the development of software for desktop computers. In both cases, the primary business challenge is identifying a consumer need, designing a solution, prioritizing tasks, and delivering the finished product to market. These are challenges of optimizing human effort to research, analyze, and make decisions. Only the build process: Factory line vs. lines of code, is distinct. And even there, the project management techniques applied to software development have frequently been adopted and adapted from contemporary best practices in manufacturing.

A 1966-era Scientific Data Systems Sigma 7 mainframe computer cost $6 million in today's dollars. Somewhat typical of computer systems at the time, it had 512k of memory and was the size of a small room.[46]

Personal computers for home use were 15 years away, and software development for these early mainframes was limited to universities, governments, and large businesses. The early commercial uses included seat reservation systems for airlines and passenger rail lines.

As was typical for corporate manufacturing projects, the development of these software applications followed a sequential pattern:

1 Create detailed specifications.
2 Divide the development work into discrete component projects.
3 Develop the individual components.
4 Assemble the components into a complete system.
5 Debug and correct errors caused by the integration of the component parts.

Known as the **waterfall** process, this linear approach has some key constraints.

1 The problem domain must be stable and well-understood. Because project specifications are decided in advance, and work is planned around those specifications, it is difficult to change elements of the design once development work has begun.
2 Because of the inflexibility of the plan, projects that last months or years cannot effectively respond to changes in customer preferences or economic pressures that occur during the development process.
3 To accommodate any unavoidable changes and to assure overall compliance to the plan, teams must maintain close communication and coordination of effort. Inevitably, some errors will be discovered in the final integration and testing stage, requiring a costly effort to fix.

Making software development more Agile

In the 1980s and 1990s, the growing ubiquity of desktop and personal computers led software engineering to the same dilemma that led to the development of brand marketing in the 1920s at Procter & Gamble. As competition increases, the business must improve its ability to listen and respond to consumer preferences.

A variety of project management techniques arose with the common hope of increasing flexibility, reducing development time, and improving the product by humanizing the process. In February 2001, proponents of Adaptive Software Development, Crystal Clear, DSDM, Extreme Programming, Feature-Driven Development, SCRUM, and Pragmatic Programming methods met at a Utah ski resort to discuss the challenge.[47]

The resulting **Agile Manifesto** was strongly influenced by the work of Demming, the Toyota Way, and the principles of continuous learning among small semi-autonomous working groups. The principles of Agile development call for development practices that value the customer, welcome changing requirements, embrace cross-departmental collaboration, and invest in continuous learning and improvement of both staff and product.[48]

The transition at Microsoft

What emerged at Microsoft in 1988 was called Program Management. The title was first held by Jabe Blumenthal, a member of the team developing Excel for Macintosh.[49] The role had evolved over several years as the complexity of projects and the growth of teams drove a need for better coordination of work.

The origin story is common: The engineering team was focused on the details of writing and testing thousands of lines of computer code and did not have time to talk to users or translate requests from marketing into working features.[50] A dedicated role was needed to support development work and integrate customer needs as well as business priorities.

Joel Spolsky, a former Microsoft program manager, describes the job as being a customer advocate, which included writing functional specifications (what a feature should do), designing user interface elements (how the user should interact with it), and coordinating efforts between teams.[51]

Product in the Valley

In the past 20 years, product managers have taken over Silicon Valley. Apple, Facebook, Twitter, Google, and Amazon all employ armies of innovators focused on setting priorities and aligning business activities to serve customer needs.

"High tech" is not a monolith, so the roles, titles, and qualifications vary. A recent search for "product manager" on Google's career portal revealed 1251 open positions across hundreds of business units, including Google Cloud, Google Nest, and Fitbit.[52]

Product management is one piece of the organizational jigsaw puzzle supporting customer focus. So, while a distinct skill set, the role is usually strongly aligned with the dominant work culture. That means many Silicon Valley product managers arrive on the job with a master's in business administration or in the fields of computer science or electrical engineering. Similarly, in news, fewer product thinkers have MBAs, and more have journalism degrees.

Product roles will vary widely depending on the size and **stability** of the business. At a startup, the founder may be CEO, product manager, and lead engineer. At Apple, there is a product manager for product customization and engraving.[53]

The principles of product management

Procter & Gamble didn't invent product management, but it did write the job description. The conditions that led to the emergence of brand and product management were also faced by many other organizations. A few universal themes are evident that are agnostic to the specific product or build process:

1 Listening to customers is the quickest path to understanding and serving their needs.
2 Organizations must be structured to enable the voice of external customers and partners to influence internal decisions.
3 Organizations must decentralize to the extent needed to maximize customer focus and the value of product-specific staff expertise.

For discussion

1 What factors define how a business organizes itself?
2 What was the core argument in Neil McElroy's request to hire a brand management team?
3 What effect can over-centralization have on an organization's decision-making?
4 Why is information processing critical to organizational success?
5 How are the HP Way and the TPS similar?
6 How is the Agile philosophy an extension of earlier organizational project and knowledge management trends?

Learn more

- *The Soul of a New Machine* – Tracy Kidder (1981). Atlantic-Little, Brown.
- *Showstopper: The Breakneck Race to Create Windows NT and the Next Generation at Microsoft* – G. Pascal Zachary (1994). Free Press.
- *The Pentagon Wars* [TV Movie] – Richard Benjamin (Director). (1998). HBO.
- *Rising Tide: Lessons from 165 Years of Brand-Building at Procter & Gamble* – Davis Dyer, Frederick Dalzell & Rowena Olegario (2004). Harvard Business School Press.
- *The HP Way: How Bill Hewlett and I built our Company* – David Packard (2007). Harper Collins.
- *The Machine That Changed the World: The Story of Lean Production* – James P. Womack, Daniel T. Jones & Daniel Roos (2007). Free Press.
- *Denial: Why Business Leaders Fail to Look Facts in the Face–And What to do About It* – Richard Tedlow (2010). Portfolio.
- *The Decision Loom: A Design for Interactive Decision-Making in Organizations* – Vincent P. Barabba (2011). Triarchy Press.

Notes

1 Jacobson, D. (1998, August). Founding Fathers. *Stanford Magazine*. https:// stanfordmag.org/contents/founding-fathers
2 Chandler, A. D. (1965). The Railroads: Pioneers in Modern Corporate Management. *Business History Review*, 39(1), 16–40. https://doi.org/10.2307/3112463
3 Chandler, A. D. (1962). *Strategy and Structure: Chapters in the History of the Industrial Enterprise*. MIT Press.
4 McCallum, D., & Henshaw, G. H. (1855). *Organizational Diagram of the New York and Erie Railroad*. New York and Erie Railroad. https://upload.wikimedia. org/wikipedia/commons/2/2b/Organizational_diagram_of_the_New_York_ and_Erie_Railroad%2C_1855.jpg
5 Chandler, A. D. (1977). *The Visible Hand: The Managerial Revolution in American Business*. Belknap Press.
6 Ibid., 96–97
7 Chandler, A. D. (1962). *Strategy and Structure: Chapters in the History of the Industrial Enterprise* (p. 292). MIT Press.
8 Staehle, W. H. (1970). A Comparison of Organization Building at Dupont and Farbwerke Hoechst. *Management International Review*, 10(6), 33–44. https:// www.jstor.org/stable/40226800
9 Tedlow, R. S. (2010). *Denial: Why Business Leaders Fail to Look Facts in the Face– And What to do About It*. Portfolio.
10 Ibid., 146
11 Fox, W. M. (1983). The Telegraph–Railroad–DuPont–General Motors Connection. *Academy of Management Proceedings*, 1983(1), 121–125. https://doi. org/10.5465/ambpp.1983.4976330
12 Sloan, A. P. (1990). *My Years with General Motors* (p. 438). Doubleday/Currency.
13 Kumar, N. (2003). Kill a Brand, Keep a Customer. *Harvard Business Review*, 81(12), 86.
14 Procter & Gamble. (2006). *P&G: A Company History*. Procter & Gamble. https:// www.pg.com/translations/history_pdf/english_history.pdf
15 Dyer, D., Dalzell, F., & Olegario, R. (2004). *Rising Tide: Lessons from 165 Years of Brand-Building at Procter & Gamble*. Harvard University Press.
16 Procter & Gamble. (2006). *P&G: A Company History*. Procter & Gamble. https:// www.pg.com/translations/history_pdf/english_history.pdf
17 McCraw, T. K., & Childs, W. R. (2001). *American Business Since 1920: How It Worked* (p. 42). Wiley-Blackwell.
18 Fulmer, R. M. (1965). Product Management: Panacea or Pandora's Box? *California Management Review*, 7(4), 63–74. https://doi.org/10/gg4kmb
19 Aimé, I., Berger-Remy, F., & Laporte, M.-E. (2017). A History of the Brand Management System. *Explorations in Globalization and Glocalization: Marketing History through the Ages*.
20 Frynas, J. G., & Mellahi, K. (2011). *Global Strategic Management*. Oxford University Press.
21 McCraw, T. K., & Childs, W. R. (2001). *American Business Since 1920: How It Worked*. Wiley-Blackwell.
22 Vantrappen, H., & Wirtz, F. (2017). When to Decentralize Decision Making, and When Not To. *Harvard Business Review*. https://hbr.org/2017/12/ when-to-decentralize-decision-making-and-when-not-to
23 Leifer, R. P., & Huber, G. P. (1976). Perceived Environmental Uncertainty, Organization Structure and Boundary Spanning Behavior. *Academy of Management Proceedings*, 1976(1), 233–238. https://doi.org/10/fw3p5j
24 Grant, R. M. (1996). Toward a Knowledge-Based Theory of the Firm. *Strategic Management Journal*, 17(S2), 109–122. https://doi.org/10.1002/smj.4250171110

25 Simon, H. A. (1947). *Administrative Behavior. A Study of Decision-Making Processes in Administrative Organization*. Free Press.

26 Van den Bosch, F. A. J., Volberda, H. W., & de Boer, M. (1999). Coevolution of Firm Absorptive Capacity and Knowledge Environment: Organizational Forms and Combinative Capabilities. *Organization Science*, 10(5), 551–568. https://doi.org/10.1287/orsc.10.5.551

27 AMA. (2017). *What is Marketing? — The Definition of Marketing*. AMA. American Marketing Association. https://www.ama.org/the-definition-of-marketing-what-is-marketing/

28 Borden, N. H. (1964). The Concept of the Marketing Mix. *Journal of Advertising Research*, 4(2), 2–7.

29 McCarthy, E. J. (1960). *Basic Marketing, A Managerial Approach*. R.D. Irwin. https://catalog.hathitrust.org/Record/006071661

30 Keith, R. J. (1960). The Marketing Revolution. *Journal of Marketing*, 24(3), 35–38. https://doi.org/10.1177/002224296002400306

31 Ford, H., & Crowther, S. (1922). *My Life and Work*. Garden City Publishing Company.

32 Jones, D. G. B., & Richardson, A. J. (2007). The Myth of the Marketing Revolution. *Journal of Macromarketing*, 27(1). https://doi.org/10.1177/0276146706296708

33 Jacobson, D. (1998, August). Founding Fathers. *Stanford Magazine*. https://stanfordmag.org/contents/founding-fathers

34 Packard, D. (2007). *The HP Way: How Bill Hewlett and I Built our Company*. HarperCollins.

35 Ibid., xii

36 Ibid., 146

37 House, C. H., & Price, R. L. (2009). *The HP Phenomenon: Innovation and Business Transformation*. Stanford Business Books.

38 Ibid., 67

39 Ibid., 67

40 Ibid.

41 Spear, S., & Bowen, H. K. (1999). Decoding the DNA of the Toyota Production System. *Harvard Business Review*, 77, 96–108.

42 Ibid.

43 Womack, J. P., Jones, D. T., & Roos, D. (2007). *The Machine that Changed the World: The Story of Lean Production - Toyota's Secret Weapon in the Global Car Wars that is Revolutionizing World Industry* (1. paperback ed., p. 100). Free Press.

44 Demming Institute. (2022). *PDSA Cycle*. The W. Edwards Deming Institute. https://deming.org/explore/pdsa/

45 Ries, E. (2011). *The Lean Startup* (1st ed.). Crown Business.

46 Scientific Data Systems. (1967). *The Sigma Family*. Scientific Data Systems. http://s3data.computerhistory.org/brochures/sds.sigma.1967.102646100.pdf

47 Beck, K., Beedle, M., van Bennekum, A., Cockburn, A., Cunningham, W., Martin, F., Grenning, J., Highsmith, J., Hunt, A., Jeffries, A., Kern, J., Marick, B.,Martin, R. C., Mellor, S., Schwaber, K., Sutherland, J., & Thomas, D. (2001). *Manifesto for Agile Software Development*. https://agilemanifesto.org/

48 Ibid.

49 Sinofsky, S. (2010). *PM at Microsoft*. Microsoft Tech Talk. https://web.archive.org/web/20100529215056/http://blogs.msdn.com/b/techtalk/archive/2005/12/16/504872.aspx

50 Iansiti, M., & Buccitelli, B. (2007). *Microsoft Office 2007 (Abridged)* (No. 607-015; Harvard Business School Case, p. 19).

51 Spolsky, J. (2009). *How to be a Program Manager*. Joel on Software. https://www.joelonsoftware.com/2009/03/09/how-to-be-a-program-manager/

52 Google. (2022). Google Careers. https://web.archive.org/web/20220223165625/
    https://careers.google.com/jobs/results/?company=Fitbit&company=G
    oogle&company=Google%20Fiber&company=YouTube&company=Loon
    &company=Verily%20Life%20Sciences&company=Waymo&company=Wi
    ng&company=X&distance=50&employment_type=FULL_TIME&hl=en_
    US&jlo=en_US&location=United%20States&page=4&q=Product%20
    Manager&sort_by=relevance&src=Online%2FHouse%20Ads%2FBKWS_TPM
53 Apple. (2022). Product Manager, Product Customization and Engraving. *Ca-
    reers at Apple.* https://web.archive.org/web/20220223164916/https://jobs.
    apple.com/en-us/details/200256186/product-manager-product-customization-
    and-engraving?team=MKTG

3 Theories of product management

In this chapter

- Product thinking vs. product management.
- Human-centered design as a business tool.
- Learning to make good decisions, despite our brains.
- Navigating complex systems.
- What is product management?

Newsrooms have a famously "learn on the job" culture. In the 100 years since the opening of the first journalism schools, there has been a tension between university-fostered professionalism and the practical wisdom of a job ostensibly accessible to anyone with an aptitude for storytelling in the public interest. As Dr. James Carey argued, the debate exists even within universities where the teaching may favor instruction in basic skills to the partial exclusion of ethics, values, and theory.[1]

What if the utilitarian approach is the correct one? As baseball player Yogi Bera said, it doesn't matter what works in theory; it matters what works in practice. And that can be a persuasive argument in a mature industry with comfortable profit margins and a stable or growing market.

But news has not been a comfortable business for decades. And the disruption of the internet has only accelerated declines in print newspaper readership that began on a per-capita basis in the 1950s in the U.S. In the digital economy, a business must constantly adapt to shifts in audience needs and the ever-present threat of new competition. To survive, much less grow, change is mandatory.

Change requires us to do new things, in new ways, for new audiences. That means the lessons of the past lose much of their **probative** value. This is a pillar in Clayton Christensen's description of disruptive innovation: Companies fail because the wisdom they earned through years of success become irrelevant in the face of new challenges.

DOI: 10.4324/9781003154785-5

Innovation requires us to develop new hypotheses, new methods to test potential solutions, and the skill to develop insights into a theory of change. So, in times of disruption, we ignore theory at our peril. We must understand the "how and why" of doing new things as a tool to guide our actions.

Often, news product managers enter the profession with years of newsroom experience but without the benefit of a degree in business or computer science. Many succeed by understanding newsroom culture and systems, pure intuition, and the skills and relationships they have built in their organization. But solving puzzles is easier if you can first see the big picture. Understanding the basics of business is something you need to learn in school, on the job, or in a book. I call that last option the "two-chapter MBA" because much of what a product manager needs to know can be learned in the opening sections of a business textbook.

Product managers tackle a lot of different jobs. We build processes, teams, products, and businesses. This chapter is an introduction to some of the theories underlying that work.

Product thinking and product management

This is a book about news product management. But the work we do is not defined by our job title. Product thinking is a problem-solving method that creates or improves processes, services, and products by identifying customer needs (including internal or external clients, communities, and individuals) and aligning resources to develop a solution.

A product manager is a job title or formal position within an organizational structure that typically pursues those same goals.

All product managers are product thinkers, but many product thinkers have other job titles: Editor, reporter, producer, developer, designer, analyst, or manager—among many other newsroom and adjacent roles.

News product managers and product thinkers believe in the same things. And the coin of the realm for both is gathering information and making decisions with an audience focus:

- Who is our community?
- What met and unmet needs do they have?
- Which of those needs align with our organizational values and mission?
- Can we develop valuable solutions?
- How will those solutions be sustained?

Those basic questions overlap with the famous "Five W's" of journalism training: Who, What, Where, When, and Why. That is because, like reporting, product thinking seeks first to understand and then to explain. In the language of product thinking: Define the need before you propose the solution.

The challenge for product management is that "understanding" requires recognizing reader needs and navigating an array of business, technical, and cultural tensions that influence organizational decisions and priorities.

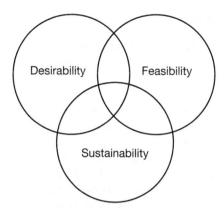

Figure 3.1 News product thinking prioritizes understanding reader needs, balanced with an imperative to build sustainable organizations to serve a community's information needs.

One way many product managers do this is with the Design Thinking innovation framework popularized by consulting firm IDEO and taught extensively at Stanford University's Hasso Plattner Institute of Design (the d.School.)

Design Thinking describes **desirability** as the quality of a product that solves a customer need. It is one of the pillars supporting a business-centric approach to human-centered design. The other two: **Feasibility** and **sustainability,** represent an organization's capacity to build a solution and its ability to develop a **subsidy** to enable the continued operation of the product or service.

The design thinking pillars (Figure 3.1) are the first layers in a stack of solutions[2] that product management must coordinate to bring an innovation to market:

Research and validation

- **Desirability** (does it solve a reader need?)
- **Feasibility** (do we have organizational capacity and skills?)
- **Sustainability** (is the business model or strategy viable?)

Design and development

- **Visual design** (is it on brand and eloquent?)
- **User experience** (is it usable and useful?)
- **Systems integration** (between disparate services and tools?)

Operation and acceptance

- **Workflow** (are employees trained in the new process?)
- **Culture** (does it align with the shared values that govern decisions and behaviors?)

An idea must pass a test at each level of that stack of requirements, from audience need to usability to organizational culture. And any failure at any level effectively vetoes an idea.

If an idea solves a reader need but is not feasible for the organization, it won't be built. If a product is researched and built but violates journalism's ethical code, the culture of the organization will reject it. These interdependencies create a complex system for new ideas to navigate.

Product managers are the architects of the user experience

Imagine you, the architect, interior designer, and owner of a new home. In one room, on one shelf, is an envelope containing a cash prize. Your goal is to help guests find their way to that gift. It is the reason they visit. But there are some challenges. The money is behind one of the dozens of doors in the house. The room is windowless, often poorly lit, and scattered with random furniture likely to trip people up. You don't personally live there, so you can't act as a tour guide. And the winning room is different for each guest. Simply posting "walk this way" signs and arrows won't work.

Everyone likes free money, so there is an incentive to visit and search the house. But your guests' interest in collecting the prize will be limited by a few assumptions:

- Their guess as to the size of the reward. (The perceived value.)
- The anticipated time and skill needed to find the room and navigate to the envelope. (The perceived effort.)
- The other tasks they must accomplish that day. (Their available time and attention.)
- The availability of cash prizes handed out on the street. (Easier solutions.)
- The time, learning, and skill required to find the room and the envelope. (The actual effort.)

Those first two constraints, perceived value and perceived effort, are gating factors. If the signals of value and usability are weak or absent, users may give up on the task before they start, judging the effort as not worth the potential reward.

Each of those factors interacts with the others. The larger the reward, the more time and effort a visitor will invest. If the actual effort exceeds original expectations, users may abandon the tasks or seek alternative, even inferior, options.

News is an **information good** (see Chapter 5), and its value can only be fully assessed after it has been consumed. Readers have limited time, and uneven interest in the news, so strong signals of value are required.

But perceived value is entirely idiosyncratic and influenced by prior experiences with your website, other similar websites, and the web in general. It is also related to the user's familiarity with the topics you routinely cover and the time they have available to read.

As a calculation: *Satisfaction = ((Perceived & Actual Value−Perceived & Actual Effort))*

A publisher has only partial control over these variables.

- A marketing campaign can explain the product and its value.
- Effective visual design can communicate quality and authority.
- The user interface can provide wayfinding signals such as section labels and navigation.
- A well-designed user experience including quality content, design, and usability.

A human-centered approach

A common theme in business and academia over the last 100 years has been the move away from purely rational and mechanistic theories of human behavior in favor of more realistic and socially constructed understandings. Rationality is not dead, but it can't fully explain the complexity of human systems and decision-making that are strongly influenced by personal experiences, incentives, context, culture, and attention.

In other words: *Why do people behave the way they do?*

The only answer: *It depends.*

The working assumptions we have used for generations to understand "how things work" and to design new businesses, tools, products, and services are imprecise at best and harmful at worst. As a result, new approaches focused on better understanding human complexities and mitigating past harms have been adopted across fields and industries.

This is evident in many of the disciplines found in and around our newsrooms. Management theory continues the shift away from Frederick Taylor's time-and-movement studies. Economics now recognizes that people do not make perfectly informed and optimized decisions. Software engineering admits the folly of writing hundreds of pages of requirements before any work begins. Design argues for the need to talk to users first. And journalism itself reckons with its historic lack of attention to audiences generally and underrepresented communities in particular.

As we will see throughout the book, the same thinking has infused psychology, sociology, and marketing. As market-based competition increases and technology empowers and changes consumer behavior, understanding customers becomes more critical to business success.

A theory of knowledge

Epistemology is the study of how we know what we know and how we prove it. It explores the process of separating justified belief from opinion, creating knowledge using methods of logic, science, perception, and attestation.

For journalism, ascertaining truth is centered on methods of objectivity, accuracy, and fairness—the definitions of which are closely debated. For product managers, the process is similar, but the goals are business-focused and more closely identified with the traditional scientific method.

1 Question.
2 Research.
3 Hypothesize.
4 Experiment.
5 Observe.
6 Answer.
7 Explain.

The job of news is to teach a community about itself. The job of news product management is to build organizational knowledge in support of business decisions that enable journalists to do their job.

How we make decisions

Have you watched the TV game show *Who Wants to be a Millionaire?* It was first broadcast in Britain in 1998 and spawned an international franchise. The premise is simple:

1 A contestant is presented with a series of multiple-choice trivia questions and must answer correctly to win a cash prize.
2 After each correct answer, you may leave with the cash or answer the next but more challenging question to multiply the prize value.
3 You have limited opportunities to ask the audience to vote on the answers, ask the host to eliminate two wrong answers, or "phone a friend" who can help you guess.
4 This process is repeated until you win the eponymous one million dollars or get an answer wrong and lose it all.

To describe that as a system:

1 Contestants operate within a universe governed by rules and constraints.
2 They face a set of questions of unknown complexity and domain.
3 Asking for help is often necessary but carries a cost.
4 There is a dynamic and escalating tension between risk and reward.

Every project in news product management inhabits this universe. We bring questions, assumptions, and goals to the table and work to gather evidence and improve the reliability of our answers. In addition, since there is no game show host with a set of neatly arranged index cards, we must also discover and define some of the questions ourselves.

To put this in **Rumsfeldian** terms:

- There are things we know and can answer.
- There are things we know we don't know, and we must research.
- There are things we don't know that we don't know and can only even discover to ask through the research process.

Though that formulation was popularized by the late U.S. Defense Secretary Donald Rumsfeld, the concept appears to have been a previous industry staple.[3] Focusing on "things we don't know to ask yet" is critical for product managers. Our personal and organizational biases cause blind spots that can lead a project to eventual failure. Product management aims not to perfect decision-making but to reduce uncertainty and limit the number of unexamined assumptions.

The cost of choice

The upkeep of a human brain is expensive. It takes 20% of our oxygen supply and calories to keep it running. And if we think too much, the brain gets tired, and performance suffers. But we make thousands of decisions daily, and as product managers, decisions are the job. So, to conserve energy, the brain takes shortcuts when it can—which is almost always.

Consider a grocery store aisle containing 200 breakfast cereal brands, sizes, shapes, and colors. How do you decide which box to purchase? Classical economics suggests we **optimize** the choice by evaluating each item on each shelf for taste, ingredients, price, and quality to make a perfectly informed choice. A more realistic assumption is we form a preference and then repeatedly purchase the same brand. **Satisficing** is what behavioral economists call our tendency to rely on past experiences and "good enough" information to limit the time and effort we spend making decisions.

The investment is related to the cost of the choice. We will spend more time and effort researching a new car than a new cereal. But no matter the deliberation, our decisions are ultimately influenced by our reliance on **heuristics**— the shortcuts the brain takes in the process.

Stories are patterns

A story is the most potent force in the universe. A good one can change people's minds or move them to action, while a bad one may paralyze them with lies. The brain loves that stories follow a predictable pattern with a beginning, middle, and end populated with a plot, conflict, action, and characters.

We can recall and retell stories better when they align with details we know from prior learning or personal experience. That sense of "connecting the dots" between old and new information helps us make sense of the story and our world.

Even simple narratives make the brain happy. What is "x" in the examples below?

1, 3, x
2, 4, x

You likely had no problem predicting that *5* and *6* were the third chapters in those short stories. Our ability to recognize patterns is a superpower. But it comes with a set of evil twins: Assumptions and stereotyping.

If the stories above were instead *1,3,3* and *2,4,8* you would wonder why and find it harder to explain. But perhaps we guessed wrong, and the story was "multiply the first two numbers." That is a different but still memorable pattern.

Other times, the pattern we learn to match against are wrong. Do you prefer "even" over "odd" numbers? Probably not, but the shortcuts the brain has learned and acted on often result in similar distortions, including stereotyping and hundreds of other biases that weaken our decision-making.

Patterns that distort

We always plan to make good decisions but are led astray by our somewhat lazy brains. A **cognitive bias** is when these mistakes arise systematically through errors of attention, perception, memory, or understanding.

This differs from a logical fallacy, an attempt to distract or appeal to emotion rather than argue the merits of a case. You might hear arguments such as:

- **The Bandwagon**—Local publishers are investing in Facebook video strategy, so we should also.
- **The Appeal to Authority**—Amazon's "buy now" button is orange; ours should also be.
- **The Straw Man**—Unless everyone in town subscribes, the redesign of our newsletter subscription form is not a success.

Cognitive bias, on the other hand, is the personalized distortion of reality that occurs when we overly rely on patterns of experience or simply fail to correct common trapdoors in our cognitive processes. Because the bias operates subconsciously, it can be challenging to recognize or avoid.

If you flip a coin nine times and count heads or tails:

T T T T T T T T T

What are the odds the 10th flip will be heads? Statistically, every chance is 50/50, regardless of the previous string of results. But the **gambler's fallacy** leads us to believe an "H" is due.

What if you were offered $150 today or $180 next month? Which would you pick? For most people, **hyperbolic discounting** incentivizes a short-term gain, even if waiting increases the payoff.

There are hundreds of similar examples:

- **Anchoring**—Our decision-making is strongly influenced by the first option presented in an array of options, especially if the choices are numeric.
- **Confirmation bias**—We tend to favor facts or ideas that align with our existing beliefs and experiences. So, we support the status quo to the detriment of new ideas.
- **Fundamental attribution error**—The benefit-of-the-doubt we give to our own actions and motivations without extending the same charity to others. This is a constant tension in any collaborative work.
- **Groupthink**—Our natural inclination to accept the majority opinion in a social setting to avoid conflict.
- **Ikea effect**—We form an emotional connection to technology projects we help build. This can be seen in teams preferring internally developed solutions vs. standardized solutions bought "off the shelf."
- **Sunk cost**—There is an often-irrational interest in investing continued resources in a failing project simply because of previous or ongoing investment. It is sometimes described as "throwing good money after bad."
- **Survivor bias**—When asking visitors to our websites their opinion of the journalism, design, and usability, the answers will inevitably be biased in favor of those with at least a moderately positive opinion. Those with an inherently negative opinion are not in the sampled group.

Systems thinking

Many product managers are systems thinkers. They solve problems first by perceiving the issue as existing within a broader series of interdependent components related by cause and effect.

Consider the control systems of the first airplanes. These were complicated machines, but the pilot flew by the use of simple mechanical levers directly connected to the wing and tail control surfaces. Pushing a pedal pulled a chain that moved the rudder left or right. If the rudder doesn't work, there are only a few connections and hinges to check and fix.

Today, commercial airliners are "fly-by-wire," with the control path almost entirely digital. When the pilot steps on a pedal, it sends an electronic signal to the flight computer, which relays a command to an electric actuator in the plane's tail that moves the rudder. If something is not working, all you can do is reboot the computer or call tech support.

It is far more difficult to intuitively comprehend the many components involved in the fly-by-wire signal: Pedals, sensors, flight computer hardware and software, wires running through the fuselage, actuators, the mechanical components of the rudder, even more sensors, and how those elements interact in a real-world environment including the performance of the plane at different weights, altitudes, and weather.

Successful evaluation of a complex system requires a fundamental understanding of each component's role and the dependencies it has for input and output signals. Adding to the challenge, many components are bundles of complex sub-systems built by domain-specific experts and then assembled, operated, and maintained by separate teams of experts.

Managing complex problems

There are four types of systems:

1 A **simple system** is stable, well-defined, and routine, with a rules-based path to the correct answer and a clear boundary between the system and the external environment. Consider a maze that exists within a single building and consists of a straight hallway. And you have a map.
2 A **complicated system** can also be well-defined with a set of known rules. But it will have multiple paths to the correct answer, and initial choices will influence later options. Like a building with a maze that has a single front door but multiple hallways of varying lengths, only some of which lead to the exit. Optimizing a solution requires trial and error and a map to document the answer.
3 **Complex systems**, on the other hand, can't be perfectly described by a set of rules. They lack well-defined boundaries and may interact unpredictably with external systems. Consider how to navigate a maze that traverses between buildings and fields with no clear paths, multiple entry and exit points, and only a partial map.
4 **Wicked systems** are entirely novel challenges that resist definition. Identifying boundaries between internal and external components is difficult, and the system itself may be in constant flux. Imagine a maze of unknown size and design with no walls, no map, and constantly shifting entry points, paths, and exits.

Understanding the level of complexity in a problem or project is essential to correctly understand the time and effort required for a solution, the level of confidence we might expect of an answer, and the tools we will want to apply in the effort.

Division of labor

In Adam Smith's 1776 *The Wealth of Nations,* he studied a pin factory, a typical manufacturer of the day:

> *One man draws out the wire; another straights it; a third cuts it; a fourth points it; a fifth grinds it at the top for receiving the head; to make the head requires two or three distinct operations...*[4]

Smith identified 18 different steps in creating a straight pin, sometimes performed by 18 different men. Describing this arrangement—each employee performs one small and distinct job within a larger process—he believed it a great efficiency. Workers needed no expert knowledge aside from the execution of a single repetitive task and could produce 90% more pins than if each had worked alone.

Smith's example of an early assembly line offers one solution to the challenge of collaborative work. A single pin-making entrepreneur requires only wire, tools, skill, and customers. But to make and sell more pins requires more staff. Five employees working together, each handling a different step in the production line, will increase productivity but at the cost of time spent managing the process. If the person cutting the wire measures incorrectly, the entire production line might be slowed or stopped.

Managers standardize each work process and train staff to follow documented procedures to reduce the risk of error or misunderstanding. In Henry Mintzberg's conception, this formalization evolves over phases:[5]

- **Mutual adjustment** is an informal collaboration possible only when a team is small enough to easily share and understand the precise details of each other's work.
- **Direct supervision** is the first step in the division of labor and may include a manager who shares in and oversees the work.
- **Job descriptions** further clarify the distinctions between employee roles and responsibilities, including guidance on tasks and processes.
- **Detailed specifications** standardize and dictate relevant elements of the work, including the required qualities of a finished product.
- **Rules and policies** that dictate employee behavior and activities, such as hours worked, safety procedures, and guidance for purchasing goods or hiring and training staff.

This formalization reduces the need for constant hands-on management oversight but creates a clear division between "thinking" and "doing" within the organization. Among Smith's pin-makers, extreme specialization results and the skill and creativity once required of a craftsperson now resides in a manager who directs every task.

The division of labor is at the heart of modern organizational design. In a large factory, the president hires vice presidents to oversee various specialties, who in turn hire directors and managers who employ staff to work the assembly line. In this traditional command-and-control structure, decisions are made at the top, and tasks are handed out to subordinates to implement with limited autonomy. This was the model of Ford's automobile factories.

Worker specialization and hierarchical management structures can be an efficient way to coordinate organizational activities. **Delegation of authority** occurs, but most decision-making still rests with what Mintzberg calls the "strategic apex," typically executive leadership. And this makes sense when the business environment is stable, the decision-making process is effectively formalized, and the production process is routinized.

But in many industries, change is now a constant. The mass production and distribution of consumer goods that began in the 1920s dramatically increased competition, necessitating the development of new products and efficient manufacturing. So instead of a stable and routinized workplace, we now manage continuous business, technical, and process innovation cycles that require ongoing reassessment and readjustment of our organizations.

Coordination of work

Mintzberg[6] opens *The Structuring of Organizations* with a parable of the pottery maker who grows her business from a basement studio to a large conglomerate headquartered in a downtown skyscraper. At each step, Ms. Raku faces the familiar dilemma: The effort required to manage the work increases as her staff grows. While mutual adjustment is practical in small groups, collaboration becomes exponentially more difficult in larger teams. This is because an effective division of labor relies on close coordination between and among specialties.

Creating a finished ceramic takes many steps over a week, including preparing the clay, shaping it on the wheel, drying it, firing it in a kiln, glazing it for color or pattern, and then firing and cooling again. The team must plan to optimize the limited availability of the kiln while also completing customer orders promptly and correctly.

Two employees can easily sustain a conversation that coordinates (mutually adjusts) their work. But seven employees, each engaged in six distinct conversations, create an unsustainable number of communication paths (Figure 3.2). As Ms. Raku's business grew, she promoted Mrs. Bisque to studio manager to directly supervise and coordinate production.

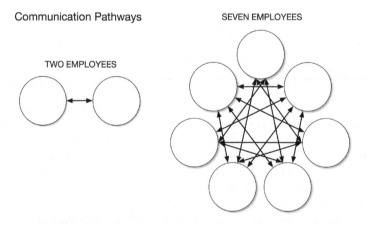

Figure 3.2 As collaborators join a project, the lines of communication multiply rapidly, making it difficult for individuals to manage the flow of information.[7]

In the pottery studio's organizational design, the growth of the business is constrained by the ability to manage the information needs required to coordinate the interdependencies between increasingly specialized roles.

Mrs. Bisque, working with two potters, a glazer, and a kiln operator, directly coordinates the team's work. Making too many or too few pots or applying the wrong glaze is expensive and wastes production time. So, Mrs. Bisque needs to juggle supplies, inventory, staff schedules, customer orders, and quality control to keep the studio running smoothly. Expertise with pottery skills and processes is a requirement, but the job itself concerns information management.

Organizations exist to process information

The more formalized and top-down an organization is, the less able it is to react to changes in the environment. A strict hierarchical structure hampers collaboration, slowing information sharing between departments.[8] And, as managers have less specific expertise and current knowledge about the work within the business than their subordinates, detail and nuance are lost as information travels upward. Organizational design is an effort to optimize **knowledge transfer** through the hierarchy to inform decision-making.[9]

Procter & Gamble's brand marketing process and Toyota's Production System were designed to shift decision-making to lower levels in the organization, closer to the daily work and customer needs. This delegation of authority flattens organizational structures and redefines job roles, enabled by broader access to information technologies and tools.

Journalism is a case study in this shift. Editorial and business teams have traditionally been kept at arm's length to maintain a polite journalistic distance from profit-driven motivations. But editors and producers are now often concerned with analyzing audience analytics almost hourly. Advertising teams coordinate revenue strategies with former print circulation departments known as "Audience." And all three groups are intertwined in support of subscription and membership initiatives. These once largely independent departments are now in an ongoing process of "reconfiguring and renegotiating their digital existence."[10]

These reorganizations focus on three goals:

1 Adapting to the demands of new and emerging market needs.
2 Optimizing the development and delivery of products and services.
3 Reducing uncertainty in decision-making.

Boundary-crossing behaviors

In disrupted industries, the business lessons that won the past may fail to secure the future. *The Encyclopedia Britannica* was unprepared for the rise of the free web—and Wikipedia—and after 244 years of expertise collecting and organizing authoritative facts, it published its last print volume in 2012.

As an organization reorients to new challenges, previously shared understandings of vision, goals, and tactics fracture. To cope with the uncertainty, employees will seek new sources of information to make sense of the changing environment. Often, this behavior includes informal discussions with other departments to gather insight into a project's status or corporate goals.

This boundary-crossing activity—reaching across internal and external organizational barriers to gather information—is a standard work practice and a foundational characteristic of product management.

Even in stable environments, organizational silos—between departments or expert domains—create barriers to knowledge transfer. Specialization and division of labor requires collaborative teams to exchange information and coordinate work. Imperfect knowledge sharing can inhibit collaboration and innovation by introducing uncertainty and risk in daily actions and decisions.

Communication implicitly carries a risk of misunderstanding or partial understanding. But knowledge transfer in a business also grapples with the domain-specific differences inherent in team boundaries. The structural complications to shared understanding include:[11]

- **Novelty**—Changes in the environment, including consumer needs and technological innovations, require the business to assess its current knowledge base and discover and integrate new understandings into the corporate culture. These changes may not be of equal concern to every team.
- **Dependence**—The more significant the mutual reliance between teams, the more each is constrained from optimizing its practices in reaction to novelty without close coordination.
- **Difference**—Increasing specialization creates divergent knowledge between groups. Each knows more about its own work but inherently less about others. This makes integrating new knowledge in situations of close interdependence challenging.

Additionally, as knowledge transfer is necessary when the current understanding between teams has diverged, the difficulty in regaining a shared understanding is related to the scope and cause of the misalignment:[12]

- **Syntactic**—A simple conversation may enable knowledge transfer when the two sides share an expertise, understanding of goals, interdependencies, and priorities.
- **Semantic**—As new challenges emerge, one side adapts more quickly, weakening the shared understanding of priorities and interdependencies. Goals remain aligned, but knowledge transfer may now require an exploration of recently acquired knowledge and of the shared context.
- **Pragmatic**—Team interests may now conflict, requiring a renegotiation of priorities and a compromise or surrender of some individual team goals.

A theory of product management

Product management requires a multi-disciplinary understanding of the internal and external faces of the organization. It is charged with bringing the voice of the reader to internal deliberations and bridging the gaps between internal teams as they renegotiate priorities in processes while considering constantly evolving business and consumer demands.

While formalization of work processes and division of labor is necessary as a business grows and adapts to new conditions, structure and hierarchy also constrain our ability to react effectively to change.

Product management works around this by crossing boundaries, facilitating information sharing, and helping internal and external experts align their understanding and coordination.

For discussion

- What is the balance between perceived value and effort in the design of a user experience?
- If we "don't know" that we "don't know" something—what is the first step?
- In your opinion, which cognitive bias is most likely to distort business decisions?
- What is required to reduce the complexity of a problem?
- What barriers exist to collaboration between departments or domain expertise in an organization?

Learn more

- *The Order of Things: An Archaeology of the Human Sciences*—Michel Foucault (1970). Random House.
- *Systems Bible: The Beginner's Guide to Systems Large and Small*—John Gall. (2003). General Systemantics Press.
- *Thoughtless Acts?: Observations on Intuitive Design*—Jane Fulton Suri & IDEO. (2005). Chronicle Books.
- *Thinking in Systems: A Primer* – Donella H. Meadows (2008). Chelsea Green Publishing.
- *The Storytelling Animal: How Stories Make Us Human*—Jonathan Gottschall. (2013). Mariner Books.
- *Misbehaving: The Making of Behavioral Economics*—Richard Thaler (2016). W.W. Norton & Company.
- *The Extended Mind: The Power of Thinking Outside the Brain*—Annie Murphy Paul. (2021). Mariner Books.
- *Subtract: The Untapped Science of Less*—Leidy Klotz. (2021). Flatiron Books.
- *Journalism Research That Matters*—Valerie Bélair-Gagnon & Nikki Usher (eds.) (2021). Oxford University Press.

Notes

1 Carey, J. W. (1978). A Plea for the University Tradition. *Journalism Quarterly*, 55(4), 846–855.
2 Kiesow, D. (2021). The Business of Digital News: Understanding the Cross-Functional Orchestra. In V. Bélair-Gagnon & N. Usher (Eds.), *Journalism Research That Matters* (pp. 131–136). Oxford University Press.
3 Newhouse, J. (1982). A Sporty Game I-Betting The Company. *The New Yorker.* https://www.newyorker.com/magazine/1982/06/14/a-sporty-game-i-betting-the-company
4 Smith, A. (2012). *An Inquiry into the Nature and Causes of the Wealth of Nations.* Wordsworth editions.
5 Mintzberg, H. (1979). *The Structuring of Organizations.* Macmillan Education UK. https://doi.org/10.1007/978-1-349-20317-8_23
6 Ibid.
7 Ibid., 1–2.
8 Simon, H. A. (1947). *Administrative Behavior. A Study of Decision-Making Processes in Administrative Organization.* New York: Free Press.
9 Grant, R. M. (1996). Toward a Knowledge-Based Theory of the Firm. *Strategic Management Journal*, 17(S2), 109–122. https://doi.org/10.1002/smj.4250171110
10 Kiesow, D. (2021). The Business of Digital News: Understanding the Cross-Functional Orchestra. In V. Bélair-Gagnon & N. Usher (Eds.), *Journalism Research That Matters* (pp. 131–136). Oxford University Press. https://doi.org/10.1093/0s0/9780197538470.003.0010
11 Carlile, P. R., & Rebentisch, E. S. (2003). Into the Black Box: The Knowledge Transformation Cycle. *Management Science*, 49(9), 1180–1195. https://doi.org/10.1287/mnsc.49.9.1180.16564
12 Carlile, P. R. (2004). Transferring, Translating, and Transforming: An Integrative Framework for Managing Knowledge Across Boundaries. *Organization Science*, 15(5), 555–568. https://doi.org/10.1287/orsc.1040.0094

4   Theories of innovation

In this chapter

- How we talk about new ideas.
- Innovation among the corn stalks.
- A bias for the next new thing.
- Understanding why innovations are adopted.
- Progress with a concern for the public good.

Innovation has drawn the interest of scholars across disciplines for more than a century.

Economists, beginning with Joseph Schumpeter in the 1920s, have studied it as the process of creating new commercial value in the marketplace. This perspective has focused on business processes that optimize and accelerate the transformation of ideas into profitable products.[1]

Anthropologists considered that cultural change in "primitive" societies was caused by external forces imposed by more "modern" external influences. That archaic view has since been replaced by a quest to understand which characteristics enable a society or group to be innovative.[2]

Sociologists are interested in how innovation and society affect each other. Several relevant schools of thought have emerged, especially in rural sociology and science and technology studies.

To flatten those distinctions: Economists are interested in business outcomes, anthropologists in how different cultures practice innovation, and sociologists in how systems within society interact with the process and products of innovation. All three traditions have been adapted by product managers in need of theories and methods to do our job.

The business of innovation

In widespread use, innovation may mean a new or exciting idea or product. But in business, a new product idea is "innovative" only when it aligns with an organizational capability and a consumer need.

DOI: 10.4324/9781003154785-6

A more technically precise usage, to paraphrase the International Standards Organization (in ISO 56000 3.1.1 Innovation management—Fundamentals and vocabulary),[3] innovation is:

> *A new or changed product, service, process, model, or method that creates or redistributes value by or for an individual or organization.*

In business, the "creation of value" is especially important as, either directly or indirectly, that is how revenue is created. But, to the disappointment of many entrepreneurs, having a "good" idea is often not enough to assure the long-term success of either the idea or the business built around it.

Two common examples:

- Betamax was a technically superior videotape format, but VHS won the consumer battle before DVDs, and streaming video supplanted it.
- The DVORAK keyboard employs an efficient key layout, the result of letter frequency and hand-motion studies. But QWERTY had an **early-mover** advantage and still prevails—though many people now type exclusively with their thumbs on a smartphone.

In each example, the cause of the commercial failure is complex. But more than 300,000 new products hit store shelves each year, according to innovation guru Clayton Christensen, and 90% fail.[4] We want to know why.

Turning ideas into products and services is a full-time job—and a primary focus of product managers. But carrying even a useful and valuable idea to market is only half of the work.

Once a product is released, there are additional hurdles to adoption, including community attitudes, perceived value, and individual awareness. Product thinking will try to minimize those gaps with research and marketing before and after launch. But sometimes, as with Betamax and DVORAK, an innovation is too late (or too early) to market or is surpassed by a better (or seemingly worse) alternative. And sometimes, despite seemingly favorable circumstances, a product never catches on for reasons that remain a mystery.

Not knowing things—uncertainty—is the enemy of business. We improve our decisions not by demanding perfect knowledge but by recognizing when even a slightly better understanding can lead to better results. For product development, we want to understand how innovations spread in a society so:

1 We can use this knowledge to better inform our research before building a product.
2 We can better understand and improve the adoption of our products after they are launched.

It may surprise those of us who think of innovation as almost inherently digital, but in the U.S., the academic study of how new ideas are diffused and adopted grew up in the cornfields of Iowa.

New corn in Iowa

In 1941, Bryce Ryan and Neal Gross were sociologists at Iowa State University in Ames, Iowa, studying when and why local farmers had adopted a newly developed variety of corn. In only ten years, the engineered "hybrid" seed had been planted in 75% of Iowa's corn fields. The two researchers wanted to understand the pattern of adoption over that time.

As a **land grant university**, the school's Agricultural Cooperative Extension Service did (and still does) play a central role in communicating and supporting farmers in adopting new technologies and methods designed to improve productivity. By technical standards, the new hybrid seed was far superior to the prior "open pollination" seed.

An open-pollination crop uses natural mechanisms, like wind or bees. The farmer retains some of the year's crop to plant the following season but lacks control over the quality of the seed. The newly engineered seed was developed to reduce that risk by assuring a more consistent and robust crop. And it did deliver a 20% improvement in yield, better drought resistance, and a strong stalk amenable to mechanical harvesting.[5] But it required that new seeds be purchased from the manufacturer every season.[6]

The prevailing theory at the time suggested that adoption of the innovation by farmers would be a "rational" economic decision for several reasons:

- The noted improvement in crop yield and drought resistance.
- The financial stress of the Great Depression made a less risky crop desirable.
- The seed is easily integrated into current planting and harvesting practices.
- The availability of scientific and observed evidence proved its high quality.

While those advantages had resulted in the rapid growth of the new product, adoption had been slower than expected, and by 1941, 25% of Iowa's corn acreage had not migrated.

To understand this dynamic, Ryan and Gross interviewed 259 farmers in two Iowa communities to track when each adopted the new seed and how the decision was informed and made. The researchers also collected a variety of personal and professional characteristics that might explain interest or resistance to innovation.

They found that while knowledge of the new seed was widespread by 1931, actual adoption trailed awareness by seven years.[7] The pair identified variables that were correlated with early adoption, including educational attainment, "trips to Des Moines,"[8] and leadership in community groups. But those are also proxies for wealth, and comfort with the financial risk of experimentation.

Even among early adopters, the researchers found cautious innovators. Farmers would often test the new seed in a small section of their fields in the first year and gradually increase the acreage over the following seasons. These early small-scale trials seemed common sense, but surprisingly, later cohorts followed a similar though compressed pattern of cautious adoption. To Ryan and Gross, this behavior appeared somewhat irrational. They believed farmers who conservatively resisted innovation needed to better "emancipate themselves" from "traditional rural techniques."[9]

Diffusion of innovation

Everett Rogers grew up on a farm in rural Iowa with a father who had been a reluctant adopter of the hybrid seed studied by Ryan and Gross.[10]

After receiving his bachelor's degree in agriculture at the University of Iowa and spending two years in the U.S. Army, Rogers returned to school for a graduate degree in Sociology. He was soon tasked with interviewing farmers in Collins, Iowa, to understand how and why they had adopted various agricultural innovations.[11] The earlier experience on his family's farm made Rogers suspicious of assumptions that the adoption of innovations was a strictly rational economic decision.[12]

His research led to the publication of *Diffusion of Innovations* in 1962. In the book, Rogers describes the adoption of innovation as a process of communication, over time, in a social system, of a "practice or object" perceived as new.[13]

In other words, adopting a new idea or product is not done with a mathematical calculation of profit and loss but with a more complex social calculation that involves the "exchange of ideas, persuasion, and personal influence."[14]

Rogers' examination of successful and failed adoptions of innovation has been a foundation for academic research and entered the public lexicon. Most famous is his classification of consumers on a continuum from innovators to laggards (Figure 4.1).

Rogers specialized in rural sociology and the adoption of health and agricultural innovations in smaller communities. In the case illustration that leads off the book, he describes an effort to encourage the adoption of boiled drinking water in a Peruvian village in the early 1950s.

A public health service worker lived in the village for two years and encouraged various sanitary improvements, including boiled drinking water. But the

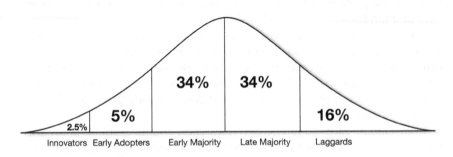

Figure 4.1 Everett Rogers found the adoption of innovations by a population resembled a Bell curve distribution.

practice failed to be adopted, not because it was a radical idea, but because it was not effectively communicated, did not convince what we might now call "influencers," and generally did not align with the social and cultural expectations of the community.[15]

That theme is repeated throughout Rogers' research and in many subsequent innovation studies. Proposing a good idea is insufficient to persuade an organization to build it or the public to adopt it.

Finding and forgetting the cure for scurvy

Before the 1800s, scurvy, caused by a lack of vitamin C in the diet, was a danger on long ocean voyages, killing as many as two million sailors in 400 years.[16] More than half of Vasco da Gama's 160 men died of the disease on the voyage around the Cape of Good Hope in 1497.[17]

In 1601, a British captain also rounding the Cape of Good Hope fed three teaspoons of lemon juice daily to the crew of one of his five ships. Few cases arose among that lucky group, while many on the other crews fell ill. But the innovation failed to be broadly adopted.

Almost 150 years later, in 1747, James Lind, a physician on the HMS Salisbury familiar with the 1601 experiment, designed a controlled clinical trial, administering six different treatments for scurvy during a voyage. Those who received citrus recovered. But the innovation again failed to be broadly adopted.

Finally, in 1795, the British Navy mandated vitamin C treatment on its ships, a year after Lind's death and almost 200 years after the 1601 experiment.

Of note, when French colonizers led by Jacques Cartier camped near present-day Québec City during a harsh winter in 1536, they and the inhabiting Iroquois fell ill with scurvy receiving a traditional cure based on a conifer tree, possibly the white cedar. The French did not widely share the secret, nor did they widely adopt it themselves.[18]

How innovations are adopted

History is littered with "good" ideas that failed or never got the chance to succeed. Rogers described five attributes of an innovation that influence the rate of adoption:

1 **Relative advantage**—Is the new idea perceived as an improvement over the currently available solutions?
2 **Compatibility**—Is the new idea perceived as aligning with the values and needs of the user?
3 **Complexity**—Is the new idea perceived as easy to understand and use?
4 **Trialability**— Is it possible for new adopters to experiment with the new idea with minimal risk?
5 **Observability**—Are the results of others' use visible by later adopters?

He also described the decision to adopt a new idea as a process of five stages, many of which are very similar to the traditional marketing funnel:

1 **Knowledge**—Becoming aware of the existence of an innovation.
2 **Persuasion**—When an initial favorable or unfavorable impression is formed.
3 **Decision**—A choice to accept or reject the innovation.
4 **Implementation**—When an individual or organization utilizes the innovations.
5 **Confirmation**—When use of the innovation reinforces the initial decision, or new conflicting information is discovered that raises the possibility of error.

Innovation as progress

The development of an innovation is often, though not always, a commercial effort. But studies of the practice are often funded or undertaken by groups interested in spreading new ideas for direct or indirect profit.

For the 1943 hybrid seed corn research, the University of Iowa and Cooperative Agricultural Extension Service was motivated to develop and popularize improvements to food production in support of local farmers. But the very nature of the university's interest imposed a **pro-innovation bias** on the research. Ryan and Gross aimed not to understand the societal costs or benefits of hybrid corn seed but to understand why the commercial innovation was not adopted more quickly.

This bias influenced the interpretation of their original data and many subsequent innovation studies. In discussing early adopters, the researchers labeled the group "leaders" while describing late adopters as "conservative beyond all demands of reasonable business methods." And the researchers expressed further disdain, writing that the motivation of the late adopters must be simply "fear of the new."[19] Even Rogers was to categorize the extremes as "innovators" and "laggards," implicitly favoring and valorizing the former. Applying judgmental labels is a bias that discounts any potentially rational and insightful motivations for reluctance. And it is in understanding such concerns that we gain insights to improve the innovation and better serve the intended community.

Innovation bias in tomatoes

Jim Hightower's *Hard Tomatoes, Hard Times* took a critical eye to the innovation bias he saw imposed on farmers in California. The book, published in 1972, critiqued the land grant university and cooperative extension service systems that had prompted Everett Rogers' interest in hybrid seed corn adoption.

Hightower argued that state universities focused too much on agricultural productivity and not enough on the social impacts of modernization and failed to consider the negative consequences of the machine-enabled "agricultural revolution."[20]

He pointed to the rise in mechanized tomato harvesting, an innovation that resulted in increased production and cheaper produce but required the development of new varieties of firmer tomatoes capable of surviving the picking. He argued researchers did not consider that mechanization would eliminate thousands of jobs and drive many farmers to discontinue the crop due to the capital investments required to compete. Hightower worried these changes benefitted larger corporate farms at the expense of small, independent, and minority farmers, as well as farm workers.[21]

While separated by 50 years and 100 miles, Hightower's complaints about innovations deployed in the Central Valley of California are not dissimilar to current criticisms of the big tech platforms, including Amazon, Apple, Facebook, and Google, and emerging technologies such as artificial intelligence. Innovation chased without regard for the broader public good creates **negative externalities**—commercial profit at the cost of societal harm.

Reinvention in innovation

This perspective that "innovation is always progress" is common in business but unproductive for product managers. As feminist scholar Cheris Kramarae wrote, most people embrace change but "want to help make the decisions," not just have them imposed by external agents.[22]

Rogers joined critics in recognizing that consumers have more influence in the innovation process than just a binary choice of adoption or refusal. **Reinvention** considers that new products are not a perfect fit in every context and might be modified by users upon adoption.[23] This modification may be a physical change to the product, the integration of it with other tools and systems, or a partial adoption that sets aside specific features and functions. In many newsrooms, the content management system is a popular object of scorn for a perceived lack of usability. Journalists often work around it, preferring to write in cloud-based tools like Google Docs before copy-pasting text into the CMS. User-designed modifications like this often highlight dissatisfactions that can inform future product improvements.

While reinvention admits users have a voice in the process of innovation and adoption, it allows it only late in the conversation. This is still a **deterministic** view—one that sees innovation as a linear and mostly one-way process. Instead, innovation is an ongoing negotiation with the inventor and society **co-constructing** new ideas and products.

The winding path of innovation

The story of innovation is often told as one of inevitability. We learn that Thomas Edison discovered the lightbulb in a flash of genius and went on to illuminate the world. But others invented the electric light prior to Edison. The race was to commercialization, requiring a complex interplay of technology, process, materials, expertise, and cost. Even for Edison's team, it took 2,773 failed attempts, competition against, and collaboration with other inventors to succeed.

The history of any technology is only inevitable and linear when seen in retrospect. But that perspective blinds us to the origins and influences that enabled success. The simple view is suitable for grade school history books but not for professional innovators who must understand and navigate the complexity of real-world projects without the benefit of knowing the answers in advance.

Innovation as intra-group problem solving

A founder of the theory of Social Construction of Technology, Wiebe Bijker documented the complex path the bicycle followed to success in Victorian-era England. In the 1880s, the now-standard two-wheeled model was viewed as just one of many divergent and competitive possible solutions. Only in retrospect was it anointed a winning innovation, with other early alternatives largely forgotten.[24]

Bijker elegantly traces this history, identifying the successful and failed experiments and the influence different interest groups exerted on the design of the machine over 30 years.

The first "Ordinary" bike, patented in 1870, had a four-foot-tall wheel in front and a 30-inch wheel in back. This left the rider sitting precariously high, with both mounting and balance a challenge. The design "worked," as it was fast and well-suited to rough roads. But it only befitted a segment of the population: Athletic, upper-class men with a tolerance for risk and injury. Social norms relegated women to tricycles, which had limitations and safety risks but allowed "lady-like" dresses on the roads.

Innovation is influenced by the tension between social groups with different needs or preferred solutions. As pneumatic tires and chain drives were developed and integrated into the symmetrically sized "safety bicycle," the solutions preferred by men and women generally aligned: Speed, stability, safety, and attire.

As these groups developed agreement on solutions for the size and design of wheels, the frame geometry, and the drive mechanism—the conflict and variability around those questions ended. This alignment of solutions brought **closure** and **stability** to the product's design, ushering in the arrival of the modern bicycle.

This constructivist mode of analysis consists of four steps:[25]

1 Define the artifact.
2 Identify all relevant social groups.
3 Understand the relevance of meaning to the artifact held by different groups.
4 Define the problems the artifact causes or solves for each group.

This is also a method of human-centered design. To create rather than extract community value, we must understand the needs of all impacted populations—not just those with political power or the ability to pay directly for our products.

Anti-cyclists influenced the development of the safety bicycle, enabling the development of an enduringly popular product. And in the case of Hightower's tomatoes—farmers and consumers are relevant groups, but so are farm workers likely to lose their jobs to mechanization. Product managers should believe in "do no harm" and work to avoid magnifying inequities already present in society.

News product management and innovation

Google describes its innovation portfolio strategy as:[26]

- 70% of our projects are dedicated to our core business.
- 20% of our projects are related to our core business.
- 10% of our projects are unrelated to our core business.

This allocation of resources is common in mature industries.[27] Most of our attention (70%) should be on not just sustaining but improving our core products and services. The middle 20% can be considered **adjacent innovation** with relatively low risk. The last 10% is for higher risk efforts at research & development in search of entirely new business opportunities.

Within that portfolio, each area of the business can be a target for innovation:

1 Products and Service.
2 Process.
3 Business model.
4 Organizational structure.

Most often, innovation efforts of any scope will cross those somewhat arbitrary boundaries. They are pliable and can be further elaborated to address the distinct needs and opportunities in journalism:[28]

1 Reporting/storytelling.
2 Audience engagement.
3 Technology/product.
4 Distribution.
5 Business.
6 Leadership/management.
7 Organization.
8 People and culture.

Disruptive innovation

Though uncommon in actual practice, disruptive innovation holds a singular fascination in popular culture. The theory, developed by Harvard professor Clayton Christensen, describes the process by which the producers of existing products and services initially scoff at and are then supplanted by newer and initially less expensive competition.

Disruption is distinguished from the more common forms of innovation because it creates a new business or market not initially recognized by incumbents.

When Apple introduced its first computer in 1976, the machine looked like a hobbyist's toy compared to the more powerful, expensive mainframes in use by big business. Before Apple, other personal computers had been developed and sold, usually with some assembly required and in relatively small volumes.[29]

IBM's domination of the mainframe hardware and software market in the 1960s and '70s[30] led to ongoing antitrust concerns and lawsuits. But by 1984, sales of personal computers surpassed mainframes[31] as the smaller and more affordable devices became ubiquitous at home and in the office.

Similar patterns of disruption have followed: The iPhone, initially considered a competitor for Blackberry or Motorola phones, turned out to be a disruptive force in the personal computer market.

Netflix, once a niche provider of a DVD-by-mail service and a competitor to rental providers such as Blockbuster, is now a disruptor of movie theaters and cable TV channels like HBO.

And Wikipedia, the crowd-sourced go-to reference guide with 10 billion English-language page views monthly, disrupted other physical and online encyclopedias—including Nupedia, a peer-reviewed project Wikipedia was originally designed to supplement.

Disruptive innovation is over-represented in discussions of new products, especially those emerging from Silicon Valley. True disruption—creating a new market and audience with a product that eventually captures a legacy market—is unusual and takes time to develop and be recognized. The news media has been a victim of the disruptive force of the Internet but is not known for causing disruption. News organizations often focus on **core innovation** that improves current products or adjacent innovation, extending distribution into new markets and platforms.

Only in rare cases has a news media company successfully competed with itself. Norwegian publisher Schibsted Media Group created a free classifieds business that dominates Europe but disrupted its own digital newspaper revenues.

Current newsroom experiments with TikTok or email newsletters might develop into self-disrupting innovations. Or, if we consider disruption is defined by a competitor that doesn't appear to be in the same business, could the next challenge come from services like Nextdoor or Facebook developing legitimate news-gathering resources; national media companies such as *Axios* developing local strategies; or non-traditional local newsrooms such as Detroit's *Outlier* or Chicago's *City Bureau* solving community needs in a new way?

In Chapter 6, we will talk about the challenges of managing innovation in journalism. One constraint is that while community information needs are always imperfectly met, they are also relatively stable and non-negotiable as an organizational mission. A newsroom may adopt new distribution channels or niche topics of coverage, but the core objectives of news gathering, reporting, and distribution remain.

Sustaining innovation

Most news product work is spent on projects not considered "innovative." These are sustaining efforts to improve existing products or services for current audiences or customers, including redesigning a website, launching a mobile app, or implementing a new video ad unit. This work also includes editorial initiatives focused on storytelling formats, news-gathering tools and techniques, and audience engagement strategies.

Because **sustaining innovation** is incremental improvement, it can lack the glamor and excitement of working on an entirely new project or platform. But do readers care about "innovation," and should journalists?

Patrick Barwise and Seán Meehan argue consumers seek "generic category benefits" from the products they purchase.[32] For news, these basic expectations include not just the quality of the journalism but of the entire user journey in any channel: Print, digital, video, audio, web, or app.

To unlock the potential value of our work, readers must first:

1 Discover it.
2 Find it usable.
3 Read it.
4 Understand it.

Reader expectations are dashed by flaws at any step in the process: Poor SEO, screen reader incompatibility, excessive page load times, confusing navigation, distracting page design, or poor writing. As digital news veteran Kim Bui said, we get distracted by "shiny object syndrome"[33] and too often chase the new instead of prioritizing audience-focused iterative improvements.

Adjacent innovation

The value of the "new" in news product is often found in adjacent innovation. These products or features include new business models or audiences but are closely related to the organization's core mission. Hiring a new team of audio journalists and launching a daily news-focused podcast is an adjacent innovation. Selling business data and insights to local companies is an adjacent innovation.

The Washington Post's Arc CMS, which it sells to other publishers, takes advantage of the people, skills, and technology the *Post* already has. The Stat-News.com newsroom has a niche focus to attract audiences and revenues distinct from *The Boston Globe's* core coverage. The *South China Morning Post* has a video unit focused on short-form documentaries that appeal to younger viewers. *Handelsblatt* launched a paid newsletter strategy targeting healthcare and real estate professionals.

For discussion

1   How did Everett Rogers' experience growing up on an Iowa farm inform his understanding of the diffusion of innovation?
2   What factors might motivate the behavior of "laggards?"
3   In product management, what is the risk of pro-innovation bias?
4   What role does society have in the development of innovations?

Learn more

- *The Social Shaping of Technology*—Donald MacKenzie & Judy Wajcman (Eds.) (1985). Open University Press.
- *Diffusion of Innovations*—Everett M. Rogers (2003, 5th ed.). The Free Press.
- *Of Bicycles, Bakelites, and Bulbs: Toward a Theory of Sociotechnical Change*—Wiebe E. Bijker (1995). MIT Press.
- *Simply Better: Winning and Keeping Customers by Delivering What Matters Most*—Patrick Barwise & Sean Meehan (2004). Harvard Business School Press.
- *Alone Together: Why We Expect More from Technology and Less From Each Other*—Sherry Turkle (2011). Basic Books.
- *The Innovator's Dilemma: When New Technologies Cause Great Firms to Fail*—Clayton Christensen (2016). Harvard Business Review Press.

Notes

1   Godin, B. (2008). In the Shadow of Schumpeter: W. Rupert Maclaurin and the Study of Technological Innovation. *Minerva*, 46(3), 343–360. https://doi.org/10.1007/s11024-008-9100-4
2   Welz, G. (2003). The Cultural Swirl: Anthropological Perspectives on Innovation. *Global Networks*, 3(3), 255–270. https://doi.org/https://doi.org/10.1111/1471-0374.00061
3   International Organization for Standardization. (n.d.). *Innovation Management—Fundamentals and Vocabulary*. ISO 56000:2020(en). Retrieved March 26, 2023, from https://www.iso.org/obp/ui/#iso:std:iso:56000:ed-1:v1:en
4   Christensen, C. M., Cook, S., & Hall, T. (2005). Marketing Malpractice: The Cause and the Cure. *Harvard Business Review*. https://hbr.org/2005/12/marketing-malpractice-the-cause-and-the-cure
5   Ryan, B., & Gross, N. C. (1950). *Acceptance and Diffusion of Hybrid Corn Seed in Two Iowa Communities*. Agricultural Experiment Station, Iowa State College of Agriculture and Mechanic Arts. https://catalog.hathitrust.org/Record/011455407

6 Ryan, B., & Gross, N. C. (1943). The *Diffusion of Hybrid Seed Corn in Two Iowa Communities. Rural* Sociology, 8(1), 15.
7 Ibid., 17.
8 Ryan, B., & Gross, N. C. (1950). *Acceptance and Diffusion of Hybrid Corn Seed in Two Iowa Communities.* Agricultural Experiment Station, Iowa State College of Agriculture and Mechanic Arts. https://catalog.hathitrust.org/Record/011455407 (p. 700)
9 Ibid., 707.
10 Singhal, A. (2012). Everett M. Rogers, An Intercultural Life: From Iowa Farm Boy to Global Intellectual. *International Journal of Intercultural Relations,* 36, 848–856. https://doi.org/10.1016/j.ijintrel.2012.08.015 (p. 849)
11 Valente, T. W., & Rogers, E. M. (1995). The Origins and Development of the Diffusion of Innovations Paradigm as an Example of Scientific Growth. *Science Communication,* 16(3), 242–273. https://doi.org/10.1177/1075547095016003002
12 Singhal, A. (2012). Everett M. Rogers, An Intercultural Life: From Iowa Farm Boy to Global Intellectual. *International Journal of Intercultural Relations,* 36, 848–856. https://doi.org/10.1016/j.ijintrel.2012.08.015
13 Everett M. Rogers. (1995). *Diffusion of Innovations* (4th ed.). The Free Press.
14 Singhal, A. (2012). Everett M. Rogers, An Intercultural Life: From Iowa Farm Boy to Global Intellectual. *International Journal of Intercultural Relations,* 36, 848–856. https://doi.org/10.1016/j.ijintrel.2012.08.015 (p. 850)
15 Wellin, E. (1955). Water Boiling in a Peruvian Town. In E. Wellin & B. D. Paul (Eds.), *Health, Culture and Community* (pp. 71–103). Russell Sage Foundation New York.
16 Price, C. (2017). *The Age of Scurvy.* Science History Institute. https://www.sciencehistory.org/distillations/the-age-of-scurvy
17 Mosteller, F. (1981). Innovation and Evaluation. *Science,* 211(4485), 881–886. https://doi.org/10.1126/science.6781066
18 Baron, J. H. (2009). Sailors' Scurvy Before and After James Lind – A Reassessment. *Nutrition Reviews,* 67(6), 315–332. https://doi.org/10.1111/j.1753-4887.2009.00205.x
19 Ryan, B., & Gross, N. C. (1950). *Acceptance and Diffusion of Hybrid Corn Seed in Two Iowa Communities.* Agricultural Experiment Station, Iowa State College of Agriculture and Mechanic Arts. https://catalog.hathitrust.org/Record/011455407 (p. 677)
20 Hightower, J. (1972). Hard Tomatoes, Hard Times: Failure of the Land Grant College Complex. *Society,* 10(1), 10–22. https://doi.org/10.1007/BF02695245
21 Ibid.
22 Kramarae, C. (2004). *Technology and Women's Voices: Keeping in Touch.* Routledge & Kegan Paul. http://public.ebookcentral.proquest.com/choice/publicfullrecord.aspx?p=166294
23 Rice, R. E., & Rogers, E. M. (1980). Reinvention in the Innovation Process. *Knowledge,* 1(4), 499–514. https://doi.org/10.1177/107554708000100402
24 Bijker, W. E. (1995). *Of Bicycles, Bakelites, and Bulbs: Toward a Theory of Sociotechnical Change.* MIT Press.
25 Bijker, W., Hughes, T. P., & Pinch, T. (2012). *The Social Construction of Technological Systems: New Directions in the Sociology and History of Technology* (W. E. Bijker, T. P. Hughes, & T. Pinch, Eds.; Anniversary ed). MIT Press.
26 Creating a Culture of Innovation Eight ideas that work at Google. (2014). https://workspace.google.com/intl/en_in/learn-more/creating_a_culture_of_innovation.html
27 Nagji, B., & Tuff, G. (2012). Managing Your Innovation Portfolio. *Harvard Business Review.* https://hbr.org/2012/05/managing-your-innovation-portfolio

28 Posetti, J. (2018). *Time to Step Away from the 'Bright, Shiny Things'? Towards a Sustainable Model of Journalism Innovation in an Era of Perpetual Change.* Reuters Institute for the Study of Journalism. http://ora.ox.ac.uk/objects/uuid:ea046265-9e51-4aa7-af82-105610f3653f

29 Ceruzzi, P. E. (2003). *A History of Modern Computing* (2nd ed.). MIT Press.

30 Ratchford, B. T., & Ford, G. T. (1976). A Study of Prices and Market Shares in the Computer Mainframe Industry. *The Journal of Business,* 49(2), 194–218. http://www.jstor.org/stable/2352248

31 Sanger, D. E. (1984). Bailing out of the Mainframe Industry. *The New York Times.* https://www.nytimes.com/1984/02/05/business/bailing-out-of-the-mainframe-industry.html

32 Barwise, P., & Meehan, S. (2004). *Simply Better: Winning and Keeping Customers by Delivering What Matters Most.* Harvard Business School Press.

33 Posetti, J. (2018). *Time to Step Away from the 'Bright, Shiny Things'? Towards a Sustainable Model of Journalism Innovation in an Era of Perpetual Change.* Reuters Institute for the Study of Journalism. http://ora.ox.ac.uk/objects/uuid:ea046265-9e51-4aa7-af82-105610f3653f

Unit II

Product management in news

5   The business of content

In this chapter

- The market failure of news.
- News as an information good, experience good, and public good.
- The actual "original sin" of digital news.
- The attention economy and aggregation theory.
- The rise and fall of digital revenue strategies.

Stewart Brand is the author of one of the most wildly misunderstood recent proverbs in journalism, "Information wants to be free." It has been used by many to argue that journalism is expensive to produce and that the "original sin"[1] of digital news was the industry's failure to require paid digital subscriptions from the outset. And it has been used by others to rightly point out that digital changes everything—as suggested when Herbert Simon invented the concept of the **attention economy** in 1971.

Brand's quote includes an important lesson that is often overlooked. It was said at the first Hackers Conference in 1984, held at an old Army base across the Golden Gate Bridge from San Francisco.

> *On the one hand, information wants to be expensive because it's so valuable. The right information in the right place just changes your life. On the other hand, information wants to be free because the cost of getting it out is getting lower and lower all the time.*[2]

Brand was talking with Apple co-founder Steve Wozniak and Bob Wallace—employee number nine at Microsoft who left in 1983 to independently develop word-processing software. Wallace popularized the **shareware** business model, mailing floppy disks of PC-Write to customers for a nominal $10 and giving them permission to use and freely redistribute the software as they saw fit. A voluntary $75 registration fee supported ongoing development.[3] Wallace

DOI: 10.4324/9781003154785-8

told conference attendees the shareware strategy was earning him $225,000 ($573,000 in 2023 dollars) a year.[4]

The ethic of the Hackers Conference was not naïvely utopian but a rather prescient recognition of the coming disruption. As Brand and others have since argued, when information becomes digital and distribution frictionless, traditional business models, laws, and regulations designed for the manufacturing and sale of physical goods will be renegotiated by society.

To update the formulation: "news is expensive but wants to be shared" reveals the tension between the inherent value of information and the challenge publishers have been trying to fully capture that value in a networked global environment.

The business of news

Journalism has always been a challenging economic venture. News is expensive to gather and has a short shelf life. Most reporting serves a small geographic region or a specific community of interest with a diminished value beyond those boundaries. Readers rarely have paid directly for news. They valued the newspaper because of the bundle of services it provided, including sports, ads, games, weather, stock listings, coupons, and comics. In print, advertising paid the bills, while subscriptions helped offset delivery costs. Broadcasters provided similar information services bracketed by abundant hours of entertainment programming, all supported by advertising.

The failing business of news

A 2019 study by the John S. and James L. Knight Foundation's Trust, Media and Democracy initiative reported that 59% of those polled in the U.S. considered their local newspaper to be an important symbol of civic pride, and 86% believed that everyone in the community should have access to local news, regardless of ability to pay.[5]

After one of my former newsrooms, the *Biddeford Journal Tribune* shut its doors in October 2019, we learned "being valued" might not save us.

> *BIDDEFORD, Maine—The mayor worries for his city because the local newspaper, the Journal Tribune, ended its 135-year run Saturday. The superintendent of the schools isn't sure how he will tell the community what's happening inside its classrooms. The head of the local food pantry is in mourning; he turned to the paper when his organization was about to be kicked out of its building.*
>
> *The three city leaders are distressed. That said, none of them was subscribing to the paper when it published its last issue.[6]*

When a valuable product or service dies of a lack of consumer support, economists consider that a **market failure**. And many scholars would argue that journalism is experiencing such a failure.[7] Exacerbating the challenge is the somewhat unique tension between profit and public service in a news organization. French economist Julia Cagé wrote:

(The news media's) primary purpose is not to maximize profits and pay dividends to stockholders but to provide a public good: the free, unbiased, high-quality information that is indispensable to democratic debate.[8]

That tension was a luxury in the U.S. as late as the 1990s when newspaper companies still earned 15% profit margins on average.[9] But in the past 20 years, as revenues have declined, survival has taken a front seat.

News is a public good

Economists categorize **commodities** based on relevant physical or financial characteristics. **Luxury goods** are expensive and non-essential. The Vacheron Constantin Tour de I'Ile wristwatch, which sold for $1.5 million, is a luxury good. **Durable goods** are products designed to be used for two years or more, like a computer or a bulldozer.

A **private good** is limited in supply, can only be used by one person at a time, or may be consumed by use. Pizza is a private good—it is eaten and is no longer available for others to share. An iPhone is a private good, a physical object designed for individual use.

A **public good** is potentially unlimited in supply, is not diminished by individual use, and is broadly available for everyone's benefit. Clean air is a public good, as are streetlights. The technical terms for these distinctions are that public goods are **non-rivalrous**: Use does not reduce the supply, and **non-excludable**: Anyone can access them.

A **club good** is non-rivalrous but excludable, such as cable TV or a private golf course.

A **common good** is non-excludable but rivalrous. A public pond may be open to fishing by all, but the supply of fish may be depleted by over-use.

Genuine public goods are typically provided by the government: National defense or the fire department—and paid for by taxes. Public goods have a **free-rider** problem as they are broadly available without direct individual payment, so some may benefit without sharing in the expense.

News is an experience good

Products that can only be evaluated in retrospect are known as **experience goods**. You might pay $50 at the hair salon, but that investment is not proven wise until you look in the mirror. Because an experience good is bought on trust, first-time customers rely on marketing and reputation and returning customers on the quality of their prior visits.

The quality and relevance of news can only be judged after consumption. Additionally, for a subscription service, you must pay and invest the effort to consume it before judging its value.

Trust in news, then, has a civic and financial impact. Both journalist and reader rely on it—as does the effort to sell subscriptions. And much of the price of a news organization when sold is **goodwill**, an accounting category that includes reputation and other intangible assets.[10]

News is an information good

A relatively new form of experience good, the **information good** is any product that can be digitized, copied, and shared. It is a creation of the online age.

News has high fixed costs of production: Reporters, photographers, and editors work to gather and contextualize facts that support knowledge and understanding. On the other hand, once an article, video, photo, or chart is published online, it can be copied and redistributed globally at no cost beyond the effort of a few clicks. This frictionless duplication commodifies the news and divorces the cost of production from the potential benefits and value of consumption.

In a classic 2009 essay, Clay Shirky recounted the Miami Herald's surprise at finding full-text copies of Dave Barry columns being shared widely by fans in the internet chat rooms of the day. The dilemma was described to him as, "When a 14-year-old kid can blow up your business in his spare time, not because he hates you but because he loves you, then you got a problem."[11]

The calculus of news

Building a valued and sustainable service requires news publishers to understand:[12]

- A community's information needs.
- The type of news and other services to be produced.
- The current competition for those services.
- The cost of staff, technology, and capital investments.
- The "public good" value to the community.
- The willingness of readers, advertisers, or other funders to subsidize the operation.

These are familiar challenges in any business. But for news, the disruption of the internet has eliminated room for error. The comfort of the advertising-centric business model of the past 100 years delayed our response to the threat of digital and reduced our capacity for experimentation and risk.

It is now universally acknowledged that a news publisher possessing a legacy business model must be in want of an easy answer. But there is no silver bullet—only shrapnel.[13] The ongoing reinvention of local journalism requires us to explore dozens of potential solutions to find the handful that will work for our community and newsroom.

The spread of news[14] and media deserts[15] means the information needs of local communities are increasingly met only in more affluent, less diverse, and more liberal zip codes.[16] However, we debate traditional newsrooms' historical strengths and weaknesses; the **market failure** and decline of local news will only worsen past harms.

Serving readers and advertisers

The first newspaper advertisement likely appeared in either a British or Dutch periodical in the 1620s.[17] In the Massachusetts colony, in 1704, *The Boston News-Letter's* first issue solicited paid advertising.[18] With that, newspapers served two audiences: Readers who came for the news and merchants who wanted to reach potential customers. Economists call that a **two-sided** market.

Advertising-supported media is a platform where readers and businesses meet to fulfill their respective goals. This model delivered a vast subsidy for journalism, with advertising revenues in the U.S. topping $48 billion in 2000 before dropping to $9 million in 2020.[19]

It is customary to blame this decline on competition from Facebook or Google, who now capture 60% of digital ad revenues in the U.S., and Craig Newmark's Craigslist, which researchers estimate earned $1 billion in 2018 from its "free" classifieds site. Classified ad revenues in the U.S. have declined 89% in 20 years.[20] But in Europe, home to a variety of digital classified ventures, notably not including Craigslist, classified revenues declined by 73% between 2003 and 2019.[21] So, while the internet giants (and Craig) are easy targets for blame, the reality is more complicated.

The videotex era

Critics have called free digital news the "original sin" of the industry, given its decades-long struggle for financial sustainability. But the epithet is ahistorical and unhelpful.

As far back as the 1970s, publishers turned their attention to text-based paid information services provided over phone and cable television lines. Dozens of publishers in the U.S. and Europe invested and experimented.[22,23]

In one of the largest tests of the technology in the U.S., Knight Ridder launched Viewtron in 1980 with AT&T and other partners. The videotex service was tested first in South Florida and included news from the *Miami Herald*, the Associated Press, and *The New York Times*. Users could also access local crime reports, school lunch menus, advice columns, personal banking, and flight schedules.[24,25]

The initial cost to consumers was $900 for a videotex terminal and a $12 monthly access fee. Subscriber growth was slow, and charges were eventually reduced first to $40 and then a $25 monthly fee, including a rental terminal.[26] The service was eventually expanded to more than a dozen markets and then shut down in 1986, despite a total investment exceeding $70 million.[27]

In the U.S., videotex failed because it was a product ahead of its time. The idea was good, but the technology was not yet. Access was expensive and slow, providing just a few sources of information. And it mainly allowed one-way communication: Newsroom to reader.[28] Videotex also faced growing competition from personal computers in the home.[29] Other online services—CompuServe, Prodigy, and AOL—gradually found a general audience, though each eventually surrendered to the world wide web.

The open nature of the web is its power—anyone can publish to it or access it. That is a boon and a threat to publishers. The cost of distribution is effectively zero, but the competition for readers is effectively infinite.

The attention economy

In 2010, 3.3 exabytes of information were newly stored on digital media every day—or 22,000 Libraries of Congress full of books.[30] By 2025, it is estimated we will create 473 exabytes of data daily—the equivalent of 3 million new Libraries of Congress every 24 hours.[31]

Not all that new data is available online, but enough is. Viewers watch 7 billion YouTube videos daily, send 700 million tweets, 4 billion Facebook posts, and 215 billion emails.[32] We still only have 24 hours in a day.

Before the arrival of the web, information was a scarce commodity. Discovering the news required waiting for the evening broadcast or the morning paper. Listening to a new hit song required sitting patiently by the radio. Finding the gross domestic product of Morocco required driving to the library (regular business hours only!) and locating an encyclopedia.

All three can now be accomplished in three clicks to CNN, Spotify, and Google.

Economics can be described as the study of the use of limited resources. But if information is no longer scarce, what rules govern this new environment?

Herbert Simon coined the term **attention economy** to highlight the shift from a scarcity of information to a scarcity in our capacity to drink from the firehose:

> *[I]n an information-rich world, the wealth of information means a dearth of something else: a scarcity of whatever it is that information consumes. What information consumes is rather obvious: it consumes the attention of its recipients. Hence a wealth of information creates a poverty of attention and a need to allocate that attention efficiently among the overabundance of information sources that might consume it.*[33]

Aggregation theory

The transformation of scarcity is at the root of the economics of digital disruption. The business of news publishing was to package advertising space and editorial content and sell into the two-sided market. Now, advertisers can bypass publishers and bid against each other to reach individual consumers, with publishers left to compete for that inventory. Ben Thompson, of the digital-economics-focused Stratechery blog and podcast, describes the implications of this change as **aggregation theory**.[34]

An economic market comprises three segments: Producers, distributors, and consumers. Profit is made by **horizontal integration** in one market segment—owning a local TV and radio station—or by the **vertical integration** of production and distribution. Prior to the web, newspapers sometimes controlled the entire publishing process: Journalism, advertising, printing, and distribution—to the extent of owning forests and paper mills.[35] In this way, newspapers reduced the overall cost of production and delivery while also creating a barrier to entry for competitors in individual markets.

But the internet has no geography or cost of distribution. So, the opportunity for profit has shifted from producers of content to online services that aggregate content—like Google or Facebook—that can scale to reach a massive undifferentiated audience.

A different original sin

Newsrooms appraised the web in the mid-1990s as an extension of earlier online experiments: A medium with obvious potential but no immediate audience or business model. Print profits were high, and the web was a risky and unknown territory. With a few exceptions, the imposition of digital subscription schemes made little sense.

Even more practically, the infrastructure that now powers frictionless online payments was not yet available. Persuading readers to pay for digital access requires an ecosystem that affords trust and convenience. But Amazon didn't sell a book until 1995, and PayPal did not exist until 1998.

So, the industry's mistake was not that it built websites in advance of a sustainable business plan. The error was in assuming the lessons learned in print would eventually light a path to digital news profits.

What is news?

The internet's arrival fundamentally changed journalism's economics and relationship with readers. In print, the business model relied on the physical delivery of news to individual doorsteps. In digital, it is contingent on the value of that news to the consumer.

Discovering how to serve and deliver that value requires a better understanding of the community's information needs.

In one way of thinking, information is "a difference that makes a difference,[36] a perceptible signal that supports a new recognition, knowledge, or action. But news has further been defined as the new, the unpredictable, and that which informs a society participating in a "common or collective interest."[37]

News is more than just information. The day's exact weather can't be known in advance, so, *It was 42°C (108°F) today* may be a noteworthy fact. However, the number is not "news" without context. *Yesterday was the fourth day of a heat wave in France, with temperatures again rising above 40°C*, is newsworthy.

Even for a weather story, making sense of today's events demands a working knowledge of yesterday. Context cues are provided in daily coverage and conversation, but developing a useful understanding of the world requires at least a semi-interested effort by the reader over time. This is more challenging in the digital environment as our attention is increasingly sought after for profit, not learning.

As journalists, we care how news is used by and valued by communities. So, we must be concerned with the quality of our reporting, the usability of our products, and the context that supports or inhibits understanding. The cost to distribute digital information is effectively zero, shifting to the consumer the burden of filtering the important from the trivial. This has implications for the design of digital news and how it produces profit. As Herbert Simon argued:

> *It is not enough to know how much it costs to produce and transmit information; we must also know how much it costs, in terms of scarce attention, to receive it. I have tried bringing this argument home to my friends by suggesting that they recalculate how much the New York Times (or Washington Post) costs them, including the cost of reading it.*[38]

Making money

News delivers benefits to readers, and it imposes costs. Money paid or personal data shared with digital ad networks is an expense. So is time spent finding, filtering, navigating, reading, and understanding the day's events.

Every software application, system, or process includes some unavoidable level of complexity. Just to create a new password, you must know and conform to the exact security requirements of the site. A goal of design and engineering is to make such tasks as easy as possible. A designer might include an explanation of the password requirements on the page. Or engineering might simplify the security policy if users routinely fail at the task. Developers call this the rule of **conservation of complexity**—any barriers to successful use should be identified and mitigated prior to being imposed on the public.

Some level of complexity in a system is necessary or desired. But every unnecessary barrier we present to readers increases the **cognitive effort** required to browse our website and understand the news. This creates a sense of frustration, reducing the perceived value of our journalism and the reader's willingness to pay for it.

The human-centered path to sustainable digital news starts with understanding the community's information needs (desirability) and includes our skill and capacity to design and deliver solutions that meet those needs (feasibility). But for any business, neither of those efforts is possible without financial sustainability.

Broadcast and print revenue models

Local newspapers traditionally offered home-delivery subscriptions and single-copy sales. But advertising income provided 60%–70% of revenues.[39] That subsidy has been under pressure for decades, as circulation declined relative to population growth since the birth of television in the late 1940s and in real numbers since 1985.[40]

For local TV broadcasters, advertising also accounts for 70% of revenues, now including broadcast and **OTT** streams. But the other 30% of local revenue comes from retransmission fees paid by cable TV carriers.[41] The ratio for some national cable TV networks, such as CNN, is closer to 50–50.[42]

The business of advertising

Before the rise of the web, every media organization sold advertising by edition: The morning paper, the weekly news magazine, and the 6 p.m. broadcast.

Regardless of medium, editions have a scarcity of space available for sponsor messages. A thirty-minute news broadcast might have eight minutes of ads; a 32-page section of the newspaper is 50% advertising. Within practical limits, once the pages or broadcast slots are filled, no more are available until the next edition. This constraint allowed publishers to exert control over advertising rates.

In addition, local media held a geographic monopoly over the mass distribution of news within their given delivery or broadcast region. Media outlets competed, but the **cost of entry** into the market was high: Buy a broadcast license or a printing press.

These conditions allowed for a profitable advertising strategy and a relatively stable competitive environment for news organizations. The internet eliminated both scarcity of inventory and geographic exclusivity.

The lack of adequate response by news organizations to recognize and adapt is as much to blame for the industry's trouble as Craigslist or Google are for recognizing and building businesses atop these new realities.

The trouble with Silicon Valley

However, the tech platforms are not beyond reproach. Google, Facebook, and Amazon now earn 64% of all digital advertising revenues in the U.S.[43] and 74% worldwide.[44]

Those revenues exceed that of every newspaper in the world combined.[45] The tech giants provide many useful and valuable services but not original journalism. The public now has instant access to almost any fact, constant communication with friends and family and trolls, and are one-click away from free shipping. But we have fewer journalists to do the work of building accurate knowledge about our local communities. This is not the fault of technology, but it is a real problem that requires public debate and policy solutions. The question is not *how do we save journalism* but *how do we support the information needs of communities*. And digital advertising is part of that future solution.

The world of AdTech

Facebook and Amazon have been frequently criticized for prioritizing profit ahead of consumer privacy and safety. But Google's domination of the digital advertising market is of particular concern to news publishers.

Advertising technology (**AdTech**) is a complex set of interconnected systems that help advertisers reach audiences through often very automated and opaque processes.

After designing the creative (a display advertisement, video, or other message), it is placed in a demand-side platform (**DSP**), which allows the advertiser to indicate the target audience, frequency of display, and budget.

The creative could be passed to an **ad network** that facilitates contracted placements with a specific publisher or an **ad exchange** that connects many advertisers and publishers via real-time **programmatic** bidding (**RTB**) for inventory.

Once an advertiser is contracted with a publisher for a specific placement, an **ad server** publishes the creative to the web page and tracks its performance.

Researchers estimate Google controls between 50% and 90% of the market at each step of that process. It "represents both the suppliers and the purchasers and also conducts the real-time auctions that match buyers and sellers and determine the price."[46]

This apparent dominance led a collection of U.S. state attorneys general to file antitrust lawsuits against Google for manipulating advertising rates[47] and collusion with Facebook.[48] Google also owns a suite of other services relied upon by publishers, including analytics and search optimization tools, adding to its complex relationship with journalism.

Fraud in the machine

In several tests, *The Guardian* has discovered as much as 70% of the ad revenue it was owed was diverted to intermediaries in the AdTech network or by outright theft.[49] By 2025, digital ad fraud will be a $50 billion global problem.

The legal and illegal siphoning of revenues away from publishers is partly possible due to the complexity and opacity of digital advertising systems. Vendors offering to target, serve, and optimize digital ad campaigns or to connect ad exchanges with publisher websites are ubiquitous. Automated systems primarily manage this vast network of transactions at a scale that leaves human oversight impractical. Experts in these markets struggle to understand the specifics of the process, and it is often unclear who paid for an ad that appears on a publisher's home page. For many news organizations, the declining promise of digital advertising has led to a new focus on reader revenues.

The carrot and stick of digital subscriptions

In 2010, only ten daily newspapers in North America had paywalls. By 2013, major metro titles, including *The Washington Post, Toronto Star,* and *Philadelphia Inquirer,* jumped on board, with more than 500 other dailies.[50] Much of that growth was driven by corporate groups such as Gannett, Lee Enterprises, and Torstar rolling out the strategy across their properties.[51,52]

Obeying the physics of digital economics, subscriber revenue is a "winner-take-most" market, with *The New York Times* and *The Washington Post* accounting for half of the reader revenues in the U.S. and *The Times* and *The Daily Telegraph* in the U.K.[53] That is a worrying trend, but it also reflects the investment in expertise and patience those organizations have applied to the challenge of converting visitors to subscribers. For local news organizations, that process begins with understanding your community as a collaborator in supporting local information, not just a checkbook.

In business, the tools of persuasion are often described as "the carrot and the stick." For a subscription product, that amounts to *please come to read and value our journalism but also pay to keep reading.* Unfortunately, most discussion of digital news subscription strategy focuses on the stick. It begins with the everyday use of "paywall" as the central metaphor—a structure designed specifically to keep non-paying visitors out. And the types of paywalls: **Strict**, **metered**, or **dynamic**, focus on the leniency a publisher allows before demanding payment. This lens encourages us to prioritize internal business needs over reader needs and motivations.

The word "paywall" by itself is harmless, but the "us vs. them" perspective it imposes on our view of readers is not without consequence. The empathy required of news product managers suggests we approach the issue with a carrot instead.

In a rewards-based framing, we invite readers to test-drive our digital news to learn more about the value it provides. In this way, the burden is on us to understand community needs and to constantly work to earn first trust, then loyalty, and eventually direct financial support. In this scenario, the paywall is a **sampling** strategy and part of a broad audience-focused product and marketing effort.

Subscriptions and membership

The two primary reader revenue models are not the same, despite the many confusing applications of the term across industries. Your favorite community news site may have a paid access program it calls a "membership," as does the gym you pay monthly and visit annually. But both are better described as subscriptions, even if extras such as local retail coupons or hot yoga classes are part of the package.

An explanatory contrast can be found between the National Public Radio membership program and the *Handelsblatt* subscription offering.

In the U.S., local NPR affiliates are famous for their canvas tote bags, given as a token of membership to supporters. NPR stations are available for free over the airwaves, so there is no explicit reason to pay for the network. But listeners value the service and treasure the NPR-branded gifts provided in return. Memberships are integral to local affiliates; for example, WNYC in New York City raises 30% of its operating budget through donations.[54]

The business newspaper *Handelsblatt* in Germany has a subscription model with a strict paywall. With limited exceptions, you cannot access its reporting if you are not a subscriber.

So, membership is a voluntary donation with benefits, while subscriptions allow paid access. Between the NPR and *Handelsblatt* examples are a variety of strategies and tactics, including subscription access programs that include other fringe benefits.

Subscription models

The Wall Street Journal went live on the web in April 1996 and followed up with a subscription paywall in August.[55] As was common among digital subscription pioneers, the Journal's business coverage attracts an audience that finds direct financial value in the journalism and may also have an expense account to pay for the subscription. The *Financial Times* in London has a similar focus and had an early paywall in 2002—first using a **metered sampling** model before moving to a paid trial strategy in 2015.[56]

The *WSJ* has also experimented with its paywall over the years, reflecting a general industry trend. The site began with a **freemium** model, letting the newsroom decide which articles could be sampled.

The paper currently uses a dynamic metering strategy directed by an artificial intelligence system. The site tracks 65 metrics and adjusts its sales strategy based on understanding a reader's **propensity** to pay.[57,58]

If the AI calculates that an additional two free stories will result in a new subscription, it will offer two more free stories. Over time, the system learns which strategies work best and acts to optimize the conversion rate.

Membership strategies

The Guardian in the U.K. is known for its commitment to provide free online access while appealing to readers for fundraising support. The newspaper is owned by a charitable trust and surpassed 1 million donating members in 2020.[59]

The Tyee is an online news magazine in Vancouver, Canada, that runs ongoing fundraising appeals and two annual membership campaigns.[60] The site is free to access but highlights its community impact and member swag—from pocket notebooks to coffee mugs.

Malaysiakini is an online news site just outside Kuala Lumpur, Malaysia. The site publishes in four languages: English, Malay, Chinese, and Tamil, and has operated for 20 years in an environment unfriendly to press freedoms. The site was initially supported by advertising, added subscriptions in 2002, and a blended membership option in 2019 that offers additional benefits while allowing "subscribers" to be less publicly in support of the organization.[61]

Zetland, a Danish news site in Copenhagen, was formed in 2012 with a focus on long-form storytelling and began publishing a handful of shorter but more regular daily stories in 2016.[62] The site redoubled its membership efforts in 2019, practicing radical transparency to engender trust and loyalty from readers—talking about its mission story and publishing its full financials.[63]

Other revenue sources

Necessity is the mother of invention, and news organizations are constantly working to diversify their revenue streams. Professor Damian Radcliffe at the University of Oregon has documented dozens of options beyond the traditional advertising and subscription access models.[64] Many bundle features and services into the core product—like a subscriber-only newsletter or podcast. But others are stand-alone efforts that can be sold outside a subscription or membership package and directly or indirectly subsidize news-gathering efforts.

The twice-weekly *The Pilot* in North Carolina owns a bookstore.

The online site *Billy Penn* in Philadelphia saw up to 75% profit margins for its local in-person events, ranging from happy hours to awards show galas. The events accounted for 80% of the site's profit in 2015.[65] *The Texas Tribune* hosts 50–60 annual events that generate 18% of the company's revenues.[66]

The New York Times earns affiliate fees when readers purchase products featured on its Wirecutter product review site.

Block Club Chicago sells coverage-themed t-shirts, an effort that raised $100,000 in 2019.[67]

Philanthropy plays an increasingly important role in supporting local journalism. Examples abound in the U.S.: The Walton Foundation provided $1.4 million to the University of Missouri to cover environmental issues in the Mississippi River Valley.

The Wichita Community Foundation promised $1.4 million to support the expansion of the *Kansas City Beacon* to Wichita. And the NewsMatch program raised $47 million, primarily for small nonprofit newsrooms in 2020.[68]

Meanwhile, Report for America placed 300 reporters in local newsrooms in 2021, and the American Journalism Project has so far raised $128 million to support 37 local news partners.[69]

The Economist has a subsidiary providing business research and consulting services. Axel Springer owns Business Insider and Politico, both of which provide business intelligence insights to premium subscribers.

And Hearst, along with many other news publishers, offers digital market-ing support ranging from SEO optimization.

For discussion

1 How are public goods prone to market failure?
2 What is the real "original sin" of digital journalism?
3 Why did the growth of the Attention Economy weaken news publishers?
4 How would you fix the flaws in the digital advertising ecosystem?
5 What are the important differences between subscription and membership programs?
6 Why were *The Wall Street Journal* and *The Financial Times* well positioned to impose early paywalls?

Learn more

• *All the News That's Fit to Sell: How the Market Transforms Information into News* – James T. Hamilton (2004). Princeton University Press.
• *The Vanishing Newspaper: Saving Journalism in the Information Age* – Philip Meyer (2009). University of Missouri Press.
• *Information: A History, A Theory, A Flood* – James Gleick (2012). Vintage.
• *The Content Trap: A Strategist's Guide to Digital Change* – Bharat Anand (2016). Random House.
• *Saving the Media: Capitalism, Crowdfunding, and Democracy* – Julia Cagé (2016). Harvard University Press.
• *Dead Tree Media: Manufacturing the Newspaper in Twentieth-Century North America* – Michael Stamm (2018). Johns Hopkins University Press.
• *Journalism Without Profit: Making News When the Market Fails* – Magda Konieczna. (2018). Oxford University Press.
• *News for the Rich, White, and Blue: How Place and Power Distort American Journalism* – Nikki Usher (2021). Columbia. University Press.
• *Abundance: On the Experience of Living in a World of Information Plenty* – Pablo J. Boczkowski (2021). Oxford University Press.
• *Saving the News: Why the Constitution Calls for Government Action to Preserve Freedom of Speech* – Martha Minow (2021). Oxford University Press.

Notes

1 Mutter, A. (2009). Mission Possible? Charging for Web Content. *Reflections of a Newsosaur*. http://newsosaur.blogspot.com/2009/02/mission-possible-charging-for-content.html
2 Levy, S. (1985, May). Discussion from the Hacker's Conference, November 1984. *Whole Earth Review*, 46, 44–55.
3 McLellan, D. (2002). Bob Wallace, 53; Pioneer in Computer Software. *Los Angeles Times*. https://www.latimes.com/archives/la-xpm-2002-sep-27-me-wallace27-story.html

4 Levy, S. (1985). Discussion from the Hacker's Conference, November 1984. *Whole Earth Review*, 46, 44–55.
5 Putting a Price Tag on Local News. (2019). John S. and James L. Knight Foundation's Trust, Media and Democracy. Knight Foundation. https://knightfoundation.org/press/releases/new-gallup-knight-study-local-news-should-be-available-to-all-yet-americans-divided-on-how-to-pay-for-it/
6 Greenberg, Z. (2019). In One Maine Town, 'Home Paper' is Gone After 135 Years. *Boston Globe*. https://www.bostonglobe.com/metro/2019/10/12/home-paper-gone-after-years/1yJKQl7FXSOM4VkAWDfHFO/story.html
7 Pickard, V. (2019). The Violence of the Market. *Journalism*, 20(1), 154–158. https://doi.org/10.1177/1464884918808955
8 Cagé, J. (2016). *Saving the Media: Capitalism, Crowdfunding, and Democracy*. Harvard University Press. https://doi.org/10.4159/9780674968691
9 Martin, H. J. (1998). Measuring Newspaper Profits: Developing a Standard of Comparison. *Journalism & Mass Communication Quarterly*, 75(3), 500–517. https://doi.org/10.1177/107769909807500306
10 Soloski, J. (2013). Collapse of the US Newspaper Industry: Goodwill, Leverage and Bankruptcy. *Journalism*, 14(3), 309–329. https://doi.org/10.1177/1464884912472016
11 Shirky, C. (2009). Newspapers and Thinking the Unthinkable. *Risk Management*, 56(3), 24–29.
12 Hamilton, J. (2004). *All the News That's Fit to Sell: How the Market Transforms Information into News*. Princeton University Press.
13 Marx, G. (2009). Q & A: Jim Brady. *Columbia Journalism Review*. https://www.cjr.org/the_news_frontier/q_a_jim_brady.php
14 Abernathy, P. M. (2018). *The Expanding News Desert*. Center for Innovation and Sustainability in Local Media.
15 Ferrier, M., Sinha, G., & Outrich, M. (2016). Media Deserts: Monitoring the Changing Media Ecosystem. In M. Lloyd & L. A. Friedland (Eds.), *The Communication Crisis in America, And How to Fix It* (pp. 215–232). Palgrave Macmillan. https://doi.org/10.1057/978-1-349-94925-0_14
16 Usher, N. (2021). *News for the Rich, White, and Blue: How Place and Power Distort American Journalism*. Columbia University Press.
17 Barrès-Baker, M. C. (2006). An Introduction to the Early History of Newspaper Advertising. *Brent Museum and Archive Occasional Publications*, 2, 1–28.
18 MHS Collections Online: The Boston Newsletter, number 1. (n.d.). http://www.masshist.org/database/186
19 Barthel, M., & Worden, K. (2021). Trends and Facts on Newspapers State of the News Media. *Pew Research Center's Journalism Project*. https://www.pewresearch.org/journalism/fact-sheet/newspapers/
20 Mir, A. (2021, July 28). The Press Now Depends on Readers for Revenue and That's a Big Problem for Journalism. *Discourse*. https://www.discoursemagazine.com/culture-and-society/2021/07/28/the-press-now-depends-on-readers-for-revenue-and-thats-a-big-problem-for-journalism/
21 Western Europe News Media Landscape Trends. (2021). https://newsmediaanalysis.s3-ap-southeast-2.amazonaws.com/accenture_analysis_WesternEuropeNewsMedia.pdf
22 Carlson, D. (2003). The History of Online Journalism. In K. Kawamoto (Ed.), *Digital Journalism: Emerging Media and the Changing Horizons of Journalism*. Rowman & Littlefield.
23 Boczkowski, P. J. (2004). The Mutual Shaping of Technology and Society in Videotex Newspapers: Beyond the Diffusion and Social Shaping Perspectives. *The Information Society*, 20(4), 255–267. https://doi.org/10.1080/01972240490480947

24 Stix, G. (1987). What Zapped the Electronic Newspaper? *Columbia Journalism Review*, 26(1), 45–48.
25 AT&T Archives. (1983). The Viewtron System and Sceptre Videotex Terminal. https://techchannel.att.com/play-video.cfm/2012/2/27/AT&T-Archives-Viewtron-Videotex-Sceptre
26 Stix, G. (1987). What Zapped the Electronic Newspaper? *Columbia Journalism Review*, 26(1), 45–48.
27 Carlson, D. (2003). The History of Online Journalism. In K. Kawamoto (Ed.), *Digital Journalism: Emerging Media and the Changing Horizons of Journalism*. Rowman & Littlefield.
28 Fidler, R. F. (1997). *Mediamorphosis: Understanding New Media*. Pine Forge Press.
29 Boczkowski, P. J. (2004). The Mutual Shaping of Technology and Society in Videotex Newspapers: Beyond the Diffusion and Social Shaping Perspectives. *The Information Society*, 20(4), 255–267. https://doi.org/10.1080/01972240490480947
30 Moore, R. (2011). Eric Schmidt's "5 Exabytes" Quote is a Load of Crap. *The Data Point*. https://blog.rjmetrics.com/2011/02/07/eric-schmidts-5-exabytes-quote-is-a-load-of-crap/
31 Desjardins, J. (2019). How Much Data is Generated Each Day? *World Economic Forum*. https://www.weforum.org/agenda/2019/04/how-much-data-is-generated-each-day-cf4bddf29f/
32 Geyser, W. (2019). 100+ Social Media Statistics for 2022 [+Internet in Real Time Live Infographic]. *Influencer Marketing Hub*. https://influencermarketinghub.com/social-media-statistics/
33 Simon, H. (1971). Designing Organizations for an Information-Rich World. In M. Greenberger (Ed.), *Computers, Communications, and the Public Interest*.
34 Thompson, B. (2015). Aggregation Theory. *Stratechery by Ben Thompson*. https://stratechery.com/2015/aggregation-theory/
35 Stamm, M. (2018). *Dead Tree Media: Manufacturing the Newspaper in Twentieth-Century North America*. Johns Hopkins University Press.
36 Bateson, G. (1970). Form, Substance and Difference. *General Semantics Bulletin*, 37. http://faculty.washington.edu/jernel/521/Form.htm
37 Park, R. E. (1940). News as a Form of Knowledge: A Chapter in the Sociology of Knowledge. *American Journal of Sociology*, 45(5), 669–686. https://doi.org/10.1086/218445
38 Simon, H. (1971). Designing Organizations for an Information-Rich World. In M. Greenberger (Ed.), *Computers, Communications, and the Public Interest* (p. 41).
39 Manduchi, A., & Picard, R. (2009). Circulations, Revenues, and Profits in a Newspaper Market with Fixed Advertising Costs. *Journal of Media Economics*, 22(4), 211–238. https://doi.org/10.1080/08997760903375902
40 Varian, H. (2010, March 9). Newspaper Economics: Online and Offline. *Google Public Policy Blog*. https://publicpolicy.googleblog.com/2010/03/newspaper-economics-online-and-offline.html
41 Jacobson, A. (2018). What's Driving TV's Revenue Riches in 2018? *Radio & Television Business Report*. https://web.archive.org/web/20180825182546/https://www.rbr.com/fangs-and-politicians-tvs-2018-revenue-drivers/
42 Walker, M., & Forman-Katz, N. (2021). Trends and Facts on Cable News. https://www.pewresearch.org/journalism/fact-sheet/cable-news/
43 Lebow, S. (2021). Google, Facebook, and Amazon to Account for 64% of US Digital Ad Spending this Year. *Insider Intelligence*. https://www.emarketer.com/content/google-facebook-amazon-account-over-70-of-us-digital-ad-spending
44 Joseph, S., & Shields, R. (2022, February 4). The Rundown: Google, Meta and Amazon are on Track to Absorb More Than 50% of all Ad Money in 2022. *Digiday*. https://digiday.com/marketing/the-rundown-google-meta-and-amazon-are-on-track-to-absorb-more-than-50-of-all-ad-money-in-2022/

45 Murphy Jr., B. (2017, June 28). Google and Facebook Now Make More from Ads Than Every Newspaper, Magazine, and Radio Network in the World Combined. *Inc.com*. https://www.inc.com/bill-murphy-jr/google-and-facebook-now-make-more-from-ads-than-every-newspaper-magazine-and-rad.html

46 Dinielli, D. C. (2020). *Stacking the Tech: Has Google Harmed Competition in Online Advertising?* (p. 14). Beneficial Technology, Omidyar Network.

47 Mickle, T., & Hagey, K. (2022). Google Misled Publishers and Advertisers, Unredacted Lawsuit Alleges. *Wall Street Journal*. https://www.wsj.com/articles/google-misled-publishers-and-advertisers-unredacted-lawsuit-alleges-11642176036

48 Bhuiyan, J. (2022). Lawsuit Claims Facebook and Google CEOs were Aware of Deal to Control Advertising Sales. *The Guardian*. https://www.theguardian.com/technology/2022/jan/14/facebook-google-lawsuit-advertising-deal

49 Pidgeon, D. (2016, October 4). Where Did the Money Go? Guardian Buys Its Own Ad Inventory. https://the-media-leader.com/where-did-the-money-go-guardian-buys-its-own-ad-inventory/

50 Borrell, G. (2013, September 16). *Why Paywalls Make Sense*. LMA Fall Conference.

51 Nowsourcing. (2012). Paywall Trends 2012. *bestcollegesonline.org*. https://www.bestcollegesonline.org/paywalls/

52 CBC News. (2013). Toronto Star moving Behind Paywall. *CBC*. https://www.cbc.ca/news/business/toronto-star-moving-behind-paywall-1.1386531

53 Fletcher, R. (2020). *How and Why People are Paying for Online News*. https://www.digitalnewsreport.org/survey/2020/how-and-why-people-are-paying-for-online-news/

54 WNYC. (2021). *WNYC Support FAQs*. WNYC. https://www.wnyc.org/support/faq/

55 Wang, S. (2016, April 29). The Wall Street Journal Website — Paywalled from the Very Beginning — Turns Y0 years Old Today. *Nieman Lab*. https://www.niemanlab.org/2016/04/the-wall-street-journal-website-paywalled-from-the-very-beginning-turns-20-years-old-today/

56 *Financial Times*. (2022). Financial Times Reaches One Million Digital Subscribers. *Financial Times*. https://aboutus.ft.com/press_release/one-million-digital-subscribers

57 Wang, S. (2018). WSJ Creates AI Paywall that Decides When Readers are Ready to Subscribe. *What's New in Publishing*. https://whatsnewinpublishing.com/wsj-creates-ai-paywall-decides-readers-ready-subscribe/

58 Seale, S. (2021, February 1). How Wall Street Journal uses Metrics and Engagement to Drive Digital Subscriptions. *International News Media Association (INMA)*. https://www.inma.org/blogs/conference/post.cfm/how-wall-street-journal-uses-metrics-and-enagagement-to-drive-digital-subscriptions

59 Bland, A. (2020). The Guardian Reaches 1m Subscribers and Regular Contributors. *The Guardian*. https://www.theguardian.com/media/2020/dec/17/the-guardian-reaches-1m-subscribers-and-regular-contributors

60 Zirulnick, A. (2020). How The Tyee Plans a Crowdfunding Campaign in a Week. *The Membership Guide*. https://membershipguide.org/case-study/how-the-tyee-runs-a-theory-of-change-driven-crowdfunding-campaign/

61 Lin, M. M. (2020). Why Malaysiakini Blended Membership and Subscription. *The Membership Guide*. https://membershipguide.org/case-study/why-malaysiakini-blended-membership-and-subscription/

62 Lichterman, J. (2017). Start Your Meetings with a Folk Song — And Other Ideas from the Community-Driven, Crowdfunded Danish News Site Zetland. *Nieman Lab*. https://www.niemanlab.org/2017/07/start-your-meetings-with-a-folk-song-and-other-ideas-from-the-community-driven-crowdfunded-danish-news-site-zetland/

63 Roseman, E. (2020). Case Study: How "Members Getting Members" Brought Zetland Financial Sustainability. *The Membership Puzzle Project*. https://membershippuzzle.org/articles-overview/zetland-ambassadors

64 Radcliffe, D. (2021). 50 Ways to Make Media Pay: 2021 Edition, Fully Revised and Updated. *What's New in Publishing.* https://whatsnewinpublishing.com/50-ways-to-make-media-pay-fully-updated-for-2021-report-download/

65 Clark, A. (2016). Amid Big Changes in Philly Media, Startup Billy Penn Sticks to its Vision. *Columbia Journalism Review.* https://www.cjr.org/united_states_project/billy_penn.php

66 Baron, S. (2020). Learn how the Texas Tribune's Live Event Strategy is Changing with the Times. *Local Media Association + Local Media Foundation.* http://localmedia.org/2020/09/learn-how-the-texas-tribunes-live-event-strategy-is-changing-with-the-times/

67 Castellano, S. (2022). These News Orgs are Boosting Revenue with Locally Themed Merchandise. *American Press Institute.* https://www.americanpressinstitute.org/publications/articles/boosting-revenue-locally-themed-merchandise/

68 Glaser, M. (2021, August 19). How Philanthropy Became a Growing Revenue Stream for Local News. *Knight Foundation.* https://knightfoundation.org/articles/how-philanthropy-became-a-growing-revenue-stream-for-local-news/

69 *Impact.* (2023). American Journalism Project. Retrieved March 22, 2023, from https://www.theajp.org/about/impact/

6 Managing news innovation

In this chapter

- Journalism has always been innovative.
- Risky business in Silicon Valley.
- Sustainable innovation for communities.
- Solving problems within the culture of news.
- How newsrooms are learning to innovate.

The word **innovation** is worn out from overuse.

In journalism and elsewhere, we too often apply it to describe any idea, good or bad, successful or not—if it is new. To the further annoyance of many, it is variously deployed as an adjective, a verb, an adverb, and a noun to describe the people, the process, the culture, as well as the outcome:

Our innovative product team, who innovate in our research & development office, innovated several new ideas this year and released an innovative new mobile app in August that was a popular innovation.

That tenuously grammatical sentence should never be spoken aloud, but it is not an unrealistic example.

We often confuse "innovation" with "invention," the intentional development of a new product or process. Indeed, an **invention** can be innovative, but only if the new product or idea is used to create societal and financial value.

That distinction is important because journalism has always been innovative, creative, inventive, and entrepreneurial. From the printing press to the penny press, broadcast airwaves to the internet, journalism has been an early adopter of new ways to tell, distribute, and subsidize the news.

Yet it is also true the industry has been slow to respond effectively to digital disruption. And journalists, especially those working in incumbent newsrooms, have a reputation for being averse to change.

DOI: 10.4324/9781003154785-9

That resistance is not necessarily irrational and might be attributed to a distrust of management, concerns about an ever-increasing workload, a lack of proper staff training and development, or the perceived threat to journalistic ethics and values.[1] After all, working journalists have been at the forefront of reporting and storytelling innovations from the inverted pyramid to computer-assisted reporting (CAR), from crowd-sourcing to live blogs, Twitter threads, and fact-checking.

Data journalism, then called CAR, was practiced as early as the 1950s, gaining popularity with the availability of mainframe computers and Philip Meyer's work at the *Detroit Free Press* in 1967. His innovative method of collecting and analyzing large data sets played a critical role in the development of digital technology in the reporting process.

The business side of news has been similarly progressive, with innovation pursued in reaction to competitive pressures and market opportunities or a desire to introduce cost-saving efficiencies. In 1846, the Associated Press delivered news of the Mexican-American war via Pony Express. In 1850, Reuters News delivered stock market prices by carrier pigeon in Germany. More recently, news organizations were early adopters of mainframe and personal computers for payroll and billing, ad layout, and newsroom typesetting of articles.[2] And publishers quickly recognized the potential of online technologies, including videotex and the web.

What can we innovate?

Innovation in news often involves a new technology: The telegraph, the radio, the smartphone. But in journalism, many projects rely on well-established technologies or are not explicitly technology-focused.

John Pavlik describes four journalistic arenas open to innovation:[3]

- The reporting process.
- The distribution of news.
- Community engagement.
- Organizational design and management.

I would add a fifth that is implicit in the above but deserves specific attention:

- Revenue strategies to subsidize newsroom operations.

All five categories reflect how we reinvent our relationship with communities, how we use new tools and processes to produce news, which mediums and platforms we use to reach readers, and how we restructure our business, teams, and individual jobs to best support those efforts.

- *PolitiFact* was founded in 2007 when political correspondent Bill Adair argued the public would be better served if newsrooms verified facts rather than just reporting what "both sides" of the issue had to say. The site won a Pulitzer Prize in 2009 and changed the way journalists think about the reporting process.

- *Outlier Media* describes itself as "on-demand service journalism" for Detroit, Michigan. The newsroom's primary product is a text messaging service that allows a direct conversation with the community to gather questions about housing and other needs, with answers and solutions provided as text messages. Traditional news stories are a secondary product written for and published in partner publications.[4]
- In Zimbabwe, *263Chat* publishes a weekday PDF edition to its 50,000 subscribers across 200 WhatsApp groups. This method allows readers affordable access to the news and enables a conversation with and among community members.[5]
- *The Wall Street Journal* began a reorganization in 2017 to become more digital and mobile-first that included adjusting digital publishing times to more effectively align with audience traffic patterns, creating a print-focused desk to remove evening production concerns from the digital workflow, and developing an operations staff for hiring and training needs, and a team to integrate digital analytics and audience data.[6]

Much of the recent revenue focus in media companies has been to optimize membership or subscription funnels. But a variety of other experiments include a dating app from *The Guardian* that closed in 2020 after a 15-year run, a wine club at *The Times* of London, and an effort at *Block Club Chicago* that launched after selling $100,000 in "Gator Watch 2019" T-shirts following coverage of an alligator discovered in a local lagoon.[7]

What motivates innovation?

Innovation is an intrinsically risky but necessary step for a business to remain viable in a changing economic environment. Like any strategy, it can be driven by:

- Market competition.
- Technological change.
- Shifting consumer preferences.
- Regulatory or policy changes.

Innovation can also be influenced or stifled by:

- Personal or corporate status-seeking.
- A simplistic mimicry of external exemplars.
- A dysfunctional workplace culture.
- A lack of process rigor.

The cost of risk

The mantra of Silicon Valley, popularized by Facebook, is to "move fast and break things," suggesting that innovation requires taking risks, making mistakes, and learning from failure. But news product managers want to "learn fast" more than "**fail fast**." And preferably, we want to do so without harming the health of the organization or the community. Because the risk of failure in the local news business is distinctly different from other industries.

- **Pets.com** failed in 2000 after raising $110 million and spending $25 million on advertising—including during the Super Bowl. The company tried to compete with local pet stores on price and convenience but lost money on every sale.
- **Juicero**, a $699 Wi-Fi-connected juice press, failed in 2017 after raising $134 million in venture capital funding. But the required proprietary juice packs could be squeezed by hand without the expensive equipment.
- The short-lived short-form video app **Quibi** collected $1.75 billion from investors before failing in December 2020 for a lack of audience interest only nine months after launch.

In these cases, the founders could not align consumer needs and organizational capabilities with a sustainable business model. But to what harm? No pets went hungry, glasses of orange juice unfilled, or videos unwatched as a result.

News organizations are often blamed for not adapting to the challenges and opportunities of the internet. And some of the criticism is fair. Publishers accustomed to 15–20% profit margins and monopoly control over news reporting and distribution in a community were often complacent in their successes. But it is difficult to place expensive and uncertain bets on new business models and new technologies if failure threatens not only the business but the civic health of the community. When a local news organization shuts its doors, it is a community loss. Often, there are few or no alternate sources of trustworthy local news. This persuades newsroom leaders to experiment too slowly and too safely.

We can't argue "newspapers," or any incumbent newsroom, are the only answers to a community's information needs. News is a valuable service; solutions will often arise to fill the gaps. But those new flowers bloom slowly and never in some communities. So, in the interim, what are the harms done? That question must be considered when weighing the risks.

Innovation in media

Innovation as the process of extracting economic value from newly invented technologies is a creation of the Industrial Age but was deified in Silicon Valley.

Journalism fits uncomfortably into that model.

News reporting is the process of turning information into knowledge. It is a creative effort and treats technology as a tool, not an object of worship. Neither the iPhone, the search engine, nor the web was created with journalism in mind. Yet all three technologies have directly impacted the reporting and publishing of news. Journalists are not trying to invent the next smartphone. But they can and do work to integrate mobile devices into journalistic practices. As such, news innovation can pale compared to the disruptive scale and success of PayPal, Uber, or Apple.

Does news need innovating? Not if we define it as risky, technology-focused projects that serve a relatively small and affluent segment of society. News needs strategies that provide new and valuable solutions to create value in our communities. That is still "innovation" but with an ethic different from many digital startups. The business of news does not require fast, limitless growth that extracts community value at the cost of trust and **sustainability**. News requires the opposite: A relationship with readers built on a collaborative creation of value.

Community-focused innovation

Ultimately, the proof of an innovation is in consumer adoption. And readers value solutions, not technology. News delivered by carrier pigeon, email, SMS, or VR is still news. Technology is just one ingredient. The innovation needed in journalism is to reorient our relationship with readers, support the community's understanding of itself, and build new models that subsidize the gathering and distribution of news and information.

For news product managers, an "innovation" is simply the successful result of an idea or service that provides this new social and economic value. A solution helps readers and supports organizational imperatives. The definition is broad:

- An idea new to us but already in use within journalism or elsewhere.
- A current product or service brought to a new audience.
- Improving an internal technology or process that supports community needs directly or indirectly.
- A new business model applied to a current product and audience.
- A novel combination of features, technology, content, audience, and business model.

Not all innovations are equal, but that framework could include projects such as:

- The development of a news talk show with a viewer call-in. (New to us)
- Launching an email newsletter with aggregated coverage of a niche topic. (New audience)
- Reorganizing newsroom shifts to publish updates during peak traffic hours. (Process change)
- The conversion of a commercial news organization into a non-profit or **benefit corporation**. (Business model change)

- Launch of a public service newsroom that publishes via SMS and is supported by donations and philanthropic grants. (A new combination of elements)

Support for innovation

Studying the operation of a large Norwegian newspaper website, Steen Steensen identified five factors that support or complicate the development of new ideas and practices.[8]

- **Newsroom autonomy**—Innovation thrives more efficiently when the relevant staff are isolated from the pressures and concerns of the legacy business. In journalism, this sometimes led to a separation of print and digital newsrooms in the early days of the web.
- **Work culture**—Traditional newsroom practice viewed readers as a passive audience, while digital journalism has increasingly understood the relationship as a conversation if not a collaboration. That leveling of the power differential between journalists and community allows beneficial new ideas and practices to develop.
- **The role of management**—Newsrooms have historically been run by command-and-control structure, a hierarchical model where goals and directions are passed down from leadership to staff. Digital innovation is easier when staff have a role both in goal setting and in self-organized management of activities within their areas of responsibility.
- **The relevance of technology**—New, expensive, or overly complicated technologies will hamper projects that do not provide the resources for training and integration necessary for staff acceptance.
- **The input of innovative individuals**—New ideas need internal champions.

Solving for needs

Theories of innovation struggle to explain the complexities of media work. Journalism is produced in a two-sided market, governed by a well-defined set of principles and ethical codes, as both a public good and an **experience good**. That complicates the pursuit of new ideas in ways not seen in other industries.

A theory of change for the business of journalism must weave together community needs, technological developments, and workplace processes and culture. Navigating such a complex system requires setting a goal and an anchor. For news, creating knowledge is the goal. Our anchor is a close understanding of the information needed for residents to make decisions and act to improve their individual and civic lives.

To effectively solve for a community need, a news product must be a desired solution and be aesthetically and functionally well-designed for that purpose. For a product to be feasible to develop and economically sustainable to invest in, a business requires the skills and time to develop it, the ability to integrate

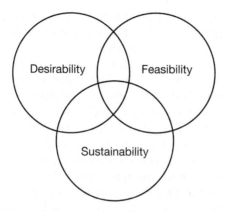

Figure 6.1 Desirability, feasibility, and sustainability must be balanced for a project to succeed.

it with existing systems and workflows, *and* the cultural support of the entire organization to accomplish these tasks.

By now, you recognize the Design Thinking Venn diagram (Figure 6.1).

- **Desirability** is the effective identification of the need and potential solutions.
- **Feasibility** is an assessment of organizational capacity to deliver a solution.
- **Sustainability** is a measure of an organization's ability to deliver a solution over time. It is often an external measure—will people pay—but it also considers strategic goals and indirect economic benefits balanced against the cost of development and support.

The three circles clearly define the areas of focus for product success but only hint at the array of complex **interdependencies** below the surface. Charting a path to product success begins with understanding community needs but includes concerns that cross internal and external boundaries and value systems.

Each crossed boundary poses new questions that a proposed innovation must be able to answer before it can be built and delivered to market, such as a paywall:[9]

1 **Desirability**—No business can succeed without a product or service the community finds of value. The greater the perceived value of the news and information we provide behind a paywall, the stronger the foundation of our strategy. *(Community need)*
2 **Viability**—While desirability is critical, the business must also operate at a profit. Understanding a reader's "willingness to pay" and optimizing revenues between subscription and advertising strategies require significant expertise and collaboration within the organization. *(Business need)*
3 **Visual design**—Effective and informative visuals that support understanding and instill trust in the brand and the confidence of an informed purchase decision by the reader. *(Aesthetics and function)*

4 **Usability**—Making digital payment forms easier to use drives new subscriptions but requires a significant investment in research, design, and development work. *(Function and usability)*

5 **Feasibility**—E-commerce is a relatively new focus for the news industry, and the complexity of the work is often underestimated. The time, skills, and priority applied will directly influence the usability and viability of the project. *(Organizational capacity including development effort)*

6 **Systems Integration**—Digital subscription fulfillment requires data to be shared with credit card companies, print circulation databases, customer service call centers, and the content management system. Any inefficiency or failure in those connections may degrade the ability of customers to subscribe or access the site. Each system to be integrated may reside in different departments or with different external vendors, adding significant complexity to the development task. *(Coordination between disparate services and tools)*

7 **Workflow**—As new systems are integrated, staff from across the company must either adapt to new business processes or managers must invest additional development time and expense to minimize the impact of process changes. *(The process for creating & publishing)*

8 **Culture**—All the above decisions and tasks must align with the company's values, beliefs, and organizational structure. A product that effectively solved for desirability, viability, design, usability, feasibility, integration, and workflow but offered a subscription product that allowed subscribers to dictate news coverage would fail as it would violate the ethical norms of the newsroom. *(The shared ethics, values, and assumptions that govern behavior)*

Culture beats strategy

The news industry has struggled for 25 years to reinvent itself online. The digital economy demands continuous change, but decades of generous and stable profitability left journalism ill-prepared. **Organizational culture** consists of the assumptions we share about what is important to the business and how we perceive our roles as individuals and teams. When a business updates an internal process, adds products, or changes strategy, some previously shared knowledge becomes obsolete. A change management process aims to help the organization learn to do new things. These efforts focus on communication, staff development, and coordination:

1 A vision and strategy set by leadership.
2 The training and development of employees in new roles, goals, and processes.
3 The actual work in pursuit of the new product, service, or organizational goal.
4 Staff-level effort to optimize communication and collaboration between people and teams.

This approach can fit any project, from the social media team adding Tik-Tok to its responsibilities, upgrading a newsroom technology, or pivoting the entire organization to a digital focus. The level of risk and uncertainty embedded in a system will dictate the time and effort required to effect change successfully.

In a *simple system*, the relevant parts are easily observed and well understood. Change may still be difficult, but it can be confidently estimated and managed. *Complicated systems* are less predictable and are subject to sometimes intractable interdependencies with other teams and processes. A *complex system* further involves unknown and unfamiliar processes, significant unpredictability, ambiguity, and risk.

Integrating TikTok into a social media engagement plan is a simple change. Assuming staff are available to do the work, the platform is well-known, the necessary tools are well-documented, and many examples of best practices are available.

The transition from analog tape to digital non-linear video editing at TV news stations was complicated, entangling multiple departments and technical domains. It required new skills, job descriptions, and deadlines. The transition was innovative to the extent it involved new technology, but most of the skills necessary to edit and broadcast the news remained unchanged.

By comparison, developing an "innovative culture" is a wickedly complex project defined by uncertainty at every step. It is difficult to predict specific outcomes; new **emergent** challenges will arise as the work progresses, and there are no "right or wrong" solutions, just "better or worse" choices.

Such projects are typically pursued only when inaction is perceived as an urgent threat to profitability and survival. At the end of the 20th century, the emerging digital disruption carried that threat. News organizations reacted by:

1 Building digital capacity in the staff needed to directly support online publishing.
2 Integrating non-digital staff and processes to the extent necessary to enable new digital initiatives.
3 Seeking online audiences and new profitable and sustainable revenue streams.

But since "culture determines and limits strategy,"[10] what we assume is possible and what we ultimately can accomplish is subject to the shared beliefs of the organization. For newsrooms, digital transformation was hindered by print-centric leadership and staff that often valued the status quo. This led newspapers in the early years of this transition, in Pablo Boczkowski's estimate, to develop a culture of innovation that was reactive, not proactive, with the protection of legacy advertising revenues prioritized over digital growth.[11]

Five waves of change

More than 30 years into the digital revolution, news organizations are in the middle of a fifth wave of how we understand the process and urgency of change. The first four waves were successful—in that each was a necessary but incomplete lesson and steppingstone:

1 Pre-web experiments. (Videotex, CompuServe, BBS)
2 The web: Technical investments with **shovelware** print-to-digital editorial and business operations.
3 Digital skills specialization and the growth of online storytelling forms and business models.
4 Digital native thinking and digital-first strategies.
5 Integration of editorial, business, and technical strategy with aligned goals.

Newsrooms did not move in lockstep through those stages, and inconsistency is still common. But forward progress is widespread, and journalism has had to continually relearn how to learn.

Training for change

Journalists have long faulted the lack of ongoing professional training in the industry. A 1993 study described the learning culture in newsrooms as "sink-or-swim"[12] with external and in-house development programs meeting only a fraction of the staff demand.

By 2002, news organizations still invested less than half as much as the average U.S. business in training. Researchers argued that the 0.07% of payroll spent was ill-preparing journalists for an increasingly complicated (and soon-to-be digital) world.[13]

And while newspapers had published on digital platforms for 20 years, the professional training offered focused primarily on the craft of reporting and writing, not digital-specific skills.

Helpful to the growth of digital journalism was the formation of the Online News Association in 1999. "We think it is up to us to encourage the best journalism possible in this new medium," wrote the organization's first president, Rich Jaroslovsky.[14] The group initially focused on bolstering the legitimacy of online reporting but evolved to support digital-native skills, including business and technical innovation.

The importance of newsroom culture and innovative thinking was further recognized in several programs funded in 2003 as part of a $10 million newsroom training initiative from the Knight Foundation.

For journalists, professional development often meant traveling to one- or two-week programs at premier locations like the Poynter Institute in St. Petersburg, Florida. These courses were popular but expensive and time-consuming for increasingly short-staffed and cash-strapped newsrooms.

To provide more affordable and accessible training, Poynter launched NewsU in 2005, offering self-guided online modules and live webinars. Upon its 10-year anniversary, the e-learning project had offered 1,223 courses to 259,052 participants on topics including news writing, leadership, innovation, audience engagement, and revenue strategy.[15]

Retraining the organization

Training for core skills is essential, but organizational-wide learning is necessary for organizational transformation. Also Knight-funded, The Learning Newsroom was a three-year research and training effort designed to enable cultural change. Run by the American Press Institute, it sent facilitators to a cohort of ten newspapers to help the organization learn how to adapt to the digital economy. The pillars of the training are given below:

- Organizational communication.
- Business strategy.
- Innovation.
- Systems thinking.
- Productivity.

The program believed newsroom culture needed to be more collaborative, community-focused, and able to learn from mistakes and failures. It taught staff to:

- Take initiative and responsibility at all levels.
- Enjoy brainstorming and trying new things.
- Learn even from failed experiments.
- Adopt "Change or Die" as a mantra.[16]

Editors reported the program supported digital progress, including increased videos and pages viewed, improved print sales, and reduced staff turnover.[17]

In 2005, API launched another business transformation effort, this one founded on Clayton Christensen's theory of disruptive innovation. It called for news organizations to urgently reinvent both strategy and culture by:

- Optimizing the core business model.
- Focusing on audience **jobs to be done**.
- Finding new audiences for news and other local information needs.
- Creating new value for current audiences.
- Building a culture capable of ongoing innovation.

The training taught a human-methods research approach, with the "jobs to be done" model a useful tool in translating consumer needs into business strategy.

Embedding innovators

Between 2012 and 2016, the Knight-Mozilla News Fellows program placed 33 creative technologists in newsrooms, mostly in the U.S. and Europe, to develop journalistic tools, write open-source code, work on data visualization projects, and bring a new perspective to the challenges facing journalism.

Efforts to foster a culture of creative technologists also arose from within as in-house media labs were formed to develop new ideas and to shepherd projects through organizational barriers. Teams at *The New York Times*, BBC, *Deutsche Welle*, and *Asahi Shimbun* were among the dozens that sprung up, mostly after 2010.

These efforts had a mixed impact on local organizational cultures and capacity for innovation. But it was a fertile training ground for many, informing fifth-generation product and innovation efforts in news organizations.

Learning by innovating

Matter VC was a media-focused accelerator that operated between 2012 and 2018, incubating media-focused startups and training the principles and methods of design thinking at news organizations and journalism schools. Matter launched eight cohorts, including startups Hearken and News Deeply, and invested venture capital seed funding in others. Startup founders spent five months learning the innovation process and applying those lessons to developing their products and businesses.

Since 2015, the Table Stakes program has asked news organizations to self-evaluate and understand if they are meeting expectations or performing above or below average benchmarks for:

- Workflow and processes.
- Skills and behaviors.
- Technology, tools, and data.
- Culture and resources.

The program takes a cohort of newsrooms and coaches each through the development of individual projects focused on one or more areas:

- Serving audience needs.
- Reaching readers where they are.
- Optimizing the subscription/membership funnel.
- Revenue diversification.
- Strategic partnerships.
- Organizational optimization via the "mini-publisher" model.

The teaching method provides detailed checklists to identify the current and potential future state of organizational processes and culture. For example, if the staff currently views their targeted readership as a homogenous mass audience, a success would be to instill a more sophisticated understanding of the community as a set of multiple audiences, each with potentially unique needs.[18]

The program is funded by Knight and is now operated by the Lenfest Foundation and API. The Google News Initiative (GNI) and WAN-IFRA partner to run Table Stakes Europe using the same methodology.

Accelerating innovation

The "train and practice" method of innovation has become increasingly popular in journalism. An array of accelerator programs have sprung up in recent years that, like Table Stakes, engage newsrooms in often year-long project-based efforts to produce real business results.

The Facebook (now Meta) Journalism Project Accelerator tackles the challenge of membership and subscription growth with local news organizations. The training outlines ten steps to reader revenue success:[19]

1 Utilize a funnel approach.
2 Obsess over user experience.
3 Get the tech stack right.
4 Make data-inspired decisions.
5 Test, test, test, and operate like an e-commerce company.
6 Treat subscribers like gold.
7 Maximize return across the demand curve.
8 Truly listen and take action.
9 Deliver value.
10 Get everyone in the canoe.

The program has worked with almost 200 publishers on six continents since 2018.[20]

The GNI Subscriptions Lab also focuses on reader revenue efforts and the rigorous and structured experimentation needed to rebuild the business of news. It proposes and teaches four phases for these data-informed projects:

1 Choosing the right experiments. (*Prioritization and planning*)
2 Laying the foundations. (*Research and assessing risks*)
3 Creating a robust design. (*Selecting test methods and goals*)
4 Analyzing your success. (*Evaluating and discussing results*)

GNI runs many other global news innovation programs, including the Innovation Challenge, which funds specific newsroom projects with up to $150,000 grants.

Learning to change

Consumer-focused product research is risky. New ideas are difficult to discover and validate. New products and services are a challenge to develop and deliver to readers. And even good products can fail to find an audience or profitability. There are no easy answers to the challenge of reinventing journalism.

But recall the eras of marketing from Chapter 2:

1 Production-focused.
2 Sales-focused.
3 Marketing-focused.
4 Relationship-focused.

Over the last 30 years, news organizations have (sometimes grudgingly) moved toward the relationship model—recognizing that understanding reader needs is the safest path to successful innovation and revenue growth.

News product management is a formal expression of that realization. The discipline brings a portfolio of proven best practices, an experimental mindset, and a culture of continuous learning. In Chapter 7, we will talk more about how product thinking works in journalism.

For discussion

1 Is journalism innovative?
2 What makes innovation in news media different than other industries?
3 What community problem is news trying to solve?
4 Why does "culture" get veto power over new ideas in an organization?

Learn more

- *When Old Technologies Were New: Thinking About Electric Communication in the Late Nineteenth Century*—Carolyn Marvin. (1990). Oxford University Press.
- *Digitizing the News: Innovation in Online Newspapers* – Pablo Boczkowski (2005). MIT Press.
- *The Myths of Innovation*—Scott Berkun (2007). O'Reilly.
- *Can Journalism Survive: An Inside Look at American Newsrooms* – David M. Ryfe (2012) Polity Press.
- *Innovators in Digital News*—Lucy Küng (2015). Bloomsbury Publishing.
- *The Lean Startup*—Eric Ries (2011). Crown Business.
- *Transforming Newsrooms: Connecting Organizational Culture, Strategy and Innovation*—Carrie Brown & Jonathan Groves (2019). Focal Press.
- *The Innovation Delusion*—Lee Vinsel & Andrew Russell (2020). Currency.
- *News Nerds: Institutional Change in Journalism*—Allie Kosterich (2022). Oxford University Press.

- *The Gutenberg Parenthesis: The Age of Print and Its Lessons for the Age of the Internet*—Jeff Jarvis (2023). Bloomsbury Academic.
- *Stratechery*—Ben Thompson. [Blog & Podcast]. https://stratechery.com/

Notes

1 Spyridou, L.-P., Matsiola, M., Veglis, A., Kalliris, G., & Dimoulas, C. (2013). Journalism in a State of Flux: Journalists as Agents of Technology Innovation and Emerging News Practices. *International Communication Gazette*, 75(1), 76–98. https://doi.org/10.1177/1748048512461763

2 Mari, W. (2019). *A Short History of Disruptive Journalism Technologies: 1960–1990*. Routledge.

3 Pavlik, J. V. (2013). Innovation and the Future of Journalism. *Digital Journalism*, 1(2), 181–193. https://doi.org/10.1080/21670811.2012.756666

4 Alo, K. (2019, May 28). The Way Things have Always been Done does not the Right Way Make: An Essay for Reporters. *Outlier Media*. https://outliermedia. org/the-way-things-have-always-been-done-does-not-the-right-way-make-an-essay-for-reporters/

5 Mugamu, N. (2021). Case Study: 263Chat (Zimbabwe). *International Press Institute*. https://ipi.media/case-study-263chat-zimbabwe/

6 Murray, M. (2018). A Mobile First Strategy at The Wall Street Journal: Interview with Matt Murray, Editor-in-chief. (Institute for Media Studies, Interviewer). http://dmn37.kvm21760.profi-server.net/wp-content/uploads/2018/02/ IFMS-Interview-with-Matt-Murray-Editor-in-Chief-Wall-Street-Journal_December 2018.pdf

7 Castellano, S. (2022, March). *These News Orgs are Boosting Revenue with Locally Themed Merchandise*. American Press Institute. https://www.americanpressinstitute. org/publications/articles/boosting-revenue-locally-themed-merchandise/

8 Steensen, S. (2009). What's Stopping Them? *Journalism Studies*, 10(6), 821–836. https://doi.org/10.1080/14616700902975087

9 Kiesow, D. (2021). The Business of Digital News: Understanding the Cross-Functional Orchestra. In V. Bélair-Gagnon & N. Usher (Eds.), *Journalism Research That Matters* (pp. 131–136). Oxford University Press. https://doi.org/ 10.1093/0s0/9780197538470.003.0010

10 Schein, E. H. (2017). *Organizational Culture and Leadership* (5th ed.). Wiley.

11 Boczkowski, P. J. (2005). *Digitizing the News: Innovation in Online Newspapers* (1. paperb. ed). MIT Press.

12 Newton, E., & Thien, R. (1993). *No Train, No Gain: Continuing Education in Newspaper Newsrooms* (B. J. Buchanan, Ed.).

13 Council of Presidents of National Journalism Organizations. (2002). Newsroom Training: Where's the Investment? A Study for the Council of Presidents of National Journalism Organizations.

14 Jaroslovsky, R. (2000). Our Mission is Simple – Yet Enormous. *Online News Association*. https://web.archive.org/web/20000815094954/https://journalists. org/

15 Kranse, J. (2015). NewsU by the Numbers (There are a Lot of Ewes). *Poynter*. https://www.poynter.org/reporting-editing/2015/newsu-by-the-numbers-there-are-a-lot-of-ewes/

16 McLellan, M., & Porter, T. (2007). Newsroom Training: Essential, Yet Too Often Ignored. *Nieman Reports*, 61(3), 90–91. https://niemanreports.org/articles/ newsroom-training-essential-yet-too-often-ignored/

17 Ibid.

18 Smith K, D., Hope, Q., & Griggs, T. (2017). *Table Stakes: A Manual for Getting in the Game of News.* Knight-Lenfest Newsroom Initiative.
19 The Meta Journalism Project Global Accelerator Program. (2021). https://www.facebook.com/formedia/mjp/programs/global-accelerator
20 The Meta Journalism Project Global Accelerator Program. (2021). 10 Steps to Build a Thriving Reader Revenue Business. https://scontent.fmci2-1.fna.fbcdn.net/v/t39.8562-6/10000000_678352799983258_1138454571661287630_n.pdf?_nc_cat=109&ccb=1-7&_nc_sid=ae5e01&_nc_ohc=QGmQ4y9Cl0QAX_I8Grn&_nc_ht=scontent.fmci2-1.fna&oh=00_AT8GAEQPs7JwslKtU_CIEwi5Qv7pXIbAG52_PgveZrMsQQ&oe=62B30524

7 The mission of news product

In this chapter

- The ethics of the business of journalism.
- Including the community in organization decisions.
- How technology disrupts ethical practice.
- Building a business for readers.
- Understanding what a community needs.

News product management exists to bridge the gap between internal business assumptions and plans and external community values and information needs. We use the scientific method to research, propose, test, validate, build, and deliver products and services to achieve our goals. We measure the success of the process at each step by asking: Does the audience value it, can we build it, and is it a sustainable solution?

But a solution to what? Why build a better app or a new email newsletter? What do journalists hope to achieve by providing information services to our communities?

An effective measure of any business activity, large or small, is how it aligns with a core organizational goal. These core goals are often expressed in a mission statement reflecting the company's vision of success.

Walter Williams, the founding dean of the Missouri School of Journalism, wrote in 1914:[1]

> *I believe that advertising, news and editorial columns should alike serve the best interests of readers; that a single standard of helpful truth and cleanness should prevail for all; that the supreme test of good journalism is the measure of its public service.*

That excerpt from the *Journalist's Creed* effectively describes the ethical and community-focused mission of both the practice and business of journalism.

DOI: 10.4324/9781003154785-10

Google's stated mission is to *Organize the world's information and make it universally accessible and useful,*[2] a phrase that effectively describes the company's search engine and related businesses.

Amazon considers success broadly, irrespective of the product sold: *Our mission is to be Earth's most customer-centric company.*[3]

Procter & Gamble takes a similar approach, holding the relationship with customers as key: *We will provide branded products and services of superior quality and value that improve the lives of the world's consumers, now and for generations to come.*[4]

And Toyota takes pains not to define itself strictly as a builder of passenger cars: *Toyota will lead the future mobility society, enriching lives around the world with the safest and most responsible ways of moving people.*[5]

Accountability reporting is often considered to be the highest calling in journalism. The work is valorized in books and on screen: Watergate at *The Washington Post,* *The Boston Globe's* Spotlight team, or the international and collaborative Panama Papers. But accountability journalism also includes coverage of the local city council, police department, or university chancellor.

If a well-designed mission statement helps define the organizational culture and inform business decisions and actions, how would we write one for news? Is it a grand pronouncement: "Democracy Dies in Darkness," as *The Washington Post's* current slogan suggests? Or something more pragmatic: "All the News That's Fit to Print" as at *The New York Times?* But perhaps neither of those is inclusive of everything a news organization provides.

In *The Elements of Journalism,* Kovach and Rosenstiel write that the role of journalism is ultimately shaped not by journalists, reporting methods, or technology, "The principles and purpose of journalism are defined by something more basic: The function news plays in the lives of people."[6] News product managers agree and believe organizational success and sustainability require an expansive definition.

Consider the bundle of services in the traditional print newspaper: Local and regional news, sports, business, and arts reporting, weather, comics, games, obituaries, stock, TV, movie and event listings, sports statistics, classified and display ads, coupons, and retail inserts. That information is now splintered across many different digital sources but is still valuable to readers as they navigate and make sense of their daily lives. That, then, is the mission of local news and the cornerstone of news product management:

Helping a community to understand itself.

Why mission matters

News is an unusual kind of product. When consumers purchase a physical good like a toaster or bulldozer, they do so in a direct **one-sided market** between seller and buyer. By contrast, news organizations facilitate two-sided markets where an audience is gathered and rented to advertisers. **Two-sided markets** are common for information products, from social media to dating apps. This model allows services like Facebook, TikTok, and Google search to be free to the public. It also enables newsrooms to deliver journalism to readers and viewers at a far lower cost than possible if subscriptions covered the entire cost of news gathering and delivery.

From a financial perspective, journalism is a **cost center**, attracting readers but without direct revenue responsibility. Conversely, advertising, circulation, and membership departments are **profit centers** without involvement in editorial decisions. This separation of duties is traditionally enforced by organizational structure and ethical codes designed to avoid conflicts of interest that could influence news coverage. It has also isolated newsrooms from the close collaboration with business and technology teams needed to develop new and innovative products and services. This, in turn, slowed many of the organizational and cultural changes essential for digital success.

But digital technologies also upended those barriers, making business tools and data broadly available across the organization. Before digital publishing, journalists had no specific understanding of how many readers or viewers they reached daily. And even in the early days of the web, the analytics team was the only source of that data. Today, everyone in the newsroom has instant access.

Organizations run on information and are structured by their access to and ability to share it. Digital technologies and the **democratization** of business data have enabled reporters and editors to accept new roles in social media promotion and the attendant monitoring of audience analytics. This has flattened organizational structures and blurred the line between departments.

As role definitions evolve and blend across disciplines, competing systems of ethical frameworks are brought into conflict. Crafting a Facebook update aligns with traditional journalistic values, but sharing responsibility for subscriber churn does not. Addressing this tension requires the organization to develop a shared set of organizational goals and values so that new ethical frameworks can be built and acted upon.

This new **North Star** is anchored in a more holistic understanding of community information needs. It recognizes that movie night planning, coupon clipping, shopping for a new car, next week's school lunch menu, and the city council story are produced by different departments, but each contributes to an individual reader's understanding of their community on a given day. And the business processes we use to identify and serve those needs are similar, whether it is a journalist or an ad salesperson responsible for the final product.

A Hippocratic Oath for journalism

Famously, the medical profession observes a code of ethics known for the directive to "First, do no harm." News has a similar responsibility, as outlined by the Society of Professional Journalists (SPJ):[7]

1 Seek truth and report it.
2 Minimize harm.

3 Act independently.
4 Be accountable and transparent.

The four pillars are inextricably linked, with minimizing harm as the keystone. A decision to publish news is unjustified if the damage caused by the report outweighs the benefits. Journalists ask, "Through this action or inaction, how will my community be better served?"

When the *Austin-American Statesman* published an hour-long video from the scene of a 2022 mass shooting, Manny Garcia included this line in his editor's note:

> *We also have removed the sound of children screaming as the gunman enters the classroom. We consider this too graphic.*[8]

In weighing its values, the Austin, Texas paper prioritized the need to seek and report the truth depicted in the footage. But by editing the audio, the staff also hoped to minimize the adverse impact on the victims' families.

Ethics are a process

Aly Colón, the Knight Chair and professor of Media Ethics at Washington & Lee University, teaches that ethical codes are not rules "written in stone" to be blindly obeyed but a statement of values to be interpreted and applied rigorously within a given context.[9] Every case is different, but deliberations should:

1 Define the question.
2 Specify the values in conflict.
3 Ask who an action might impact and how.
4 Identify diverse voices and concerns not already represented.
5 Develop scenarios and their potential outcomes.
6 Explore **edge cases**, the "unlikely, but what if?"
7 Select values to act upon.
8 Seek options to mitigate harm.
9 Determine a plan of action or actions.
10 Self-evaluate and seek feedback.

The goal of the process is to understand the stakes of a decision, describe all potential stakeholders, reveal biases, and then weigh the most ethical options.

A seat at the table

News product thinking, like journalism, requires us to consider the civic impact of our organizational decisions. And product managers are said to represent the **reader's voice** and the interests of the community. But **implicit** or **explicit bias** can negligently constrain our definition of community, often excluding:

- Non-subscribers.
- Historically excluded populations.
- Less frequent news readers.
- Younger audiences.

When we fail to engage with segments of our audience or are selective listeners, even an otherwise rigorous ethical process will deliver inequitable journalism, products, and services. You cannot make an ethical decision without asking, "Who isn't getting a voice?" says Jill Geisler, the Bill Plante Chair in Leadership & Media Integrity at Loyola University Chicago.[10]

Consider the simple task of making dinner plans. When choosing between a Brazilian steakhouse or Texas-style barbecue, we might simply assess the cost and location before making a reservation. But if a group member is a vegetarian, restaurants with a more flexible menu must be considered.

Assuming every diner—or reader—has the same preferences and needs harms the business and the community. Disability activists say, "Nothing about us, without us." And for news organizations, ethical decisions are possible only in collaboration with all stakeholders.

President Lyndon Johnson established the Kerner Commission to study and recommend solutions in response to racial violence in U.S. cities in the three years before its founding. Its landmark report, released in 1968, devoted a chapter to the role of the media in perpetuating harm in Black communities. And the lack of diversity in newsrooms and editorial leadership was noted as a direct cause. In the archaic terms of the day:

> *The journalistic profession has been shockingly backward in seeking out, hiring, training, and promoting Negroes. Fewer than 5 percent of the people employed by the news business in editorial jobs in the United States today are Negroes. Fewer than 1 percent of editors and supervisors are Negroes, and most of them work for Negro-owned organizations.*[11]

How much has changed since 1968? Look around the room the next time you are at work or school. Who is missing?

If you are in a typical four-year college classroom in the U.S., you are already out of the ordinary. Only 33% of residents earn a bachelor's degree.[12]

That number is strongly correlated with family wealth. Students from the top quintile of household incomes are 50% more likely to enroll in college than those in the bottom quintile.[13]

More women than men have earned a bachelor's degree in the U.S. each year for the past 40 years. That advantage is growing and now stands at 14 points, 57%–43%.[14] The gender gap in the overall U.S. population is 51%–49%.

The average classroom is likely to be 71% white, 10% Asian, 8% Black, and 8% Hispanic or Latino. The actual population percentage for those groups is 60%, 6%, 13%, and 18%, respectively.[15]

So, who is missing from your classroom? Well, 70% of the country. But on average, Black and Hispanic or Latino residents, and generally people from lower income groups, are distinctly under-represented among those pursuing four-year degrees.

The disparities are even starker in U.S. newsrooms which are 58% male and 83% white.[16] That gap is wider among editors and executive leaders. And almost 80% of newsroom employees have at least a bachelor's degree.[17]

Even the largest newsrooms in some of the largest cities in the U.S.—Washington D.C., Los Angeles, and New York underrepresent their communities by 20% for racial and ethnic diversity on staff.

The lack of diversity in newsrooms is not unique to the U.S. A 2020 study by the Reuters Institute for the Study of Journalism found that across 200 media outlets in ten international cities, only 23% of top editors were women.[18] A similar study looking at editorial leadership in 100 newsrooms on four different continents found that 85% of top editors were white, though the general population of the countries studied was 42% non-white on average.[19]

What is the cost of the lack of diversity? In the U.S., 59% of recent Pew Research Center survey respondents believed that the news media did not understand them or "people like them."[20] More than three-quarters of the U.S. believes the news media should reflect the country's diversity.

But that majority opinion is further evidence of the challenge facing media trust and diversity efforts. In the Pew research, liberal and Black residents favored more racial and ethnic diversity in newsroom hires. At the same time, conservative and white respondents wished to see more diversity of political views reflected.[21]

The ethics of product management

News product ethics are an extension of the journalistic codes used in reporting. Editorial teams work on tight deadlines, and the risks of a published or broadcast misstep are real and immediate. News product teams work on projects lasting weeks or months. But once launched, a digital feature might remain in use and unchanged for years. And like news, product design choices can create **asymmetric harms**, disproportionally targeting or excluding portions of the audience. For example:

- Subscription models that make news unaffordable for parts of the community.
- Web design that fails accessibility standards.
- A lack of language options for non-English-speaking local populations.
- Story forms and features that amplify stereotypes (e.g., police mug shot galleries).

- Revenue strategies that might confuse or deceive readers (e.g., some native advertising or sponsored content units).

Building a digital business strategy is a complex web of cause and effect. Identifying and mitigating harm requires an understanding of systems thinking and a diverse team with an intentional and comprehensive practice of audience engagement.

The ethics of computer code

In the digital age, our business, editorial, and technical strategies dynamically co-exist in the reader's web browser. Ads are selected and served on demand from thousands of networks. Lists of recent, related, and recommended stories change by the minute. And the web page itself is compiled on-the-fly from hundreds of different services worldwide. As a result, some of what is delivered to readers may be a surprise to editors. Beyond the reported article, photos, or videos, the news story page is an algorithmically-driven **black box** that no one can fully explain in detail.

A subscription offer that pops up may obscure article text, a newsletter sign-up form may break because of an unrelated JavaScript change, or an ad for luxury travel to the Caribbean may appear next to an article describing a recent earthquake in that exact location. The complexity of the systems, and the crossing of departmental boundaries, impose an uncertainty of cause and effect that makes identifying root causes and prioritizing solutions difficult.

Even when the technology works as intended, there are unintended consequences. Advertising, audience, and editorial tactics are often at odds, and product managers are asked to reconcile those differences to achieve mission and goal alignment. If left unresolved, the conflicts are inflicted on readers as a bad user experience.

Restaurant workers refer to the concept of **front** and **back of the house** to denote the business operations that are (or are not) exposed to customers— for instance, the dining room vs. the walk-in-freezer. In the age before digital news, we might have similarly considered journalism as the "front," while business and technical operations were in the "back" and mostly invisible to the community.

But digital has flattened those distinctions, much as it has blurred the lines between skills and departments. In 1983, what ethical concerns could the community have about your source of newsprint, advertising billing system, or the microphones used on set? But in 2024, advertising and publishing systems and the terms of service of every partner platform are exposed to readers. This creates new ethical concerns for both journalists and consumers.

For example, the auto-playing of videos increases **pre-roll** ad inventory and boosts advertising revenue. But this tactic is typically unpopular with readers. So, the organization must balance the competing values of financial gain vs. user satisfaction. This debate is often decided in favor of the immediate quantitative revenue metric rather than user satisfaction, a long-term qualitative measure.

But auto-playing video is less often discussed as an ethical concern. To evaluate, it helps to consider the extreme cases:

a What are the potential harms if, without their express consent, readers are presented a two-minute video of a group of playful kittens?

   Is it fair to say that no readers would be troubled by this?

b What are the potential harms if readers are exposed to a video of a police officer shooting a 13-year-old boy, as in the case of Chicago's Adam Toledo in April 2021?

   Few editors would purposefully inflict that video on readers without warning.

But, on websites that auto-play news videos, that decision is taken out of the newsroom's hands.

The introduction of technology as a mediator in the news experience—web servers, algorithms, video players, programmatic advertising—changes the ethical discussion in news organizations. It introduces an abstraction between cause and effect, making potential risks appear unlikely or distant and less important. And it reduces the **agency** of journalists to exercise editorial judgment when a conflict of values occurs on deadline.

Similar issues of harm, distanced from the initial ethical decision-making process, arise for advertising-based tracking and data collection, click-bait headlines, and the distorting effects of algorithmic recommendation systems.

The ethical implications of business and technological choices must be addressed early in the development process and in consideration of all relevant internal and external stakeholders. Compromise solutions are often possible, like allowing editors to turn off auto-play on specific sections or stories. But other non-technical possibilities also abound. The nonprofit *Block Club Chicago* published two versions of the Adam Toledo story, one without video. Co-founder Jen Sabella told NiemanLab.com, "The whole *Block Club* team is passionate about telling the stories of Chicago—the good and the bad—without causing further harm to communities that have been misrepresented in the media for decades."[22]

Shared values and practices

Digital news projects inevitably cross departmental boundaries. Redesigning a story page, launching a podcast or an email newsletter require editorial, advertising, and membership teams to work together to create value and avoid harms. And to do this, community must be the shared focus.

No, the ad sales staff need not pledge adherence to the Society of Professional Journalists Code of Ethics. But, in a digital-first, audience-first organization, business and editorial teams must explicitly share a mission and apply humane values to create, not extract, community value. Much as Walter Williams said in 1914, everything a news organization produces should "serve the best interests of readers."[23] Every department and team must:

- Make a sincere effort to listen to and empathize with the needs of readers.
- Respect the principle of creating, not extracting value from a community.
- Seek rigorous-enough answers to reduce uncertainty and provide strategic guidance.
- Use methods applicable in practice for both editorial and business projects.

Entrepreneurial journalism

The sometimes challenging collaboration between editorial and business concerns is not a creation of the digital age. Instead, it has been part of the entrepreneurial model of journalism since the time of the first newspapers in the 17th century. Those early news publishers wore many hats as founders-salesmen-editors-printers-reporters. But along with the growth of the industry through the 20th century came well-intentioned lines separating business and news operations.

Entrepreneurial journalism re-emerged as an area of academic study and teaching after 2010 in the U.S., as the newspaper industry emerged from the economic recession, having lost 23% of its advertising revenues almost overnight.[24]

As a playbook to launch new businesses, entrepreneurialism serves a pressing need for journalists trying to find new solutions for the information needs of their communities. It is also in demand from the ranks of freelance journalists managing a staff of one.

At the City University of New York Graduate School of Journalism, Jeff Jarvis began teaching the business of news in 2006, an effort that became the Tow-Knight Center for Entrepreneurial Journalism in 2010. "Journalists must now take on the urgent responsibility of building the future of news."[25] The study and teaching of the practice blossomed in the decade after.

Two of the leading membership organizations now supporting innovative news enterprises, the Local Independent Online News (LION) Publishers and the Institute for Nonprofit News (INN), have seen their membership rolls double in recent years. And dozens of smaller initiatives are also available, providing best practices for startup funding, technology platforms, business development, and audience engagement.

In his 2012 book *Entrepreneurial Journalism*, Mark Briggs describes the process of launching a news business in five phases:[26]

- Understanding the news ecosystem.
- Developing a business plan.
- Learning to innovate.

- Turning ideas into actions.
- Launching.

In the introduction to *Media Innovation and Entrepreneurship*, a textbook edited by Michelle Ferrier and Elizabeth Mays, Jan Schaffer describes the business side of news as:[27]

- Understanding digital tech and culture.
- Identifying opportunities.
- Engaging audiences.
- Developing data insights.
- Pitching ideas.
- Growing revenues.

Journalists don't need to launch a startup to be innovative risk-takers. In the same textbook, veteran journalist and consultant Mike Green describes an entrepreneur as "someone with a market-driven pursuit of a conceptual idea, who seeks a viable business model that succeeds in a target market."

But, closer to the typical product manager role is the intrapreneur, "an employee who innovates and thinks entrepreneurially to develop new lines of business, programs or products within an existing organization or corporation."[28]

That supports a convenient definition for us to consider:

> *News product thinking is a set of tools and methods used by both entrepreneurs and intrepreneurs to develop innovative and sustainable information products and services.*

Entrepreneurs use these methods to identify a market need, develop a business plan, and build a company. Product managers use the same methods but often within an already existing organization. First and foremost, both are concerned with understanding reader needs and translating potential solutions into sustainable products and services.

What readers want

In his theory of Disruptive Innovation, Christensen argues that since 90% of new consumer products fail, the process of marketing and innovation must be at fault.[29] Traditional marketing campaigns target consumer **demographics** (age or income) or **psychographics** (personalities or interests). Christensen's **Jobs to Be Done** (JTBD) approach looks to develop and sell better products by first identifying the gaps experienced by a consumer between need and solution.

In journalism, two years before API's 2006 Newspaper Next adopted JTBD methods, researchers at Northwestern University similarly theorized about the factors influencing the acquisition or cancellation of newspaper subscriptions. The study did not translate "jobs" into specific products and services. However, it effectively described many basic expectations and frustrations felt by news consumers, which are still relevant 20 years later.[30]

Reader satisfaction correlated with a belief the publication could:

- Inform me.
- Entertain me.
- Save me money.
- Give me something to talk about.
- Look out for my interests.

Reasons for dissatisfaction included:

- Wasting my time.
- Drowning in news.
- Lacks distinction.
- Lack of local focus.
- Poor service.

The list of positive attributes aligns with the mission of local news and offers a launchpad for discussing new products and services. But the negative attributes detailed in the Northwestern study are also instructive. Innovation, practiced ethically, involves an affirmative duty to develop a new economic and social value for the business and community. And it imposes a responsibility to avoid intentional or unintentional harms.

The JTBD framework is an increasingly popular tool to translate reader needs into unified strategies in news organizations. *The Wall Street Journal*, *The Atlantic*, and *The Conversation*, among others, have used versions of the method.

Dmitry Shishkin pioneered the approach at the BBC World Service and described six needs he originally used in supporting digital transformation there:[31]

- Update me.
- Keep me on trend.
- Give me perspective.
- Educate me.
- Inspire me.
- Divert me.

According to Shiskin, user needs must be **actionable**—the jobs they describe must translate to achievable business or editorial strategies. In 2016, the broadcaster realized it was producing many "update me" stories that received relatively few page views compared to other categories. A re-balancing of editorial focus led to fewer articles published but overall page view and article growth. By better understanding JTBD, the newsroom's output was more effectively aligned with the needs and expectations of the audience.

For discussion

1 Is news a business or a public service?
2 How is the technology underpinning the business of journalism now imposed on readers?
3 In your opinion, what is the mission statement of journalism?
4 How does "Nothing about us, without us" apply as an ethical principle in news coverage and news product thinking?
5 If we understand reader needs, does that ensure we produce ethical products?

Learn More

- *The Invention of Journalism Ethics: The Path to Objectivity and Beyond*—Stephen J. A. Ward (2004). McGill-Queen's University Press.
- *Entrepreneurial Journalism: How to Build What's Next for News*—Mark Briggs (2012). CQ Press.
- *Media Innovation and Entrepreneurship*—Michelle Ferrier & Elizabeth Mays (Eds.). (2017). Rebus Community. https://press.rebus.community/media-innovation-and-entrepreneurship/
- *Reckoning: Journalism's Limits and Possibilities*—Candis Callison & Mary Lynn Young (2019). Oxford University Press.
- *Democracy Without Journalism?: Confronting the Misinformation Society*—Victor Pickard. (2020) Oxford University Press.
- *Community-Centered Journalism: Engaging People, Exploring Solutions, and Building Trust*—Andrea Wenzel. (2020). University of Illinois Press.
- *The Elements of Journalism: What Newspeople Should Know and the Public Should Expect*—Bill Kovach & Tom Rosenstiel (2021, 4th ed.). Three Rivers Press.

Notes

1 The J-School Legacy. (2023). *Missouri School of Journalism*. https://journalism.missouri.edu/the-j-school/the-j-school-legacy/
2 Google. (2021). *About Google, Our Culture & Company News*. https://about.google.com/
3 Amazon. (2021). Who We Are. *About Amazon*. https://www.aboutamazon.com/about-us
4 P&G. (2021). *Purpose, Values and Principles*. https://us.pg.com/policies-and-practices/purpose-values-and-principles/
5 Toyota Corporation. (2021). *Vision & Philosophy*. Toyota Motor Corporation. https://global.toyota/en/company/vision-and-philosophy/global-vision/index.html
6 Kovach, B., & Rosenstiel, T. (2014). *The Elements of Journalism: What Newspeople Should Know and the Public Should Expect*. Three Rivers Press.

7 SPJ Code of Ethics. (2021). *Society of Professional Journalists.* https://www.spj. org/ethicscode.asp

8 Garcia, M. (2022). Why the Austin American-Statesman Chose to Publish Video from Inside Robb Elementary. *Austin American-Statesman.* https://www.states man.com/story/opinion/columns/2022/07/12/uvalde-shooting-video-austin-american-statesman-editor-investigation-publish/65371937007/

9 Conversation with Aly Colón. (2022, July 18).

10 Geisler, J. (2022, May). *Don't Just Talk Diversity. Lead Inclusively.* Journalism Institute. https://www.pressclubinstitute.org/2022/05/16/dont-just-talk-diversity-lead-inclusively/

11 National Advisory Commission on Civil Disorders, T. (2016). *The Kerner Report* (National Advisory Commission on Civil Disorders). Princeton University Press.

12 Selected Social Characteristics in the United States. (2019). https://data.census. gov/cedsci/table?d=ACS%201-Year%20Estimates%20Data%20Profiles&tid= ACSDP1Y2019.DP02&hidePreview=false

13 College Enrollment Statistics [2021]: Total + by Demographic. (2021). *EducationData.* https://educationdata.org/college-enrollment-statistics

14 Fry, R. (2019). *U.S. Women Near Milestone in the College-Educated Labor Force.* Pew Research Center. https://www.pewresearch.org/fact-tank/2019/06/20/u-s-women-near-milestone-in-the-college-educated-labor-force/

15 Selected Social Characteristics in the United States. (2019). https://data.census. gov/cedsci/table?d=ACS%201-Year%20Estimates%20Data%20Profiles&tid= ACSDP1Y2019.DP02&hidePreview=false

16 Arana, G. (2018). Decades of Failure. *Columbia Journalism Review.* https://www. cjr.org/special_report/race-ethnicity-newsrooms-data.php/

17 Grieco, E. (2018). *Newsroom Employees Earn Less than Other College-Educated US Workers.* Pew Research Center. https://www.pewresearch.org/fact-tank/2018/ 10/04/newsroom-employees-earn-less-than-other-college-educated-workers-in-u-s/

18 Andı, S., Selva, M., & Nielsen, R. K. (2020). Women and Leadership in the News Media 2020: Evidence from Ten Markets. *Reuters Institute for the Study of Journalism.* https://reutersinstitute.politics.ox.ac.uk/women-and-leadership-news-media-2020-evidence-ten-markets

19 Robertson, C. T., Selva, M., & Nielsen, R. K. (2021). Race and Leadership in the News Media 2021: Evidence from Five Markets. *Reuters Institute for the Study of Journalism.* https://reutersinstitute.politics.ox.ac.uk/race-and-leadership-news-media-2021-evidence-five-markets

20 Gottfried, J., & Barthel, M. (2020). *Black, Hispanic and White Adults Feel the News Media Misunderstand them, But for Very Different Reasons.* Pew Research Center. https://www.pewresearch.org/fact-tank/2020/06/25/black-hispanic-and-white-adults-feel-the-news-media-misunderstand-them-but-for-very-different-reasons/

21 Holcomb, J., & Stubbs, H. (2020). *In U.S., Views of Diversity in News Vary by Party ID, Race.* Knight Foundation. https://knightfoundation.org/articles/ in-u-s-views-of-diversity-in-news-vary-by-party-id-race/

22 Scire, S. (2021, April 16). Block Club Chicago Offered Two Versions of the Same Breaking News Story — With and Without a Horrifying Video. *Nieman Lab.* https://www.niemanlab.org/2021/04/block-club-chicago-offered-two-versions-of-the-same-breaking-news-story-with-and-without-a-horrifying-video/

23 The J-School Legacy. (2023). *Missouri School of Journalism.* https://journalism. missouri.edu/the-j-school/the-j-school-legacy/

24 Chen, S. (2009). Newspapers Fold as Readers Defect and Economy Sours. *CNN.* https://web.archive.org/web/20090326040522/https://www.cnn.com/ 2009/US/03/19/newspaper.decline.layoff/index.html

25 Jarvis, J. (2012) Introduction. In Briggs, M. (2012). *Entrepreneurial Journalism: How to Build What's Next for News.* CQ Press.
26 Briggs, M. (2012). *Entrepreneurial Journalism: How to Build What's Next for News.* CQ Press.
27 Schaffer, J. (2017). The Case for Learning about Media Entrepreneurship: An Important Gateway to Your Future. In M. Ferrier & E. Mays (Eds.), *Media Innovation and Entrepreneurship.* Rebus Community.
28 Green, M. (2017). Developing the Entrepreneurial Mindset. In M. Ferrier & E. Mays (Eds.), *Media Innovation and Entrepreneurship.* Rebus Community.
29 Christensen, C. M., Cook, S., & Hall, T. (2005). Marketing Malpractice: The Cause and the Cure. *Harvard Business Review.* https://hbr.org/2005/12/marketing-malpractice-the-cause-and-the-cure
30 Calder, B. J., & Malthouse, E. C. (2004). Qualitative Media Measures: Newspaper Experiences. *JMM: The International Journal on Media Management*, 6, 123–130. https://doi.org/10.1080/14241277.2004.9669388
31 Shishkin, D. (2022). What Engagement Reporters & User Researchers can Learn from Each Other: User Research. https://docs.google.com/presentation/d/1t89qCD0C00e97NdD3dHOMpqBLS-gMo0TyZhp2niD9KQ/edit#slide=id.gf2a4424586_0_113

Unit III
Making news products

8 Product is research

In this chapter

- Three frameworks to understand product management.
- Evaluating ideas for new products and services.
- Using surveys and interviews to understand community needs.
- Building organizational empathy for readers.
- Avoiding bias in decisions and products.

News product management aims to deliver sustainable solutions for a community's civic, commercial, or lifestyle information needs. For a solution to succeed, its origin story must be:

- Reader-oriented.
- Data-informed.
- Process-driven.

That story might begin with a vague idea mentioned at a staff meeting, a discovery while talking to readers, or an idea spotted on a competitor's website:

- I wish we could use all the audio collected for this investigative story.
- I wish we could launch an election newsletter.
- I wish we could attract more national advertising.
- I wish readers would make more use of our news archives.

Turning a wish into reality involves a series of informed decisions, and in product management, the theory and practice of making those decisions can be summarized in three frameworks:

1 **The Design Thinking Venn diagram**
    News products are built with an understanding of audience needs, aligning organizational capabilities to meet those needs, and developing a

DOI: 10.4324/9781003154785-12

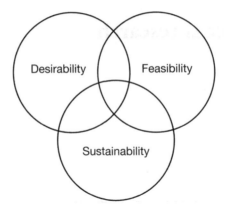

Figure 8.1 The three pillars are an inclusive umbrella of any research question that can be asked in the product development process.

business model that supports a sustainable effort over time (Figure 8.1). A project will fail unless all three requirements work in balance.

2 The continuous learning loop

Core to every business is the allocation of time, money, and staff to the projects with the best strategic and economic potential. But the uncertainty and risk inherent to new ideas make assessment and investment decisions difficult.

Silicon Valley startup culture suggests failing fast—testing ideas quickly and cheaply to find out what does not work—as the most efficient way to innovate. Mark Zuckerberg called this "move fast and break things." But we want to learn fast, not fail fast, and the **scientific method** of research is our template:

1 **Hypothesis**—Start with a testable idea and limited evidence.
2 **Analysis**—Study individual elements of the problem.
3 **Synthesis**—Reintegrate the elements to build a helpful understanding of the case.
4 **Theory**—Develop a proposed plan rooted in the evidence.

Despite the name, "build" is the third step in the *Build-Measure-Learn* loop (Figure 8.2) popularized in *The Lean Startup*.

1 **Prioritize** the known risks and assumptions.
2 **Identify** the information needed to support additional investment.
3 **Build** an experiment.
4 **Measure** and analyze the results.
5 Apply what we **learned** to the next experiment.

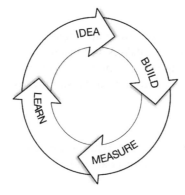

Figure 8.2 The Build-Measure-Learn loop follows the scientific method of hypothesis-analysis-synthesis to develop rigorous theories of audience needs and product value.

3 The phase-gate process

A product development process (**PDP**) (Figure 8.3) divides work into four to six distinct phases, with a decision "gate" between each. The total number of steps can vary, but follow a similar template:

- Research.
- Design.
- Develop.
- Launch.

Within each stage, we apply the continuous learning loop of experimentation and evaluation to improve our understanding of a project's potential, and, at each gate, decide:

1 The idea is not feasible. (*Abandon it*)
2 More investigation is needed. (*Recycle the loop*)
3 Proceed to the next stage. (*Advance*)

Figure 8.3 Product development follows a path from concept to delivery, and in a formal process, the stages are defined with a review and approval checkpoint in between.

In practice

Product ideas frequently arise within an organization because staff members have direct access to decision-makers and insight into half of the process: Potential solutions. Managing these internally generated proposals requires a method to collect and structure the early assumptions. We want to know:

- What is the product?
- What audience will it serve?
- How will it generate revenue or create strategic value?
- How does it align with current goals and objectives?
- Why will it work?

At *The Daily Beast* in 2017, Emma Carew Grovum used a suggestion form that asked seven questions, including:[1]

- Goal: Describe the precise problem we want to solve with this project or experiment.
- Hypothesis: What's our test statement? What belief are we experimenting with, challenging, or trying to prove?

At *The Texas Tribune*, Becca Aaronson used a ten-question survey featuring:[2]

- Success metrics: What are the specific goals you'd like to reach, and what metrics will you use to measure success?

These early-stage evaluations occur at the **fuzzy front end** of innovation—the unstructured collection of discussions, emails, notes, whiteboard sketches, executive questions, and customer feedback that are not yet ready for formal investment. Proposals at this stage are strewn with guesses and often predicated on past organizational successes. *The newsletter we launched last year did well; we should produce another.* The role of product thinking is to transform these ideas into testable hypotheses.

Requests of any quality from any source can be effectively evaluated if the process (1) balances audience and organizational needs, (2) undertakes rigorous research and analysis before investment, and (3) stipulates important decision-making milestones.

For example:

I wish we could use all the audio collected for this investigative story.

Since our wish list contains many ideas, the initial due diligence must be time and energy-efficient. Binary "yes or no" answers supporting a clear "advance or abandon" recommendation are preferred.

- Is the quality of the collected audio sufficient for a podcast? (Yes/no)

- Do we have the staff and equipment necessary to produce audio projects? (Yes/no)
- Do we have time to build an audio project before publication of the investigative package? (Yes/no)

The advantage of such **red flag** questions is they can be quickly enumerated, researched, and applied to decision-making. At this stage, we are not engaged in a nuanced evaluation of reader needs but a ruthless prioritization to filter out obviously unworkable proposals.

The three pillars: Audience needs, organizational capabilities, and business sustainability, are addressed when a project advances into the full formal PDP. But in the early stages of research, a simple value vs. benefit analysis might find:

- Low audience interest and low revenue potential—the project is abandoned.
- Medium interest and revenue—advancement if the cost of development is practical.
- High interest and revenue with low development cost—very likely to advance.

Increasingly time-consuming and expensive evaluation is needed as our investment in a project escalates. But the general pattern repeats: In each phase, what minimum but effective research effort is merited by the project costs and risks being considered.

Readers first

The value of a product can only be proven in the market. Does the community find it helpful to solve a need? We conduct research to propose solutions that achieve a **product-market fit**.

For **information goods** like news, a solution bridges the gap between *I want to know* and *Now I understand*. It might be a simple need: "I am a football fan. Did Liverpool win on Wednesday?" Or, more complex: "I am a local taxpayer. Why is the city expanding the highway through downtown?"

That broad range of needs and potential solutions is a challenge and an opportunity for news organizations.

A sports score is a singular fact of interest to a potentially global audience. A local policy decision is a complex narrative that develops over time and is of interest in a specific region. The research process and finished product or service we deliver will be as different as the audience and the value of the problem being addressed. But we ask similar questions along the way:

1 **Needs**—What is the problem being solved?
2 **Context**—How, where, and when will the product be used?

3 **Requirements**—How does the product or service need to behave in the relevant contexts?
4 **Design/Develop**—How do the requirements manifest in the appearance and operation of the service?
5 **Validate**—How can we ensure the development process maintains fidelity with the identified needs and requirements to create a successful solution?

Time is money

The investment in reader-focused research must be proportional to the project's potential value and level of risk. Before a project of any size is begun, we ask:

- What is the cost of development?
- What is the cost of potential failure?
- Is there any likelihood of harm to the community?
- Is there a possible reputational risk to the company?
- What is our experience with similar products?
- What relevant data is already available?

Even for a product as relatively straightforward as an email newsletter, the costs include:

- Organizational time and effort spent on research and analysis.
- Contracting an email management service (EMS) such as MailChimp or HubSpot.
- Design and development of the email template.
- Design and development of marketing and sign-up forms.
- Integration of analytics, advertising, and content management systems to populate the email template.
- Producers and editors to manage the content.
- Administrative effort to assure compliance with policies, including **CAN-SPAM.**
- Reporters and producers to deliver the news.

In an organization with none of the required processes or technologies, launching a newsletter could be an expensive and time-consuming project. That cost imposes significant risk if the strategy fails and merits a considered investment in research and analysis.

But, in an organization with experience producing and delivering newsletters, the costs and risks are marginal. In that case, the cheapest research might be simply to launch and measure the results.

That calculation of time and risk involves repeatedly asking, "how do we know?" It does not assume a product that is inexpensive to launch will succeed (or vice versa); it just guides our understanding of the cost of failure. The larger the risk, the more valuable an investment in research will be.

Learning about needs

A business understands the outside world through signals that cross its boundaries carrying details of consumer attitudes and behaviors:

- Sales reports.
- Digital analytics.
- Reader comments.
- Calls to customer service.
- Conversations in the community.

These signals are numerous but are often **low bandwidth**, carrying data but not the information and insights needed to inform strategy.

- **Data** consists of raw collected facts, often numbers but also text.
- **Information** is data that has been organized and processed for human interpretation.
- **Insights** are the result of analyzing information and developing theories applicable to business activities.

Product management is the process of collecting data from relevant sources and transforming that raw material into insights. Each formal or informal reader **touchpoint** is an opportunity to further develop a rich portrait of the needs and motivations of our audience.

Talking to people

Our most common research tools: Interviews, focus groups, and observation studies, are **qualitative** methods. This is distinct from **quantitative** research, which uses numerical data, and both approaches are common in industry and academia. (Online surveys have both qualitative and quantitative elements.) Qualitative studies collect data on human attitudes and behaviors to develop insights and solutions. In contrast, data sources such as web analytics tracking are quantitative—telling us the "what" of reader characteristics and activity.

To understand the "why," qualitative research methods commonly require:

- Well-defined research goals.
- A target audience.
- The scripting of questions.
- Collection of data.
- Analysis with business goals in mind.

Reader surveys

Designing a good online **survey** is like writing a news story—inside out.

In the reporting process, journalists perform interviews and follow up on interesting answers. In a survey, the quality of the collected responses depends on the precision of entirely pre-scripted questions.

To write a news story, journalists organize their research and reporting into a structured narrative. In an audience survey, we organize and structure questions to turn the answers into research data.

To use a reader survey and inform a business strategy, we:

- Define the research question.
- Design the research instrument (survey or interview script).
- Recruit subjects.
- Deliver the survey.
- Collect and analyze the data.
- Develop insights.
- Follow up.

Each step in the process should help amplify useful data embedded in the collected answers. That means:

- Matching the insights we seek with the correct research methods.
- Asking the questions of the right audience.
- Organizing the questions to reduce **cognitive load** for respondents.
- Collecting the appropriate number of responses.
- Drawing prudent conclusions by recognizing the weaknesses inherent in the method and process.

Surveys in practice

In a recent senior capstone project at the Missouri School of Journalism, students designed and deployed a survey for a large national publisher interested in their audience's use of Instagram for news. The research question was, *How can we engage more effectively with readers on Instagram?* and the first draft of the script began with:

---

1 How do you scroll through a specific news outlet's Instagram feed?
2 How much time do you generally spend on Instagram per day?
3 What is your purpose for using Instagram? (I.e., keeping up with friends, funny videos, getting the news, etc.)
4 What features do you use the most on Instagram? (Stories, IGTV, feed, messaging, Discover page, etc.)
5 Do you follow any news organizations?
6 How often do you tap on news organizations' Instagram stories?
7 How often do you interact with content from news stations?

Each question has flaws that would dilute potential insights. We cannot assume that:

1 Everyone who receives the survey link uses Instagram. (*Poor audience targeting*)
2 People can accurately remember or estimate app usage times. (*Excess cognitive load*)
3 "Purpose" can be accurately described in a short answer format. (*Weak question*)
4 Users of the app are familiar with the formal names of different sections. (*Cognitive load*)
5 Our definition of "news organization" is the same as the respondent's. (*Misaligned mental models*)
6 The respondent has an immediate recall of interacting with a news organization. (*Cognitive load*)
7 Free-form answers from 1,000 respondents will be comparable for analysis. (*Wrong question format*)

Beyond the imprecise language, our draft survey also lacks a narrative focus. The questions do not provide context or build understanding. Much like the lead of a news story should highlight a primary news value, a survey must progress toward a single-minded insight. Ask, "What is the most important thing we want to learn?" Then, design the script to lead inevitably to that answer. This is an issue of both content and organization.

The alignment of a research goal, questions, and audience is an art, not a science. To make a quick assessment, develop a set of hypothetical "best possible" survey responses and evaluate what findings might result. From our first draft, we might only learn that our audience uses Instagram several times daily to watch funny videos; they follow two news organizations and occasionally click on the videos. Those are anecdotes, not insights.

In the second draft, the student team took a more structured approach. First, by limiting responses to **qualified** respondents to improve the signal-to-noise ratio:

---

1 Is Instagram installed on your phone? (SELECT: YES/NO)
SKIP REST IF NO

We talk to readers because they are the experts of their own lives and habits. So, asking non-Instagram users about the app is futile. When designing surveys and interviews, we can improve the quality of the data collected by asking only qualified respondents, either recruiting readers with specific experiences or by using screening questions that help them self-select. We reach readers by:

- Using a general email list of subscribers or members.
- Maintaining a reader advisory group willing to participate in research.

- Renting a pre-qualified list from an external research service.
- Collaborating with community partners to reach their members.
- Promoting the survey via ads on our digital platforms or social media.

The demographic or psychographic characteristics we filter for depend on the type of research and the insights we seek.

- **Generative** or exploratory research is designed to broadly explore reader needs and preferences to guide the identification of solutions.
- **Evaluative** or explanatory research supports the design and development of a solution to ensure it correctly addresses the need.

Generative and evaluative are roughly equivalent to "open-ended" and "closed-ended" questions: *How do you feel about Instagram* vs. *Do you use Instagram—yes or no?*

The student-led survey was meant to be more generative than evaluative. It asked about a single app but was meant to probe a limited **use case**, not investigate specific features. The team correctly assessed that those answers would be found among loyal users interested in the news. So, the questions were rewritten to filter for and engage with that cohort.

A research question seeking deep insights should be addressed to a narrow group of expert readers. And one seeking broad feedback should be tested with a general audience.

Sports podcasts are a well-known product, and speaking to a small group of loyal fans would help us understand the value of a product and prioritize feature development.

Augmented reality is still an emerging technology, and talking to a large general audience would inform our understanding of future opportunities but not specific solutions.

In the class project, after screening for Instagram use, students proceeded to simplify the questions, further probe for expertise, and use a **controlled vocabulary** in the allowed answers to ease analysis:

---

2 How many accounts do you follow on Instagram? *(ENTER: ##)*
3 How often do you open Instagram? (SELECT ONE: Daily, Weekly, Many times per day...)
4 Which features of Instagram are you familiar with? (SELECT MULTIPLE: Main feed, Stories, IGTV, Messaging ...)
5 Do you follow any news organizations on Instagram? *(SELECT: YES/NO)*
   SKIP REST IF NO

After only five questions, we understand several key attributes of each respondent: How invested and engaged they are with the app, how familiar they are with its features, and if they knowingly follow any news accounts. We have also had two opportunities to disqualify the subject if they neither use Instagram nor follow a news account. After two more screening questions, we can be confident our remaining respondents are qualified to answer the research question before we start the main body of the survey.

---

6 How often do you notice photos or videos from news organizations? *(SELECT ONE: Daily, Weekly, Many times per day ...)*
7 When was the last time you remember interacting with a photo or video from a news organization? *(SELECT ONE: Today, Yesterday, This Week, This Month, Never)*
SKIP REST IF NEVER

Assuming readers have an attention span of 5–6 minutes, we have time to ask another 7–8 questions focused entirely on news use in the app. These will be a mix of multiple choice, ranking, and short answers designed to generate insights.

---

8 Do you follow any of these newsrooms on Instagram? (*SELECT MULTIPLE: List of competitors*)
9 Instagram is a useful platform to discover news. (RANK *AGREEMENT: 1–7*)
10 What do you find most valuable about our news feed on Instagram? *(SHORT ANSWER)*

A block of demographic questions can be inserted at the top of a survey if those answers are needed to filter respondents or branch the survey. They may also be placed at the end if required only to segment responses for analysis.

Before you launch a survey

- Assume no respondent will take more than 5 minutes.
- Use standard survey language when possible.
- Write simple questions—avoiding ambiguity.
- Don't **lead the witness** by writing questions that bias responses.
- Turn more complex ideas into multiple questions.
- Cluster related questions to provide context.
- Support **recognition, not recall**.
- Test drive your survey—multiple times—before deployment.
- Consider incentives (especially for longer surveys), such as a random drawing for a gift certificate.

In-depth interviews

Though a popular tool, online surveys can only tell half the story of "why." Surveys allow us to capture and make sense of feedback from hundreds or thousands of readers, but more context is needed to produce **deep insights**. We can recruit subjects for follow-up in-depth interviews (**IDI**) if we collect names and email addresses.

An IDI is typically a semi-structured discussion, with a **moderator's guide** of pre-scripted questions providing consistency while allowing the researcher to probe for insights. For instance, the answer to an open-ended question can be shepherded by subtle prompts:

1 What do you find most valuable about our news feed on Instagram? (PROMPT FOR: Entertaining, Shareable, Timely, Factual)

The follow-up prompts should be drawn from hypotheses developed in the survey or other prior research. Readers might address the topics unprompted, but if not, the moderator can gently direct the discussion to gather specific feedback that might help prove or disprove an idea.

We aim to question without unduly influencing the answer:

That is interesting, and do you ever share those videos on or off Instagram?

Each pre-scripted IDI question should include several prompts, which may be revised as subsequent interviews strengthen or weaken individual hypotheses.

Focus groups

While an IDI is a conversation between moderator and subject, a focus group can involve several moderators and a room of 6–10 subjects engaged in a dynamic but focused discussion.

Participants are typically chosen for demographic similarities or interests and experiences. As with the other qualitative methods, the profile of the recruiting pool will be dictated by the primary research question.

Focus groups can be helpful early in the research process (generative phase) when gathering thoughts, feelings, and anecdotes from readers will be useful in defining the job to be done. Later in the development process, the discussions can be an effective tool for gathering feedback (evaluative phase) to understand the effectiveness of a proposed solution.

Focus groups can be challenging to moderate. Some participants, by nature of their personalities, will want to contribute more, crowding out or swaying the opinions of others. But the highly interactive nature of the focus group conversation can also prompt participants to provide personal insights they may not articulate in other settings. It is helpful to set ground rules at the beginning of the session so the group understands the expectations of the format.

> *Thank you all for coming today. We appreciate your time and look forward to hearing your thoughts. There are no right or wrong answers. We are interested in your personal perspectives and experiences. Feel free to react to or disagree with other participants, but politely. We want to hear from everyone, so we will occasionally interject with questions or call on people who have not spoken recently.*

Even with a collegial group, a second researcher can help watch for non-verbal cues among participants and to participate in note-taking and post-session analysis.

Observation

As anthropologist Margaret Mead did not exactly once write: "What people say, what people do, and what people say they do are entirely different things."[3] Often, the most effective way to understand how our products are used "in the wild" is simply to watch. As a method, direct observation can provide insights a survey or interview is ill-suited to offer.

A member of a family of methods that includes **ethnography**, direct observation can help researchers understand the user journey and provide context for product design discussions. The technique can be done quickly and inexpensively in formal and informal settings.

When developing a mobile app at *The Boston Globe* in 2012, I would seek out commuter rail passengers browsing the morning headlines. At the time, many were still reading Kindles or paperback books, not skimming our website on their iPhones. In an office context, a researcher may watch as an **expert user** works with a software system, taking note of their habits and workarounds.

Observation in the user's everyday environment can reveal the complexities of multi-tasking between different screens or applications, the use of sticky notes with passwords and shortcut key combinations, or the user's struggles with the interface due to patchy Wi-Fi connectivity. Any of those findings might lead to the development of new features or new products. But most importantly, each of those rich details helps internal teams gain empathy for the needs and struggles of the user.

Recognizing use cases

Understanding how and when your readers are using your website, or app will directly influence the design of your product. You have probably noticed that streaming music apps such as Spotify have two primary UX design patterns:

1 Not in the car.
2 In the car.

Smart recognition of those two contexts allows the app to provide the most appropriate user interface for each case. For news, you might be able to list hundreds of other potential contexts, including:

- On a smartphone.
- On a PC or laptop.
- At home on Wi-Fi.
- Around town, on 5G.
- While driving.
- When notified by a push alert.
- In the morning.
- At night.
- In school.
- At work.

Not every context requires a unique interface design and user experience, but some might—like *driving* or *not driving*. Identifying those cases and designing for them reduces barriers to use, making your product more valuable.

Personas and profiles

Personas are deeply-researched, though still hypothetical **archetypes**[4] developed using a broad mix of data sources to represent segments of your audience.

Alan Cooper is credited with creating the methodology in 1998. As Cooper argues, **personas** enable an organization to focus on its audience by allowing it to envision "just one person"[5] it is designing and developing a product for. This critical use is why the process of creating a persona must be rigorous and well-understood by each relevant department.

A factually informed fiction

A persona represents an amalgamation of details about a group of readers crafted into a coherent narrative used to inform team discussions and decisions. The goals of a persona project are to:

- Understand and group your users into relevant cohorts.
- Describe as accurately as possible a "real" person who uses your products.
- Identify their activities, needs, and motivations for using your products.
- Share those details within your business to focus attention and effort.

UX teams may develop several personas for a given product—but a single persona should be the target audience for any prioritization of features.

Persona development begins with a review of web analytics to generate initial hypotheses, audience surveys that allow readers to self-categorize, and in-depth interview sessions for final validation.

In 2012, *The Boston Globe* reexamined its Boston.com personas during strategic planning for the site. Researchers identified five archetypes as categorized by their information-seeking behaviors. The primary persona consisted of readers who checked in frequently to scan the homepage for new stories:

The headliner

- Represents: 46% of visitors.
- Age: 35–64.
- Gender: 64% male.
- Loyalty: Visits multiple times daily.
- Popular sections: Business, local, health, technology.
- Motivation: A need to stay informed.
- Obstacle: Knowing when new articles are posted.
- Opportunities: Offer highlights, executive summaries, text alerts, and customization.

By clearly defining motivations and obstacles—and comparing those to other validated personas—business teams can envision possible product solutions to serve each type of reader. Researchers will often apply alliterative names, "Harry Headliner," and include a representative stock photo of the persona to aid team discussion.

Developing useful profiles

When a designer or product manager says they are working with a "persona," they often mean they have a **profile**, a working sketch of a segment of their audience—not a deeply researched and validated biographical description. A profile typically includes demographic and behavioral details, including geographic location, age, gender, and web activity. Profiles do NOT explain the "why" of a user's motivations, but they can help illuminate the differences between the different audience segments using your products.

Profiles are best used in low-risk scenarios like survey design or early product strategy discussions. If the proposed product is an email newsletter focused on the local school district, several hypothetical profiles can be crafted:

- Our core audience for this product is approaching middle age, lives in our city, and is a homeowner. They have two school-age children and work in a white-collar or another professional setting. They actively follow both local and national news events.
- A key secondary audience are retirees who no longer have school-age children but have an interest in the district and are sensitive to modifications to changes in local real estate tax rates.
- An adjacent audience we would like to reach and serve better are younger adults who may be renting and have no children or children too young for school. They are just beginning to take an interest in schools and funding.

- A potential audience are people thinking about relocating to our city and are interested to know more about schools and city government.

We don't know the validity of those profiles. But by explicitly discussing and documenting our assumptions, we can develop research questions, prototypes, and other experiments to improve our understanding of the target audience.

Bias in qualitative research

All forms of research are prone to distortions imposed by the researcher or the method. No process involving human beings is free of bias, but recognizing the common pitfalls can help us mitigate the impact on our decisions. A few of the cognitive biases that commonly arise in research:

- **Confirmation bias**—We see patterns in the data that support a favored pre-existing hypothesis, but we fail to recognize or accept contradictory facts.
- **Ethnocentrism**—We write questions and interpret responses through our own cultural knowledge and experiences without understanding how others might understand or respond.
- **Question order bias**—Respondents are influenced in their understanding or response to questions by prior questions. To minimize this effect, begin surveys or interviews with broad questions and progress to more specific questions.
- **Leading questions**—The wording of a question implies a specific perspective or preferred answer.
- **Social desirability bias**—Respondents will seek approval by answering questions in a way they think aligns with the researcher's expectations.
- **Survivor bias**—It is a form of selection bias, the inclusion or exclusion of participants that inherently skew research results. When seeking to understand customer feedback, it is easy to talk to current users of your product without recognizing past customers or non-customers are likely to have differing opinions. If the goal is to improve the retention of existing subscribers, listening only to that audience can help. But if you are concerned with acquisition and retention, targeting and identifying respondents makes a difference. Never-subscribers will have needs and interests very distinct from those who have been loyal readers for 15 years.

Does it work?

The **usability test** is a fundamental research method in product management. In these sessions, a reader is given specific tasks to complete on a website or app, and a moderator observes the results. Hints may be provided when a task poses unexpected challenges, or the reader may be asked to talk through the problem aloud.

Sessions may be held in person or remotely, and any product or service can be the subject of a usability test. The goal is to identify user interface or design problems that inhibit task completion or to gather **evaluative** feedback about perceived value. Generative insights can also be collected by exploring a competitor's website or sites in a related industry.

Prototyping

When developing the first Palm Pilot (a personal digital assistant circa 1996), company founder Jeff Hawkins took notes, created calendar entries, and answered calls on a block of wood.[6]

Hawkins used the block, carved into the size of the proposed device, to understand the appropriate weight and shape that would be practical to users and to act out the routines of its expected functionality. He demonstrated that a Palm Pilot could comfortably fit in his shirt pocket and be useful in a business context. This form of prototyping, now known as the **Hawkins Block**, is a popular method to explore the design of physical products.

A block of wood is cheap to design and modify, allowing rapid cycles of testing and improvement. It doesn't function like a real Palm Pilot, but any version of an idea you can make accessible for interrogation and learning will improve the final product.

A prototype could also be a detailed verbal explanation, a paper sketch, a set of cards representing user actions, or a roughly designed interactive website. A prototype does not offer a polished user experience, especially early in the design and development process. And the goals for the test dictate which elements of the eventual final design are presented:

A **horizontal prototype** depicts the full scope of a product, from navigation menus to individual pages and features. But it is presented at low fidelity, typically as wireframes with minimal visual design. The goal is to understand how users interact with the product and to gather insights into **information architecture** and expected features.

A **vertical prototype** focuses on a specific feature or function and should depict as closely as possible the final design, interactivity, and systems integration for that one element. This narrow but deep view of the product allows teams to test technical feasibility and explore the feature's usability.

For discussion

1 What is the purpose of dividing a project into phases, as in the Product Development Process?
2 How do we decide who to talk with to optimize human-centered research results?
3 What is the difference between generative and evaluative research? Which comes first in a project?

4 In your opinion, what is the best research method?
5 Why is "defining the question" the most important step in a research project?
6 How or why are readers "experts?"

Learn more

- *The Machine in the Garden: Technology and the Pastoral Ideal in America* – Leo Marx. (1964). Oxford University Press.
- *The Inmates are Running the Asylum* – Alan Cooper (2004). Sams – Pearson Education.
- *Living with complexity* – Don Norman (2011). MIT Press.
- *The Design of Everyday Things* – Don Norman (2013, Revised) Basic Books.
- *Interviewing Users: How to Uncover Compelling Insights* – Steve Portigal (2013). Rosenfeld Media.
- *Design Thinking for Entrepreneurs and Small Businesses* – Beverly Rudkin Ingle. (2013) Apress.
- *Just Enough Research* – Erika Hall (2014, 2nd ed.). A Book Apart.
- *Value Proposition Design: How to Create Products and Services Customers Want* – Alexander Osterwalder, Yves Pigneur, Gregory Bernarda & Alan Smith. (2014). John Wiley & Sons.
- *Doorbells, Danger and Dead Batteries: User Research War Stories* – Steve Portigal (2016). Rosenfeld Media.
- *Measure what matters: How Google, Bono, and the Gates Foundation rock the world with OKRs* – John Doerr (2018). Portfolio/Penguin.
- *Escaping the Build Trap: How Effective Product Management Creates Real Value* – Melissa Perri (2019). O'Reilly.
- *Building for Everyone: Expand Your Market with Design Practices from Google's Product Inclusion Team* – Annie Jean-Baptiste. (2020). John Wiley & Sons.
- *Imagined Audiences: How Journalists Perceive and Pursue the Public* – Jacob L. Nelson (2021). Oxford University Press.

Notes

1 Carew Grovum, E. (2017). *The Daily Beast Product Project Request Intake*.
2 Aaronson, B. (2017). *Texas Tribune Pitch Guide*.
3 Ewing, S. (2011). *Architecture and Field/Work* (S. Ewing, Ed.). Routledge.
4 Cooper, A. (2004). *The Inmates are Running the Asylum* (p. 124). Sams – Pearson Education.
5 Ibid.
6 Kahney, L. (1999). The Philosophy of the Handheld. *Wired*. https://www.wired.com/1999/10/the-philosophy-of-the-handheld/

9 Product is prioritization

In this chapter

- The need for a shared organizational vision.
- Using Objectives and Key Results (OKRs) to align mission and tactics.
- Evaluating and comparing business and product opportunities.
- Informing decisions to improve outcomes.
- The importance of good storytelling in business.

News organizations are a nearly unlimited source of product ideas.

- For our next project, should we launch a new email newsletter or work on optimizing the membership funnel?
- Should we add a homepage customization tool or an article-text-to-voice feature?
- We need a public event strategy, is a book festival or a series of public forums with local candidates better?

Ideas (even the best ones) are a dime a dozen. But our time is precious. To prioritize, we use the three pillars of desirability, feasibility, and sustainability to rank projects by potential value. That research and deliberation requires babysitting information, insights, and decisions across the organization. Effective management of the organization is as important as the quality of the original idea.

Many online tech companies use **OKRs** to align corporate goals with team activities. First practiced at Intel and later popularized at Google, OKRs are a formal performance-tracking process that pairs specific goals with quantifiable metrics. This is stated as:

We will achieve OBJECTIVE as measured by RESULTS.

DOI: 10.4324/9781003154785-13

In a media company, that formula might translate into a team or departmentmental OKR of:

- We will increase our newsletter readership by 30% as measured by:
- *Key Result One:* Launch two new topic-focused newsletters.
- *Key Result Two:* Increase open rate among all subscribers by 15%.
- *Key Result Three:* Reduce subscriber **churn** by 10%.

Those key results would be further supported by individual OKRs, and tactics shared among product managers, developers, journalists, and marketers contributing to the project.

This approach is an evolution of the methods of scientific management that date back to Frederick Taylor in the early 1900s and includes the development of management by objective (**MBO**) as part of the HP Way in the 1950s and 60s.

As a rule, OKRs:

- Originate at the team level.
- Are set and reviewed quarterly.
- Are flexible if the business situation changes.
- Are aggressive—not every goal will be met.
- Should help manage success, not punish failure.

The philosophy behind OKRs and MBOs is described broadly as "goal alignment." Often, the relevant difference between methods is the level of autonomy given to line employees to set their own goals that complement organizational strategic objectives. In strictly hierarchical command-and-control organizations, employee goals are set by managers. But a more enlightened practice of a 50–50 balance is recommended.

What's the plan?

A business is a machine designed to organize people and resources in pursuit of a goal. OKRs and similar methods are helpful tools in that alignment. But as Lewis Carroll's Cheshire Cat once told Alice, if you don't know your destination, it doesn't matter in which direction you walk. Finding our way begins with a shared vision of success and then developing the strategy and tactics required.

- A **mission statement** describes our vision but not how we intend to achieve it.
- A **strategy** is a plan that describes the major initiatives to be pursued.
- **Tactics** are the detailed tasks that support an initiative.

Google's original (see Chapter 7) mission statement, *Organize the world's information and make it universally accessible and useful,* says nothing specifically about the web, search engine design and development, nor the creation of the Android mobile operating system.

The Keene Sentinel, a daily newspaper in western New Hampshire, similarly says nothing specifically about the tools or platforms it will use to achieve its mission:

> *The reader of The Keene Sentinel will feel a sense of belonging and will be inspired and empowered to engage in community. This is made possible by an innovative, caring, proactive and responsive news organization that serves as a trusted source and civic partner.*[1]

Vision is the art of knowing where you want the business to be in five years. But management is about knowing what you need to do tomorrow. We often focus too much on the first part—the grand idea—and not enough on the second part—how to achieve it.

The executive suite typically develops and sets forth a company's strategy. Tactics are then identified by middle management and carried out by staff. In a large business, those are distinct groups of people possibly working in different locations. In a small organization, one person might be responsible for every step.

Where to start?

The path from organizational objective to an individual task is a continuum between long-term and short-term goals. And the work of aligning ideas and activities flows down through adjacent levels of an organizational hierarchy, so we often describe it as a linear process:

- Developing a vision and mission (*A focus of the CEO and leadership*)
- Connecting mission and strategy (*Leadership and managers*)
- Aligning strategy and goals (*Managers and teams*)
- Assigning goals and tactics (*Teams and staff*)

But in business, what comes first? The vision or the strategy, or the tactics? Is it the chicken or the egg or the omelet making? The answer is: *Yes.* Continuous iteration is a circle with no distinct beginning or end. It matters less where on the circle the discussion starts if the loop is repeated until a useful answer is discovered.

Every business decision follows this pattern, starting life as a hypothesis to be informed and updated as we travel the loop and gather insights. But vision and mission are foundational building blocks and must be accepted as validated theories before strategies and tactics can be fully developed and acted upon. This is partly due to the time horizon each tier observes and the practical effects of organizational hierarchy.

A **mission statement** is intended to guide the organization for 7–10 years. Frequent major revisions would paralyze productivity as employees struggled to understand and reorient to each new direction. In startup technology companies, this shift called a "pivot" is more common as the business chases a **product-market fit**. Twitter (now X) began life as an MP3-sharing service before shifting to focus on its current short-messaging platform strategy. But newsrooms don't "pivot" in that same way. Journalism is inherently mission-driven, and the goal of serving community information needs is non-negotiable. Instead, news entrepreneurs focus on strategy and tactics: Finding an audience and diversifying revenues.

A business **strategy** is typically a 3- to 5-year plan guiding an organizational investment of time and resources. A business will pursue multiple strategies in support of its mission. The design of each strategy must reflect organizational capacity, consumer preferences, and current and future economic trends and policies. Some risks can be fairly estimated and accounted for in strategic planning, and others cannot.

- In 2018, the General Data Protection Regulation (GDPR) complicated the widespread collection and sharing of customer data between publishing partners and vendors in the European Union. That policy change came after years of discussion, giving publishers time to reconsider their strategic plans, though many did not.
- In 2020, live event strategies had to be paused or abandoned in the face of the global COVID-19 pandemic. Until then, events had been an increasingly important source of community engagement and revenue for many local publishers. But the global shutdown of in-person gatherings could not have been predicted. Goals are set quarterly or annually as progress is made or circumstances change. So in Q2 of 2020, any goals focused on ticket sales and revenues were adapted to measure attendance and engagement instead.

Tactics are sometimes updated monthly as the needs of a project change. The activities required to support a paid live event include picking a venue, processing ticket sales, arranging food and beverage, renting audio-visual gear, and arranging travel for speakers and guests. For an online event, ticketing might be built into the video-conferencing tool, and no travel is required. On an incremental basis, tactics also evolve naturally as a staff and organization learn what works and course correct.

Alignment and focus

Imagine your newsroom has a niche focus, reporting on the election process in your city. A simple *vision, mission, strategy*, and *tactic* set might be:

- **Vision**: The city would be better served if citizens understood more about the candidates and offices.
- **Mission statement**: A better city with better elections.
- **Strategy**: To provide more opportunities for office-holders and those running for office to meet voters.
- **Tactics**: We will provide a job-sharing program that allows voters to hold elected office "for a day" while a candidate for that office covers their job.

Notice the strategy and tactics are increasingly specific and support the founding vision. Of course, the proposed service in this case (job sharing) is impossibly fanciful, a fact that would be revealed early in the research process.

In the real world, a strategy proposes a practical solution while considering:

- Long-term goals.
- External customer needs.
- Alignment of organizational resources.
- Tactical planning considers.
- Shorter-term objectives.
- Specific goal-oriented activities.
- Coordination of day-to-day organizational efforts.

At a team and individual level, tactics become increasingly detailed and specialized. In Chapter 10, we will discuss the process of defining development tasks and estimating the time and cost necessary to evaluate and produce a product or service.

Seeing the future

Strategic planning concerns itself with the risks and opportunities apparent within a 3- to 5-year window. But we are often inattentive to longer-term changes and threats. It is easier to plan for a future that looks like today—but with bigger smartphones—than it is to prepare for a change as disruptive as the world wide web continues to be. But history tells us that Artificial Intelligence, Quantum Computing, or Fusion Reactors might change the world and economy in the next 15–20 years in ways we can't currently imagine.

Media-focused futurist Amy Webb calls for leaders to consider the potential for unexpected changes a decade away. Her time horizons for business strategy are:

- 1- to 2-year range for planning and adjusting tactics.
- 2- to 5-year window for setting and following a specific strategy.
- 5 to 10 years before updating an organizational vision.
- 10+ years to prepare for a systems-level evolution of culture and technology.

Webb notes the rise of the smartphone as an example of publishers failing to plan for the opportunities presented by the new devices, despite being aware of the technology well in advance of mass public adoption.[2]

Strengths and weaknesses

A standard tool for evaluating strategic opportunities is the **SWOT** matrix: Strengths, Weaknesses, Opportunities, and Threats. The grid helps identify the internal and external factors relevant to the success of a project or strategy.

As a discussion starter, it can be completed in a 20-minute brainstorming session. For more critical uses, it can be the summarized output of long-term planning discussions.

- Strengths: What do we do well? What is unique about our product?
- Weaknesses: How can we improve? What skills or resources do we lack?
- Opportunities: What trends are favorable? Are there underserved audiences or markets?
- Threats: How will competitors react? What broader economic trends are a challenge?

A SWOT analysis can be applied to a project as well as a business. A quick study of a news subscription plan (Figure 9.1) would explore the organization's capacity to pursue the strategy.

SWOT analysis - paywall strategy

Strengths

- Well-known and trusted organization
- Largest newsroom in the region
- Declining but still robust advertising revenues

Weaknesses

- Significant competition for digital attention
- Constrains access for some communities
- Our digital sign-up flow is unfriendly

Opportunities

- Increasingly accepted consumer model
- More consistent revenue forecasts
- Enables creation of value-added bundles of content and services

Threats

- Local TV stations will never use a subscription model
- Digital news start-ups might pursue memberships
- Decline of advertising revenues might outpace subscription gains

Figure 9.1 A SWOT analysis can be used to evaluate a business, strategy, or product.

Porter's five forces

A consultant and professor at the Harvard Business School, Michael Porter outlined a set of influences in the development of corporate strategy:

- Competitive rivalry.
- Threat of substitute products.
- Bargaining power of buyers.
- Threat of new entrants.
- Bargaining power of suppliers.

All apply to the business of media, but two are most relevant to the digital disruption facing journalism and threaten the position of incumbent media organizations:

- The rise of the internet as a distribution platform for news also provides consumers unlimited access to substitute products—either as alternative sources of information or entertainment.
- The low marginal cost of digital distribution significantly reduces the cost for new newsrooms to enter the market, compared to the previous expense of a printing press or broadcast license.

External threats

While the SWOT and Five Forces models balance a view of internal and external factors, **PESTEL** examines the larger macroeconomic pressures that influence strategic planning. These are forces a business might support or oppose but which they cannot directly manage:

- Political—Including quality of governance, taxes, and trade.
- Economic—Trends, interest rates, unemployment.
- Socio-economic—Population growth, culture, lifestyle.
- Technology—Innovation, automation, research & development.
- Environmental—Climate, weather, regulations.
- Legal—Labor laws, antitrust, copyright, health & safety.

For a media company, each of these categories holds both opportunities and threats. For instance:

- In the U.S., the Journalism Competition and Preservation Act, proposed but not passed in 2022, was like laws in Australia and Canada requiring internet giants, including Facebook and Google, to negotiate with and pay news organizations for content shared on social media and in search results.
- The lack of regulation constraining Facebook and Google from leveraging their core social and search platforms to capture much of the global digital

advertising economy. Conversely, the imposition of the GDPR in the European Union has influenced the decline of third-party tracking of consumer behaviors.

- The ongoing uncertainty about Section 230 of the Communications Decency Act in the U.S. that shields internet service providers (including news publishers) from responsibility for user-generated content such as tweets or article comments.
- The rise of unionization in newsrooms and the growing trend toward remote work for many white-collar employees.
- The constantly shifting relationship between Journalism and Big Tech (like Facebook) has led to recurring cycles of newsroom investment in initiatives (like video), resulting in newsroom losses and layoffs when the platform later abandons the strategy.

Any initiative approved or launched that relies on an assumption of stability in those (and numerous other) external factors will inevitably fail when the variables change. Strategic decision-making must weigh that risk and be prepared to update or discard a strategy or tactic that threatens to become untenable.

Dogs and cows and harvests

There are dozens of variations of the matrix decision-making framework. The Boston Consulting Group (Figure 9.2) is known for a four-box grid that categorizes business opportunities:

- Stars have a high growth potential.
- Question Marks exhibit high growth but do not maintain pace with the competition.
- Cash Cows grow slowly but dominate their market.
- Dogs both grow slowly and perform poorly against competitors.

The GE-McKinsey NineBox Matrix (Figure 9.3) expands on that analysis of investment or divestment opportunities.

Translating a strategy into a product

The continuous improvement loop (Build-Measure-Learn) guides the process of designing and aligning organizational mission and goals, as well as the work of product research and development. In theory, these are sequential efforts:

- Mission—Strategy—Goals.
- Needs—Solutions—Assessment.

In practice, the efforts are interwoven and continuous, like a Möbius loop (Figure 9.4).

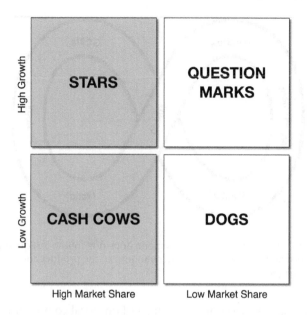

Figure 9.2 The two-by-two matrix is a popular analysis tool. This version from the Boston Consulting Group frames the discussion of business opportunities relative to market share and growth.

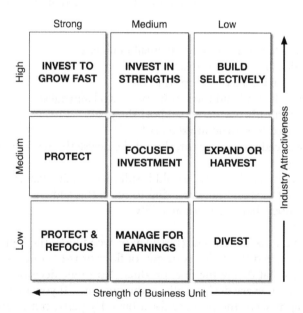

Figure 9.3 A McKinsey-developed matrix also considers business opportunities for investment or divestment.

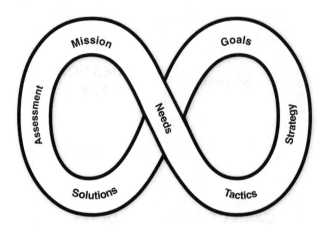

Figure 9.4 The work of product management does not follow a sequential path but loops and overlaps as our understanding of the product and audience needs develops.

If our mission is to serve and inform all of our local communities. And one goal is to improve outreach and engagement with Spanish-speaking residents. A specific strategy could be to better deliver coverage of interest to those readers.

We might propose a product solution: *A Spanish-language email newsletter.*

Our journey through the research questions then circumnavigates the Möbius loop:

• Do these readers want or need an email newsletter?
• And how does it support our strategy?
• Should it be bilingual or in Spanish only?
• Do we have the staff and time to support two languages?
• Will a Spanish-only newsletter support the goal?
• Or do we need to restructure the goal?
• To improve reader engagement, should the newsletter be manually curated and written?
• If it were automated instead, would it still meet reader expectations?
• Do we need to expand our reporting to reach this audience?
• If so, how does that affect sustainability?

Like baking a cake, the event (birthday or wedding?), the ingredients (do we have sugar?), and the recipe (one cup of flour or two?) offer opportunities and limitations that define the final product. No single decision ensures success or failure, but every decision affects the outcome. If you are low on flour, a cupcake might serve the purpose for a birthday party, but scrambled eggs might not.

Evaluating opportunities

Before investing in a new email newsletter, a newsroom will want:

- An internal assessment that design and development work is practical and will cost $100 (in hypothetical dollars).
- Research that validates reader interest and forecasts 500 subscribers.
- A business analysis that estimates an initial $5 in monthly advertising revenue that increases to $10 at the 500-subscriber goal.
- An understanding that ongoing support and maintenance will cost $3.75 a month.

With that information, we can forecast first-year revenues of $60 against $145 in expenses. But in year two, annual costs fall to $45, and revenue improves to $120. If the subscription goal is met early, a $10 total profit might be realized over two years.

Deciding to decide

In business, the goal of research is to inform a decision. A good product management team helps to define the questions and processes needed to investigate and propose an answer. So, when it comes to the final deliberation of our email newsletter proposal, you might argue $10 is a reasonable profit. "Trust the numbers!" But humans are prone to errors of both commission and omission. So, trust is a subjective process informed by our perception of the process, the quality of prior recommendations, and the culture of the organization. Without trust, every analysis is open to criticism about potential bias or questions not asked. And it is the nature of decision-making that any question left unaddressed, no matter how irrelevant, will be highlighted by critics:

> *How can we possibly finalize our product roadmap without first discussing the Q4 commodity futures for apple juice concentrate?*

The other side of that skepticism is an assertion the research is taking too long:

> *How much more time and how many more answers do we need before we can make a decision?*

These tensions often flare late in the process because decision-making is a series of steps toward reducing uncertainty. Along the way, unresolved risk constantly collects in the corners of the discussion and must eventually be cleared out before a consensus can be reached.

Decision-making support

Even when we follow a rigorous process, poor decisions can still be made as the result of:

1 Simple misunderstandings.
2 Incorrect assumptions.
3 Lack of agreement on the facts.
4 Misalignment of goals or incentives.
5 Individual self-interest (or self-preservation).
6 Cognitive biases.

In a binary decision (yes or no) with non-overlapping choices, there are three possible outcomes:

1 A false yes.
2 A false no.
3 A correct yes or no.

Among statisticians and researchers, the false results are known as **Type 1** and **Type 2** errors, respectively. In a courtroom setting, a Type 1 error would result in the conviction of an innocent person; a Type 2 error would set a guilty person free. In business, that would mean investing in a bad idea or rejecting a good one—errors of commission or omission.

Former Amazon CEO Jeff Bezos describes some business decisions as "one-way doors," meaning they cannot be reversed once a decision is made.[3] While every decision is important, our investment in reducing uncertainty must be calibrated to risk. A two-way door with nominal cost or risk involved might merit little research. In contrast, a one-way door with a complex problem and potential million-dollar risk should receive significant attention and debate before making a decision.

Deciding

For the newsletter project, our diligent research and analysis suggests the newsletter is, at best, likely to gain a modest audience and income. Should we:

• Approve the project as likely profitable?
• Reject it as not profitable enough?
• Delay a decision because the level of uncertainty in the data supports either option?

In product and strategy deliberations, success is a flexible metric. It can mean:

• Direct financial profitability.
• Indirect profitability, including as a **loss leader**.
• Value in offensive or defensive efforts against competitors.

Before we make a decision, we need to consider the goal of the newsletter project, which was agreed to at the beginning of the initiative:

1 Audience engagement. (Improving the loyalty and retention of current readers is most important.)
2 Audience growth. (Acquisition of new readers is secondary.)
3 Revenue growth. (Advertising and attributed membership/subscriptions.)

Collecting and analyzing those metrics will take months, and retention is difficult to attribute to a single cause. To make our decision before launch, we must decide how much to trust our predictions of:

- Development cost and time estimates.
- Revenue estimates.
- Reaching 500 subscribers in the first year.

Ultimately, not every question can be answered with quantitative certainty. As much as we try to transform conflicting motivations and incomplete insights into neat and tidy frameworks and spreadsheets, human subjectivity can't be fully domesticated. Instead, it is the purpose of a rigorous and well-documented research and analysis process to provide transparency, facilitate trust, and help us recognize when the quality of additional information tips toward **diminishing returns**. Any final decision will inevitably rely on human intuition and interpersonal power dynamics—informed by rigorously collected reader-focused research and data.

How the *why* convinces us

Because the human brain is attracted to a good story, explaining the "why" of a decision is a more powerful tool than simply offering a spreadsheet of consumer demographics or purchasing behaviors.

If our weekly sales report shows a spike in umbrella sales last week, we might welcome the news: *Sales increased 45% week-over-week!*

Reviewing the weather report might remind us it rained for several days, hinting at a motivation for the purchases: *The spike in sales is likely due to recent inclement weather.*

But talking to consumers (and local salespeople) is required to understand the full story: "I was eating lunch downtown, and a freak thunderstorm hit. Luckily, I spotted a large sign on the sidewalk across the street advertising a sale on umbrellas."

If you are in the business of selling umbrellas, you can't make it rain more often. But understanding the context and consumer need driving an increase in sales makes the raw numbers **actionable**, helping us to plan. Next time the thunderclouds roll in, we will be prepared to take advantage.

Clayton Christensen introduced his theory of consumer needs and motivations with "Jobs to be Done" in 2005 and a story about milkshakes. But the idea goes back at least as far as the 1950s, and another Harvard professor, Theodore Levitt, used to tell his marketing classes: "People don't want to buy a quarter-inch drill. They want a quarter-inch hole!"[4]

Levitt's axiomatic advice reflected his belief that companies and marketers must focus more on customer needs to remain competitive. He argued that growth industries eventually fail because executives mistake the business they are in. Railroad executives believed they were in the train industry. But the competition from cars and planes in the 20th century showed railroads were part of the broader transportation sector.

As told by Christensen, the McDonald's fast-food restaurant chain wanted to improve sales of their milkshakes.[5,6]

The company had a sophisticated and data-rich marketing operation and developed a profile of a typical milkshake customer. As is common marketing practice, the company identified look-alike customers and interviewed them to understand their preferences. Would they buy more milkshakes if the drink was "Chocolatier, cheaper chunkier (or) chewier?"[7] But sales and profits were unaffected despite testing and deploying changes based on this feedback.

The company turned to Christensen's consulting group. A researcher spent 18 hours in a restaurant noting the time, what each customer ordered, what they were wearing, whether they were alone, and if they ordered take-out or eat-in. He noticed an unexpected pattern: Nearly half of the milkshakes that day were sold before 8:30 a.m.[8] And those morning customers had many similarities: They often arrived alone, bought only a milkshake, and drove away with their purchase.

The following day, the researcher positioned himself outside the store and intercepted and interviewed customers emerging from the store with a milkshake.

Customers are not always able to articulate specific purchasing motivations. If you were to ask, "What did you buy a milkshake?" they might rightfully answer, "I was thirsty."

Instead, a product thinker works to elicit deeper insights:

- Do you purchase a milkshake every day?
- Think about the last time you were in a similar situation but did not buy a milkshake; what did you purchase instead?
- What was the advantage or disadvantage of that other product compared to a milkshake?

This style of questioning encourages subjects to reflect on their behaviors and motivations in a new way. Standing in the parking lot. The researcher discovered customers had in the past "hired" a variety of other products to "do the job" also served by a milkshake:

- Bagel.
- Donut.
- Candy bar.
- Banana.

For the consumer, each of those solutions had a drawback. It is a challenge to spread cream cheese on a bagel while driving; one donut is not filling; a candy bar feels like an unhealthy choice; and a banana is consumed too quickly to be satisfying.

As it turns out, the early-morning milkshake drinkers were on their way to work, had a "long, boring commute,"[9] wanted something to do while driving, and needed a snack that would hold them until lunchtime.

Given the job to be done, hiring a milkshake makes perfect sense. It can be easily held in one hand, takes considerable time to drink, and is filling.

The other half of milkshake customers purchasing in the afternoon were hiring the drink for an entirely different reason. These parents were buying meals and waiting while their children struggled to consume the cold, thick drink through a narrow straw.[10]

"People drink milkshakes because they are thirsty" is a superficial answer that lacks actionable insights. But *morning commuters may drink a milkshake because it is filling and convenient when driving* is a deep enough insight to inform new strategies.

Where the prior marketing research had profiled an average milkshake customer through the aggregation of demographic characteristics, the jobs-to-be-done framework revealed that the customer need, not their age, gender, or income level, was the distinguishing motivator.

With those two distinctly different jobs in mind, McDonalds targeted its morning customers by making the milkshake thicker, adding fruit, and providing a quick "self-serve" option with a prepaid card for a conveniently located milkshake dispenser for on-the-go commuters.

Feature planning

After approving our new email newsletter strategy, the work shifts to prioritizing the wish list of product features:

1 An automatic content feed with the ability to customize.
2 Three top stories, two each from two other categories.
3 Integration of advanced analytics.
4 Mobile-friendly template.
5 Privacy policy requirements.

Understanding readers' context, needs, and motivations helps us prioritize those features. And like strategy setting, we use decision frameworks to routinize and inform the process.

There is no perfect feature prioritization process, though each tries to balance:

• Cost of investment.
• Value and benefits.

- Time to deliver.
- Return on investment.
- Time to recoup the investment.

Understanding a project's potential time and cost is always the first step, and **T-shirt sizing** is a popular estimation strategy in Agile development environments. It sorts product and feature requests into relatively sized categories based on the development time required. The estimates use the metaphor of T-shirt sizes (in the U.S. measuring system) from extra small (XS) to extra large (XL).

Using a handful of categories allows the estimation process to proceed more intuitively than possible if more precise categories were required. The length of time implied by each size is agreed to within the group. So, an XS might represent a one-hour task and an XL one year. Or one week and one fiscal quarter. These estimates are used in value vs. effort and similar prioritization processes and inform the **work in progress (WIP)** estimates that help the development team manage and forecast their workload.

Prioritization methods are often selected by random luck, organizational structure, tolerance for formal processes, and the influence of the development team's project management processes. So, which is best? It depends.

A **MoSCoW** prioritization can help build consensus across teams within an organization. The tool's output is not a precise ranking of features but a categorization of items in the backlog.

- **Must haves** are non-negotiable features that cannot be left out of the product.
- **Should haves** are important but not necessarily critical.
- **Could haves** should be included but will have less impact if left out than the two categories above.
- **Won't haves** are features that the team decides are low priority and will not be considered for development at this time.

Value vs. effort and **value vs. complexity** are similar **heuristics** that evaluate the potential cost and success of features (or products). A series of expense and revenue variables are assessed and assigned a single numeric value to be charted onto a matrix for discussion. Value vs. effort focuses on development effort, while value vs. complexity considers overall risks and costs. The calculation can include:

- Revenue or strategic value.
- Benefit to current or potential customers.
- Impact on business goals.
- Cost or time to build.
- Development and implementation effort.
- Cost of ongoing support & maintenance.
- Risk.
- Complexity.

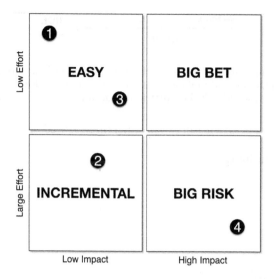

Figure 9.5 Prioritization tools are always used to compare two or more projects. Here, projects 1,2,3,4 are charted by their estimated relative value.

- After assigning each feature a score on both dimensions, the results are charted (Figure 9.5) for discussion and prioritization.

Both methods allow for a broad clustering of feature ideas to help simplify the ranking of items in a backlog but do not dictate a precise ordering of the work.

The Weighted Shortest Job First (**WSJF**) method used within the Scaled Agile Framework (**SAFe**) also considers economic value and development time to evaluate the cost of delay (CoD) relative to other jobs. The "weighted" portion of the equation includes consideration of consumer and business value, the interdependence of the work with other ongoing tasks, and its overall strategic value. Identifying the "shortest job" is also an estimate of job size and time (JST) to complete, and the two variables are assigned a number (sometimes from the Fibonacci sequence of 1,2,3,5,8...) to produce a ranked prioritization.

Jobs with a high cost of delay will be prioritized, but so will jobs with a short duration. The calculation works to balance those two extremes.

So, if WSJF = CoD/JST, then job two would be prioritized:

- Job One: $3/2 = 1.5$.
- Job Two: $5/3 = 1.6$.

A **RICE** prioritization (Figure 9.6) also attempts a ranked output by assessing:

- **Reach**: The number of customers expected to be attracted to or served by a feature or product.

$$\frac{\textit{Reach} \times \textit{Impact} \times \textit{Confidence}}{\textit{Effort}} = \begin{array}{l}\textbf{RICE} \\ \text{Score}\end{array}$$

Figure 9.6 Assigning a score comprised of several related estimates is a valuable tool in comparing and ranking projects. Still, it can also lead to compounding errors if the individual estimates are inaccurate.

- **Impact**: The value of a feature or product often scored on a scale of 0.25–3.

    3 = maximum impact

    2 = high

    1 = medium

    0.5 = low

    0.25 = minimal

- **Confidence**: The level of risk perceived in the decision

    100% – No risk

    80% – Average risk

    50% – High risk (no better than a coin flip)

- **Effort**: The investment of staff effort measured by a "person month."

The **Kano model** prioritizes consumer needs and preferences over cost and value alone. It is formally joined with a quantitative survey of your audience, asking them to assess a series of potential features from your backlog:

How would you feel if your email newsletter was formatted for mobile devices?

- I would like it.
- I would expect it.
- I would be neutral.
- I would tolerate it.
- I would not like it.

The survey responses are then analyzed and sorted into five categories:

- **Threshold features** are those expected or required to make your product competitive.
    A news product must include news, likely chronologically ordered and sorted by category.

- **Excitement features** are those expected to delight your readers and can provide key distinctive value.
  A popular advice columnist or a word game unique to your site.
- **Performance features** directly increase customer value in response to your investment.
  A reduction in cost or the addition of new and relevant news coverage.

Product development should avoid:

- **Indifferent features** that are irrelevant to the interests of readers.
  Syndicated wire service stories or low-quality and irrelevant advertising.
- **Dissatisfaction features** are those likely to annoy readers.
  Pop-over notifications that cover articles or auto-playing videos.

For discussion

1 What is the result of having misaligned or misunderstood goals in an organization?
2 What is the rationale for pairing a goal and a metric in the setting of OKRs?
3 Are tactics set by the bottom or top of an organization?
4 Why do businesses use so many 2 × 2 matrix decision-making and prioritization frameworks? (i.e., SWOT, Stars, cost-value.)
5 How does a "why," like in the Christensen milkshake example, make a strong argument in product strategy deliberations?

Learn more

- *Crossing the Chasm: Marketing and Selling High-Tech Products to Mainstream Customers*–Geoffrey A. Moore (2001). PerfectBound.
- *The Power of Habit: Why We Do What We Do in Life and Business*—Charles Duhigg. (2012). Random House.
- *The Innovator's Solution: Creating and Sustaining Successful Growth*—Clayton Christensen & Michael Raynor. (2013). Harvard Business Review Press.
- *Building Insanely Great Products: Some Products Fail, Many Succeed?*—David Fradin. (2016). CreateSpace Independent Publishing Platform.
- *Measure What Matters: OKRS—The Simple Idea That Drives 10x Growth*—John Doerr (2017). Penguin Business.
- *Inspired: How to Create Tech Products Customers Love*—Marty Cagan. (2017). Wiley.
- *Experiment-Driven Product Development: How to Use a Data-Informed Approach to Learn, Iterate, and Succeed Faster*—Paul Rissen. (2019). Apress
- *Testing Business Ideas* - David J Bland & Alexander Osterwalder. (2020). John Wiley & Sons, Inc.
- *Continuous Discovery Habits: Discover Products that Create Customer Value and Business Value*—Teresa Torres. (2021). Product Talk LLC.

- *Radical Focus: Achieving Your Most Important Goals with Objectives ad Key Results*—Christina Wodtke (2021, 2nd ed.) Wodtke.

Notes

1 About Keene Sentinel. (2022, February 1). *Keene Sentinel.* SentinelSource.Com. https://www.sentinelsource.com/site/about/
2 Webb, A. (2019). How to Do Strategic Planning Like a Futurist. *Harvard Business Review.* https://web.archive.org/web/20220923230859/https://hbr.org/2019/07/how-to-do-strategic-planning-like-a-futurist
3 Bezos, J. (2016). *Letter to Amazon Share Owners.* https://www.sec.gov/Archives/edgar/data/1018724/000119312516530910/d168744dex991.htm
4 Levitt, T. (1960). Marketing Myopia. *Harvard Business Review, July-August,* 45–56. https://hbr.org/2004/07/marketing-myopia
5 Christensen, C. M., Cook, S., & Hall, T. (2005). Marketing Malpractice: The Cause and the Cure. *Harvard Business Review.* https://hbr.org/2005/12/marketing-malpractice-the-cause-and-the-cure
6 HubSpot (Director). (2019, November 8). Clay Christensen: The "Job" of a McDonald's Milkshake. https://www.youtube.com/watch?v=Stc0beAxavY
7 Phoenix University. (2016). *Understanding the Job.* https://www.youtube.com/watch?v=sfGtw2C95Ms
8 Christensen, C. M., Cook, S., & Hall, T. (2005). Marketing Malpractice: The Cause and the Cure. *Harvard Business Review.* https://hbr.org/2005/12/marketing-malpractice-the-cause-and-the-cure
9 Ibid.
10 Ibid.

10 Product is building

In this chapter

- How product managers and software engineers work together.
- Reducing risk in the product development process (PDP).
- Estimating effort and setting schedules.
- Empowering Agile teams to deliver better products.
- Documenting and managing software development.

Product managers work with almost every team inside (and outside) of our organizations throughout all phases of a project. Talking to readers is vital, but from the early idea-generating discussions, representatives from editorial, business, marketing, and engineering, as well as design, product, and research, should be in the conversation.

But the first two phases of the product development process (**PDP**): identifying and validating ideas, support the third phase: building and launching a product or service. Proving the value of a proposed product only matters if we can deliver it to readers. And the engineering team is often the most critical component.

Not every new product requires software development. A live event strategy is (usually) held in person, relying on marketing and logistics. Even an email newsletter may depend on a code-free tool we buy, not build. But many other projects, and most of the longer and more complicated initiatives, rely on a team to program, test, and maintain software and servers.

Product management teams are often structured around the assumption of close collaboration with engineers. And that means being familiar with the motivations, tools, technologies, and rituals observed by those teams. Moving into Product from a newsroom-focused role can feel like arriving in a new country where you don't speak the language. But developers feel the same way when working with journalists.

DOI: 10.4324/9781003154785-14

Who are software engineers?

There are a variety of often overlapping engineering roles in media organizations: front-end and back-end development, web, and mobile apps, systems
architecture, DevOps, quality assurance, and operations security, to name a
few. Their skills might range from HTML, CSS, JavaScript, Python, R, and
Swift, or understanding the development and administration of Linux servers
and Amazon Web Services.

The arrangement of those roles and responsibilities (**division of labor**) will
differ widely between companies. Brian Boyer, formerly of Tribune Co. and
National Public Radio, schematically describes teams as having either a horizontal or vertical orientation.

A vertical structure is suitable for a small or very focused team. A single
developer might generate a story idea, collect the data, build a simple database, design the visualization, and write the accompanying article. As the size
of the team grows, new hires will also be generalists supporting individual
projects from start to finish.

In a horizontal structure, team members are more specialized. Instead of a
single data-savvy journalist-developer, the team might consist of several pro-
grammers, a designer, and a reporter. In a large organization, multiple cross-
functional teams would work on separate projects.

The high cost of development

You will learn four things after working on a software development project:

1 It took longer than the early estimates assumed.
2 The engineering was more complicated than initially expected.
3 The developers were not involved early enough in the process.
4 Writing code was the most expensive part of the process.

It is a mistake to waste anyone's time launching the "wrong" product. But
when we engage software engineers to build a feature or product that readers
do not want, it is exceptionally costly.

The annual mean wage in the U.S. is $56,000. For journalists, as a broad
category, it is $66,000. But for developers working in the software industry,
it is $129,410.[1] And for a developer at a high-tech company in Silicon Valley,
compensation might start at $150,000 and easily exceed $500,000.[2]

That salary differential means it can be difficult and expensive for news organizations to recruit and retain software engineers. As a result, these teams
are often understaffed compared to the demand for their services. But this
"shortage" is equally true of *The Washington Post* (with an engineering team
of 500) and Miami-based startup Whereby.us (which has had as many as
25 total staff, including a handful of software developers). A truism in business is that the number of projects requested by leadership will always grow to
exceed the time and staff available.

Building the right things right

Previous chapters discussed the research and prioritization needed to understand audience needs and assign a business and community value to individual products and features. Those tasks operate within the larger framework of a **new** PDP.

A typical PDP (Figure 10.1) follows a five-step risk-mitigating **phase-gate** format:

1 Ideas & Prioritization → *Decision Gate.*
2 Research & Specifications → *Decision Gate.*
3 Build & Deliver → *Decision Gate.*
4 Monitor & Measure → *Decision Gate.*
5 Learn & Improve → Ongoing Evaluation.

Each step is designed to inform the design and specifications of a product and improve the organization's understanding of its potential value, reducing the potential risk in our decision to approve or reject it at the next gate.

Each round of approvals commits the business to new tasks, staff time, and escalating investment. While the early research may require two or three staffers, developing an entire app or website demands a sizable cross-functional team. Those costs increase as we pass each gate, and the burden of proof to move forward also increases. When I worked for the McClatchy Co., we developed a version of the PDP that defined the phases and gates as:

1 Investigate → Executive sponsor review.
2 Plan → Executive committee review.
3 Design → Design review.
4 Develop → Technical review & Executive review.
5 Measure → Ongoing evaluation.

As a project progresses, executive leadership approvals assessing the strategic value of the project are required. The gates also allow all stakeholders to validate that the original specifications (including desirability, feasibility, and sustainability) are still being met.

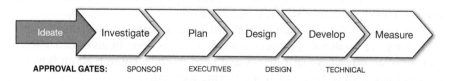

Figure 10.1 A phase-gate process organizes activities and approvals to minimize organizational investment until the potential value of a project is understood.

Schedules and estimates

In business, every project has a deadline. This is to be welcomed, as a project with no timetable is a hobby. In Scott Berkun's book about **project management**, he describes the benefits of imposing a schedule:[3]

- It makes a public commitment.
- It clarifies and makes concrete individual roles and contributions.
- It is a **forcing function** to impose focus and accountability.

An accurate project schedule allows managers to develop strategic roadmaps, assign staff and resources, and set quarterly and annual goals. An inaccurate schedule guarantees a cascade of delays and unexpected costs across the organization.

- Making a plan requires:
- Effective prioritization.
- Agreement on strategy and goals.
- A transparent accounting of team skills and availability.
- An understanding of the required tasks and interdependencies.
- The process and skill to collect and synthesize information and develop estimates.

As with any hypothesis, a schedule is an informed guess meant to be adjusted as new facts are discovered. To minimize surprises, project timetables are best set at the end of the planning phase after the project's scope has been detailed. The cost and schedule inform the final decision to move a project into active development.

Managing what and how

The similarities between project and product management can be confusing, especially in organizations with small teams or poorly-defined job descriptions. Both roles manage processes and timelines to deliver consumer and organizational value. But while Product is responsible for the "what and why," Project is charged with the "how and when."

A common joke is, "The job can be done well, quick, or cheap. Pick two." And like desirability, feasibility, and sustainability are a focus of product teams, project managers balance scope, time, and cost.

You might be lucky enough to work with a great team of project managers. If so, they are invaluable partners in getting things done in an organization. But we often don't have that luxury and need to know enough about how to organize and plan to keep our work moving forward.

The modern history of project management began in the 19th century with the expansion of the railroads in the U.S., the management studies of

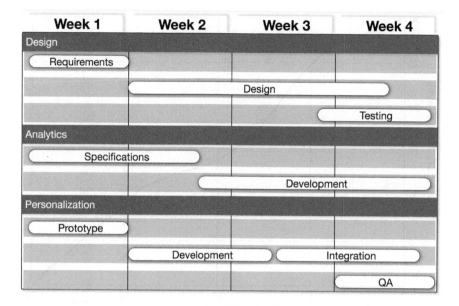

Figure 10.2 Project schedule visualizations allow the team a shared understanding of timelines and interdependencies.

Frederick Taylor, and the use of visual planning systems like the one popularized by engineer Harvey Gantt in the early 20th century.

Gantt's scheduling diagram depicts the timing and length of individual activities and the required resources, interdependencies, and the progress to date. This allows users of the **Gantt chart** (Figure 10.2) to analyze and manage the complexities of a project more effectively and to update forecasts and deadlines as needed.

The Gantt chart is one version of a **work breakdown structure** (WBS) detailing the activities and resources required to complete a project. A WBS can be displayed as a timeline, a tree, a spreadsheet, or a list, with each format informing different aspects of the project, from scheduling to task definition and team assignment.

The **Critical Path Method** (CPM) of project planning was developed in the 1940s at DuPont, with an early iteration used in the Manhattan Project's development of the atomic bomb. While the Gantt chart depicts all relevant activities and resources, the "critical path" is the sequence of the most essential tasks and dependencies. This analysis sets the expected maximum length of the project and allows other "noncritical" activities more flexibility in the scheduling process.

The very similar Program Evaluation Review Technique (PERT) method was developed by the U.S. Navy in the 1950s. Instead of defining the activities and timeline of one path, it estimates three: the longest, shortest, and most likely project timeline scenarios.

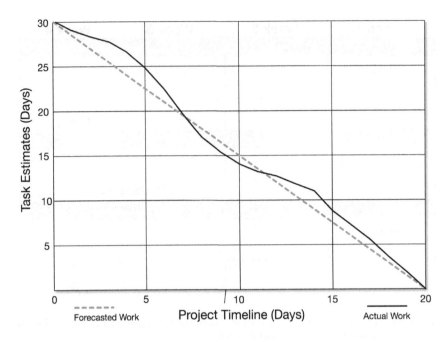

Figure 10.3 Visualizations of forecast vs. accomplished work help the team track progress and are also used to improve the future estimation of work.

A **burndown** chart (Figure 10.3) is a simple visualization that estimates a project's progress toward a deadline. The tool forecasts a team's productivity and expected milestones, represented as a diagonal line from the start to finish dates of the project. A second line traces actual progress, allowing easy comparison.

Software changes everything

Designing and building a new car is a five-year project, with research, design, specification, and manufacturing as sequential phases of development—all prior to the first new model reaching the sales floor. In the early decades of software development, project managers adopted these well-known processes. Called the **waterfall** approach, the output of each stage—rich documentation and specifications—flows into the next before manufacturing begins.

Software is a digital product, but mainframe computers in the 1960s sold for $40 million in today's dollars and weighed more than 1,000 pounds. Only governments, and a few large corporations, could afford them. The cost and scarcity warranted a continued use of slow and sequential project management techniques.

As personal computers and the web emerged in the 1980s and 1990s, the business and consumer demand for software applications grew. Software publishers needed to accelerate **time-to-market** and release more frequent software updates to be competitive. Developers began to look for more efficient ways to work; a movement was memorialized by the **Agile Manifesto** signed by 17 people in 2001.[4]

> We are uncovering better ways of developing software by doing it and helping others do it. Through this work we have come to value:
>
> - Individuals and interactions over processes and tools.
> - Working software over comprehensive documentation.
> - Customer collaboration over contract negotiation.
> - Responding to change over following a plan.

That open and adaptable philosophy has evolved into a sometimes inflexible regime of training and doctrine. But in reality, there is no such thing as a *typical* Agile development practice. Each team will adapt the rituals and processes according to their organizational structures and cultures. The flexibility of the method, and the devolution of authority in an Agile system, means the development team is empowered to solve problems, not just "push code."

The philosophy of Agile

Product managers need to understand the basic premise of **Agile** development, but you should expect to receive some formal or informal training when you arrive at a new job. Agile is a philosophy integrated into many similar project management frameworks with different methods and terminologies. What they usually have in common is:

- The documentation of user stories as a fundamental unit of work.
- The management of two- to four-week-long sprints constructed to deliver specific and forecastable value-creating improvements.
- The use of daily stand-up meetings to facilitate transparency and collaboration.
- An insistence on incremental development where every release is useful and an opportunity to learn.
- The use of retrospectives at the end of projects to identify lessons and process improvements.

In Chapter 9, we discussed the organizational alignment of vision, mission, strategy, and tactics. In Agile development, that process adopts its own vocabulary: themes, initiatives, epics, and user stories (Figure 10.4).

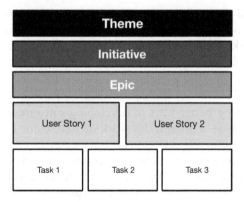

Figure 10.4 The hierarchical categorization of work in Agile represents the relationship of individual development tasks to larger organizational goals.

Organizational objectives or **themes** are broad areas of focus shared by everyone within a company. A theme will not dictate specific solutions but will inform and help align the creation of those plans.

One theme within a news organization might be to *better serve and retain loyal readers.*

Departmental strategies or **initiatives** broadly describe a specific product or service to be developed and are directly connected to a theme. These efforts often require collaboration across the company and might be the focus for several fiscal quarters or a year.

Editorial, development, and marketing teams may work together to *create an email newsletter personalized to the specific interests of individual subscribers.* That initiative aligns with the organizational theme to target loyal readers.

Team tactics or **epics** are a logically grouped collection of features that, when released in coordination, provide consumer value. These collections of work are defined by the development and product teams and prioritized to optimize the efficiency of that value creation. A group of epics might be completed every few months.

An **initiative** will contain multiple **epics** arranged by date of release: Newsletter: *March 2023* or a set of related features: *Newsletter: Topic-based User Configuration.*

Developer tasks or **user stories** are informally worded descriptions of a software feature that take the consumer's perspective. A group of Stories contribute to an Epic and inform the technical requirements developers use to define and build the feature. The subtasks required to complete a Story should be completed within a two-week sprint.

In Agile development, the grammar of a user story is standardized: As a (*persona*), I want to (*need*) so that (*purpose*).

As a loyal reader, I want to customize the articles that appear in my email newsletter so I may save time by only receiving topics of interest.

The persona + need + purpose (journalism's who + what + why) format maintains a focus on the customer throughout the product and development process. This formulation allows the development team to better understand the user's needs and how a product or feature should solve that need.

Documentation

In contrast to waterfall, a feature of Agile methods is the minimization of overly-detailed specifications developed at the start of a project. Agile does not ignore the need to document a product's vision, goals, features, functionalities, audiences, and timelines. But instead, it favors understanding project objectives, with specifications evolving as the team discovers audience needs and proposes solutions. In Agile, the rule of thumb is that documentation should be "just good enough" and developed **just-in-time** (JIT) to support development needs.

Each company culture has a different tolerance for the volume and formality of specification paperwork. Organizations will tend to develop idiosyncratic habits, reflecting the needs of the team involved in the development process. But each will assemble some abridged, expanded, or remixed version of a standard set of requirement documents.

A **product roadmap** (Figure 10.5) is the strategic summary of your product's planned features, functionalities, and timeline, often displayed visually. It is used to provide transparency to internal stakeholders as well as customers.

A Business Requirements Document (**BRD**) describes the problem a given product is designed to solve and the risks and constraints, offering a persuasive argument for investment. It can be a one-page executive summary or a lengthier and more formal document.

Roadmaps / 2024 Product Strategy

	Q1	Q2	Q3	Q4
Subscriptions	New payment processor		iOS app integration	
		Social media sign-in	Dynamic metering	
		Funnel optimization		Android app
Email	New newsletter			
		Paid subscriptions		
Web	Redesign			Share tools
		Personalization	Recommender tools	

Figure 10.5 Organizational goals are planned 6–12 months in advance and must include the detail necessary to allocate staff time, considering all relevant priorities and interdependencies.

A Product Requirements Document (**PRD**) is a standard template in waterfall development but is also used in more flexible project management methods. It includes a list of objectives, stakeholders, and **key performance indicators** (KPI), a description of the intended users, and the features and functionalities required to solve an audience need.

On some teams, a Functional Requirements Document (**FRD**), which takes more of a technology- and system-focused perspective, may be used instead of a PRD.

The varieties of Agile

First used in 1993, **Scrum** is the most popular project management methodology using Agile principles and was created by two of the original signatories to the Agile Manifesto. There are a dozen others, of which Kanban, Lean, and Scaled Agile Framework (SAFe) are commonly encountered in media organizations.

Roles within Scrum

The **development team** includes software engineers but also anyone who contributes to the defined tasks, including designers, researchers, and writers. The team owns the Scrum process, accepting organizational objectives as problems to be solved and proposing, designing, and delivering work that delivers value.

A **product owner** is a formally defined role within Scrum, and the name often leads to confusion. None of the Scrum roles are job titles but identify specific responsibilities within the process. So, a product manager can hold the product owner role, but it is not a requirement. The product owner sets the direction for development work by balancing customer needs and business requirements to prioritize tasks.

The **scrum master** is a coach and facilitator, helping the product owner prioritize and deliver value and supporting the development team to manage the work and constantly improve the process.

How Scrum works

As a project management system, Scrum provides tools to guide a development team and enforce team ownership of the process.

Developers self-organize their work into two- to four-week-long **sprints**. The design of each work period occurs during a **sprint planning** meeting where the team reviews the task **backlog** and assigns **story points** defining the amount of time and effort each will require. Tasks forecasted to need more than one sprint are divided into smaller parts and assigned across multiple periods. Any jobs not scheduled for a specific sprint remain in the backlog.

The goal of each sprint cycle is to have completed work that can be shown to meet business and consumer requirements before the team moves on to the next round. To ensure this, the team requires **acceptance criteria** to be defined and attached to the user story before work is added to a sprint. This criterion describes the specific conditions that must be met and what tests need to be completed for the work to be considered done.

During each sprint, the development team meets near the beginning of each day to review progress in the work, identify roadblocks, and coordinate understanding and solutions. In a **daily scrum**, three questions are asked and answered by each participant:

- What did I do yesterday?
- What do I plan to do today?
- What are the obstacles?

A similar meeting, the **stand-up**, is sometimes also held but may include stakeholders and serves to provide status updates.

At the end of the round of work, a **Sprint Review** is held to review the completed work and provide feedback. This informal meeting typically involves the development team and relevant business stakeholders. Team members might demonstrate newly delivered features, discuss the release plan, and identify the next steps.

A **Sprint Retrospective** is a more formal meeting involving just the development team. While a Sprint Review examines the output of a specific work period, a retrospective is designed to identify process improvements. The team will identify elements of the sprint that went well or need attention, including collaboration between people or teams, the accuracy of story points, or code quality. Specific solutions are discussed to be implemented in future sprint planning.

Planning with signs

Kanban originated with the automotive industry in Japan. It means "signboard" and was originally a literal billboard in Toyota's factories that visually represented the status of the parts and inventory in the system. This shared reference allowed individual sections of the assembly line to self-optimize the flow of materials throughout the plant.

In Agile environments, the Kanban board displays cards identifying development tasks that progress between columns representing stages of work, including "To Do, In Development, Technical Review, Blocked, and Done." Kanban does not impose time boxing (like two-week sprints) as Scrum does, so teams often impose **work-in-progress** limits on each column to manage team workloads and scheduling.

More about Lean

Similarly, **Lean Agile** is an extension of the production processes first developed at Toyota. In a factory, the Toyota Production System (TPS) minimizes manufacturing waste, including errors. In software development, a team focused on Lean principles invests in continuous improvement of its processes to deliver value to consumers more effectively. Lean methods are utilized within SAFe, which attempts to apply the benefits of Agile development in large enterprises.

The book *The Lean Startup* also adapts TPS methods, with a focus on entrepreneurial digital companies. It features the Build-Measure-Learn loop and minimum viable product (**MVP**) as methods to understand and serve consumer needs but is a business framework, not a project management method.

Launch day is not the end of the work

Launching a new feature, product, or service can be unsettling, even at the end of a well-run project. No matter how many prototypes are tested, or beta versions released, or how many readers are interviewed, there is no perfect product and no guarantee of immediate success.

To avoid or manage surprises, the days and weeks before launch are the time to make a list of "what could go wrong" and sketch action plans prioritized by the potential risks.

Launch day best identifies the team's untested assumptions and "unknown unknowns." When it comes to learning, the days and weeks after launch are an opportunity like no other.

There are a lot of ways for a product launch to go astray:

- Failure of technical components. (*The site or app crashes*)
- Failure of internal processes and training. (*Staff don't know how to support it*)
- Failure of design and usability. (*Readers don't know how to use it*)
- Failure of product-market fit. (*Readers are not interested*)

The entire PDP is designed to avoid or at least minimize those risks. But sometimes, reality doesn't respect the plan.

Sometimes the mistakes are expensive, like the $1.75 billion spent on the Quibi short-form video platform that few consumers wanted. Or, the errors can be more tactical and manageable, like these launch-day oversights shared on the News Product Alliance Slack:

- Forgot to allow enough time for the DNS to propagate.
- Changed the credit card form without warning Customer Care.
- Did not load test the servers.
- Did not clear the caches at the Content Delivery Network (CDN).
- Failed to test the new site on a mobile device/browser combination used by "only 15%" of customers.

The launch plan should include a checklist that details what internal and external signals will be monitored and who will be checking to validate nominal operations or to raise a warning flag. For instance:

- Crash and bug reports.
- Content audit.

- Audience analytics.
- Revenue projections.
- Customer feedback.

Every project is different, but it is better to over-communicate rather than assume you can predict the interests and dependencies of other teams. The **RACI** chart (detailing who in a project is Responsible, Accountable, Consulted, and Informed in decision-making) is invaluable. It is a handy communication checklist to be used in the days and weeks before and after launch.

Troubleshooting complex systems

In a truly complex system, many asynchronous, false, or irrelevant signals will work to confound analysis and hinder an accurate diagnosis of problems. Understanding how the system works and how to troubleshoot it is required.

If an incorrect headline appears online after a homepage redesign, what is the cause? The first step toward an answer is categorizing "how" the headline is wrong.

- Is it an outdated or print-specific version?
- Is it the correct headline but with misspellings?
- Are there incorrect characters in the text instead of the expected letters and numbers?
- Is it the headline for a completely unrelated article?
- Is the headline missing entirely?

Each of those faults likely has a different **root cause** ranging from operator error, a text encoding mismatch, or a flaw in the CMS database containing article and headline text.

A product manager who understands the system is well-positioned to identify the cause by starting at the source of the information (the content management system) and following the data through the workflow steps to determine where the error occurs. Some sections of that data flow are open to inspection, and others (the database) require domain expertise to peer inside the black box.

And repeat

After a launch, the work of managing the product begins. Every product that is developed and released must have OKRs or KPIs. Those metrics must be monitored, objectives evaluated, and decisions made. Early in the development process, OKRs are set that align the work with larger corporate goals.

We will increase our newsletter readership by 30% as measured by:

- *Key Result One:* Launch two new topic-focused newsletters.
- *Key Result Two:* Increase the open rate among all subscribers by 15%.
- *Key Result Three:* Reduce subscriber churn by 10%.

Each element of the OKR might also be linked to one or more KPIs designed to measure progress toward the success of specific business objectives. In the example above, the KPIs are almost perfectly defined by the OKR:

- *KPI One:* How many topic-focused newsletters have we launched?
- *KPI Two:* What is the rolling 30-day open rate for our newsletters compared to the prior month, the same month last year, and the average open rate over the previous six months?
- *KPI Three:* What is the monthly churn rate for our newsletters compared to the prior month, the same month last year, and the average over the previous six months?

To monitor those KPIs and provide updates to a dashboard shared by the team and relevant stakeholders, the product manager would track launches and rely on Google Analytics or an email service provider for the other two metrics.

At regular weekly, monthly, or quarterly intervals, the product manager should review the performance of the product and provide a business recommendation:

- **Maintain**—The product is performing as expected, and we are on track to meet our goals. Continue to monitor.
- **Improve**—Metrics are below expectations, or the product is performing, but increased growth is possible.
- **Potential solutions** have been identified and are being defined for consideration in the next development sprint.
- **Terminate**—The product is not performing, and the team believes it cannot be salvaged.

The decision to improve or terminate a product involves the same calculations as the original prioritization process: the current and potential value of the product and the current and potential cost of ongoing support.

For discussion

1 What are the three roles within Agile Scrum?
2 Why is a Sprint Retrospective meeting reserved for development team members only?
3 How does a phase-gate process reduce risk in the PDP?

4 What are the benefits of setting a project schedule? When should a timetable be set?
5 What makes Agile a better project management framework than waterfall for digital, consumer-focused organizations?

Learn more

- *Making Things Happen: Mastering Project Management*—Scott Berkun (2008). O'Reilly.
- *Coaching Agile Teams: A Companion for ScrumMasters, Agile Coaches, and Project Managers in Transition*—Lyssa Adkins (2010). Addison-Wesley Professional.
- *Agile Product Management with Scrum: Creating Products that Customers Love*—Roman Picher. (2010). Addison-Wesley Professional.
- *Why We Make Things and Why It Matters: The Education of a Craftsman*—Peter Korn. (2015). David R. Godine.
- *Innovation Management and New Product Development*—Paul Trott (2017, 6th ed.). Pearson.
- *The Product Book*: How to Become a Great Product Manager—Josh Anon & Carlos González de Villaumbrosia (2017) Product School.
- *The Art of Agile Product Ownership: A Guide for Product Managers, Business Analysts, and Entrepreneurs*—Allan Kelley. (2019.) Apress.

Notes

1 National Occupational Employment and Wage Estimates. (2020, May). *BLS.gov* https://www.bls.gov/oes/current/oes_nat.htm#15-0000
2 Leswing, K. (2019). Here's How Big Tech Companies Like Google and Facebook set Salaries for Software Engineers. *CNBC.* https://www.cnbc.com/2019/06/14/how-much-google-facebook-other-tech-giants-pay-software-engineers.html
3 Berkun, S. (2008). *Making Things Happen: Mastering Project Management.* O'Reilly.
4 Beck, K., Beedle, M., van Bennekum, A., Cockburn, A., Cunningham, W., Fowler, M., Grenning, J., Highsmith, J., Hunt, A., Jeffries, R., Kern, J., Marick, B., Martin, R. C., Mellor, S., Schwaber, K., Sutherland, J., & Thomas, D. (2001). *Manifesto for Agile Software Development.* https://agilemanifesto.org/

11 Product is learning

In this chapter

- Product managers fill gaps in existing processes and knowledge.
- The digital economy requires constant change and learning.
- Organizations learn and adapt when employees do.
- Formal change-management efforts must focus on the human element.
- Emotional intelligence is needed to empathize with others and manage our own reactions to change.

In an exemplary organization, with perfect knowledge and precise decision-making, developers and designers who consummately understand consumer needs and business objectives and have instant access to the tools and time to do their work would always manage and deliver top-quality products ahead of deadline. In that sublime reality, product managers are not needed.

But we live in the real world. Gaps exist in our understanding of consumers. Budgets and competing priorities constrain our focus. Our decisions are distorted by imperfect knowledge and both organizational and individual bias.

Product management exists to cross the boundaries between internal and external stakeholders to improve the organization's understanding of the world and to fill any gaps that hinder collaboration and progress within the business. These challenges differ between organizations, teams, and initiatives. So, each new project affords three increasingly complex levels of work:

1 Guide the research and prioritization needed to develop better products.
2 Support the optimization of organizational skills, processes, and collaboration.
  And, maybe most importantly:
3 Help the organization change over time.

DOI: 10.4324/9781003154785-15

Change management

Change is difficult for everyone. It creates a discomforting gap between our current and future selves. It demands we learn and adapt, implying we are imperfect humans and employees. And it is complicated by concerns about status and career goals. Every effort at change is a people-focused project.

The formal practice of **change management** addresses the human implications of strategic, technical, process, and organizational disruptions of the institutional and personal status quo. This differs from traditional project management, which delivers value to the organization through the on-time and on-budget delivery of new products or services.

The future is not predictable. Change can occur by plan or accident, and change efforts can and often do fail. But as professional rationalists, we prefer planning over guessing or wishing.

Intentional change allows us to align needs, goals, and resources in pursuit of a favorable outcome. A plan, even if it fails, offers a learning opportunity. Unplanned change lacks the benefit of preparation or strategy, though it may be "domesticated" through ad hoc interventions to steer it toward productive ends.[1] But neither the success nor failure of an unmanaged process offers us the opportunity to learn, iterate, and improve the outcome.

A good process with a good outcome is always a success (Figure 11.1). A poor process with a poor result is both a failure and a missed opportunity to learn how to do better next time.

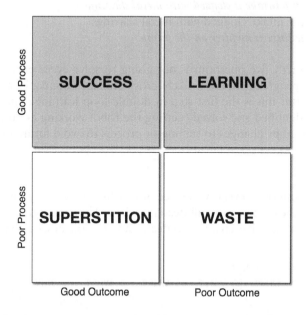

Figure 11.1 Product management works with rigorous and documented processes to learn and improve as a result of either success or failure.

How does an organization change?

Journalism has a culture of learning. Newsrooms value collaboration, editing, and feedback on editorial projects. And reporters are called on to be "instant experts," researching and explaining a topic that only hours earlier was new to them.

Across the organization, there are processes to avoid or at least learn from mistakes. But these efforts are often narrowly focused, designed to address an immediate flaw: The misspelling of a source's name, a poorly designed payment form, or a bug in the code. Recognizing and fixing these mistakes is important, but they are examples of single-loop learning. The inquiry and remedy are often limited to the minimal efforts needed to achieve an immediate project objective and not the changes necessary to avoid future errors.

In the Toyota Production System, the **five whys** (Figure 11.2) method of inquiry digs deeper to identify the root cause of a problem. Its inventor Taiichi Ohno described the process:[2]

1 "Why did the robot stop?"
    The circuit has overloaded, causing a fuse to blow.
2 "Why is the circuit overloaded?"
    There was insufficient lubrication on the bearings, so they locked up.
3 "Why was there insufficient lubrication on the bearings?"
    The oil pump on the robot is not circulating sufficient oil.
4 "Why is the pump not circulating sufficient oil?"
    The pump intake is clogged with metal shavings.
5 "Why is the intake clogged with metal shavings?"
    Because there is no filter on the pump.

Asking exactly five questions is not going to solve every problem. And as the "whys" progress, they will likely cross domain boundaries and grow in complexity. But this is the first step in double-loop learning. The immediate problem is identified and solved (getting the robot working as quickly as possible), followed by changes to staffing or process to avoid future breakdowns.

Small fixes

Change is common in every workplace. Journalists switch assignments, rewrite leads, update headlines, and shift deadlines daily. Those changes are not always easy and many involve creative conflict. But the job descriptions, technical

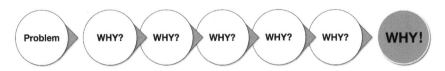

Figure 11.2 The "Five Whys" provide a simple framework to push a discussion beyond surface insights.

systems, and processes common to newsrooms have been implicitly designed to support that work. Those tasks are performed within **normative**, predictable, and stable boundaries. We can call this **routine change**. In the context of a product or development initiative, it would be incremental change or continuous improvement. It is built atop current proficiencies and improves but does not directly challenge the status quo.

Big change

The more difficult challenge is a longer-term and more comprehensive **transformative change**. The transition of news onto digital platforms required adopting new ways of thinking and working that had a metamorphic and ongoing enterprise-wide impact. Digital has forced us to reimagine almost every aspect of news production, from publishing schedules to technology, job titles, and business models. Transformative change is only needed when our desired goals (in 1993, the demand to publish online) conflict with the current and accepted way of doing things (no one here knows HTML).

But more minor transformations: Moving office space, restructuring the organizational chart, installing a new software system, or even developing and launching a new product, can disrupt the status quo in unexpected ways.

Doing anything new imposes unexpected demands on people and processes. Often, a novel idea will face cultural resistance within the business or simply struggle against the constraints of organizational design. Confronting those obstacles is almost always required of truly innovative projects.

Alex Watson, the former head of Product at the BBC, describes transformation change as "the re-allocation of power" within an organization.[3] It is the task of negotiating who has the authority to make decisions and take action to support new strategic goals.

Remember our jigsaw puzzle from Chapter 1? Now imagine it divided across multiple teams in a business. For 20 years, the enterprise has profitably solved this puzzle, constructing a picture of a lighthouse on a scenic rocky coast. But now the puzzle has changed, and the different departments can't agree on what the new picture is meant to look like. One group insists it is still a lighthouse, while another argues it now more resembles a spaceship. As a result, collaboration breaks down, and teams are reluctant to share their puzzle pieces and let another group take the lead.

It is easy, but unproductive, to write this disagreement off as the result of one group being unwilling to "keep up with the times." Those expressing resistance to change usually feel they do so for good reasons.

- The vision for change has not been fully communicated.
- The vision has been shared, but not persuasively.
- The plan itself has irreconcilable flaws.
- The systems and processes to implement the plan are insufficient.

Each roadblock to change carries with it a different cause and a different resolution. In the jigsaw puzzle project, it may have been the CEO who decided to abandon the traditional scenic lighthouse without clearly explaining to the staff what the new picture was. Or maybe not every team has received their new puzzle pieces yet.

Changing the organization

Successful organizational change begins with the recognition of:

1 A beneficial opportunity.
2 The risk of inaction.

In 1975, some within Eastman Kodak foresaw the future of photography and developed a prototype of the first digital camera. But the company could not muster the urgency to make the required investment and instead kept its bet on the traditional film business. Thirty-five years later, Kodak was bankrupt. Change happens with or without your approval. Doing nothing is not a strategy, but doing anything requires overcoming institutional inertia and bias against the "new."

Acknowledging the need for change is not an indictment of past strategies or successes. It is a recognition that our old hypotheses need to be updated as the world changes. The skills we have developed and the organizations and products we build are designed in the past for the needs of the past. Few will survive uncontested into the future.

The question is not "why do we need to change" but "what, how much, and when?" To act requires that:

1 *We have a theory of change.*
    What is the goal, and how will our actions help us achieve it? Explaining "how this will work" requires understanding the people, processes, and incentives in the system being changed.
2 *We can define and describe the things to be changed in specific enough terms to be understood and accepted by stakeholders.*
    Every project requires a shared understanding of the vision, strategy, and tactics involved to receive buy-in. But projects perceived as requiring "change" face harsher scrutiny than more routine initiatives. Faced with the potential for disruption, people will ask, "how will this affect me?" The level of detail or proof they will demand is proportional to the scope of the perceived personal impact. This tension is at the heart of change management and, by extension, product management. The more urgently changes are needed, the more resistance may be faced.
3 *We have control over the things requiring change.*
    Everyone complains about the weather, but no one ever does anything about it. Within individual news organizations, we control the business and

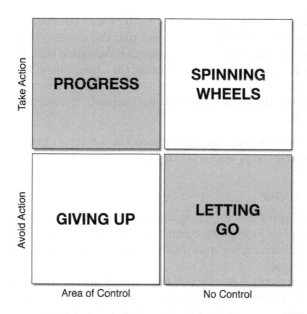

Figure 11.3 Organizational focus requires us to actively avoid projects that fall outside our ability to influence.

product choices we make, the stories we publish, and our relationship with our community. We do not have control over the news, the competition, the big tech platforms, or the broader economy.

Product management lives in the top left quadrant of the control matrix (Figure 11.3), practicing the "art of the possible."[4] The top right corner is also essential, but for the opposite reason. Any meeting involving phrases such as "I wish Facebook would ..." are **red flags** that we are spinning our wheels instead of moving forward.

The bottom two corners offer a similar contrast. Quitting is a super-power if done for the right reasons. Giving up on a task within our control wastes an opportunity. But, to let go of a task outside our area of control is to free up time and resources better spent elsewhere.

4 *We can measure progress in a way that informs our tactics.*

Change is not an explicit goal of product managers but is often a require-ment. Ultimately, the success of a business objective is the best **summative** assessment of change. But, to manage the project, **formative metrics** are also needed, and employee perception surveys, the number of training ses-sions delivered, or an assessment of skills gained are common measures.

5 *We understand the risks and effort required.*

The TROPICS test developed by Paton & McCalman uses a seven-step evaluation of the complexity of a change management project:[5]

- **Time scale**—Is it a short-term or long-term effort?
- **Resources**—Is the investment fixed and defined or still undefined?

- **Objectives**—Is the goal tactical and objective or visionary and subjective?
- **Perceptions**—Is there an agreement that this change is necessary?
- **Interest**—Is the project and its group of stakeholders well-defined, or not?
- **Control**—Does the group proposing the change have the authority to enact it?
- **Source**—Is the catalyst for change internally developed or externally imposed?

The more well-defined and constrained the answer in each category, the more manageable the project will likely be.

Learning to change

For adults, the process of acquiring a new skill or new way of thinking at work inflicts a temporary feeling of incompetence and unease. To start and continue in a project of learning, we must first understand the personal or career benefits that will result.

Organizations only learn when its employees learn; the new knowledge and skills are made routine through process and practice[6] and then spread widely through **knowledge transfer** between individuals and teams.

The ability to make learning and change a continuous and productive process is the cornerstone of a true learning organization. (see: Learning Newsroom in Chapter 6.) Peter Senge popularized the term in his book *The Fifth Discipline* and described five contributing practices.[7]

1 **Personal mastery** of the ongoing adaptivity and growth required in a continuously evolving business.
2 Self-awareness of the **mental models** that influence our perception of the organization and co-workers that affect our decisions.
3 A **shared vision** among staff and management that enables decisions and actions to effectively contribute to company goals.
4 A **team learning** environment where the collective growth exceeds that of the individual.
5 **Systems thinking** integrates the other four practices into an understanding of the business as a collection of **tightly-coupled** components.

Four phases of change

All change is personal. Managing a team or project through the process requires preparing for and accepting the human reactions likely to be experienced (Figure 11.4). Understanding where you and the team are in the process of adopting a change can help diagnose reluctance from recalcitrance. The reluctant can be persuaded; the recalcitrant cannot always be.

1 **Denial** is the insistence that the required change is not needed, not urgent, or will not happen.

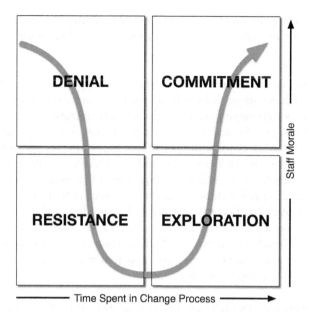

Figure 11.4 A successful journey through change management process is not a straight
line.

2 **Resistance** can be either passive disengagement or active dissension in discussions, meetings, and training.
3 **Exploration** is the eventual recognition that a change will occur and may
bring some benefits.
4 **Commitment** is understanding that the change was necessary and beneficial.

It is all about people

News product management is about building valuable products for our communities. And solving for reader needs often requires us to persuade colleagues
to adjust how they think about and do their own work. And that inevitably
requires organizational change. So, despite our best intentions, sometimes
adding a text field to the CMS requires us to redesign the organization first.

Nothing is easy about that process; the only way to sustainably manage it is
to develop real empathy for readers, co-workers, and ourselves. Psychologists
define three kinds of empathy:[8]

1 **Cognitive** is knowing how a person feels and what they might be thinking.
This awareness helps us tailor our communication by recognizing what is
important to others in the conversation.
2 **Emotional** is the ability to recognize and understand another person's feelings, enabling us to build a connection that includes mutual understanding
and trust.

3 **Compassion** is the most profound form of empathy and leads us to deeply identify with and take action to help another person or group achieve their goals.

Product managers are concerned with all three types, but our job is to help the business achieve its goals by helping readers achieve theirs. So, *compassion* is our aim, although *empathy* remains the broadly operative term.

That prioritization for studying and better understanding the human element extends beyond readers to both co-workers and ourselves. Beginning in his 1995 book *Emotional Intelligence* (EI) and a series of works since, psychologist and science journalist Daniel Goleman has argued that understanding our own emotions and recognizing those of others is a powerful tool for career success.[9]

Goleman's work has been widely adapted, extended, and criticized, but his four categories of EI are a helpful framework for product managers. Much of what we have already noted that product management is—listening, learning, understanding, and collaborating—are skills that make success in journalism, business, and technology possible.

1 **Self-awareness**—research has shown that 95% of us think we can accept feedback, understand other perspectives, and fairly evaluate our own performance. Only 10%–15% of us can.[10]
2 **Self-regulation** is essential, allowing us, even in imperfect moments, to control our emotions and avoid disruptive or harmful statements or actions.
3 **Social awareness** is required for us to recognize how other people are feeling and reacting to events, especially interactions with us.
4 **Relationship management**—packaged together, these skills help us be more effective and influential managers, coaches, and co-workers by maintaining strong lines of communication and collaboration at work.

For discussion

1 What is the first step in enacting change in an organization?
2 Why is a sense of urgency a required element in making change? And how does an organization achieve that shared urgency?
3 If organizational change also relies on personal change among employees, what is the best way to manage that buy-in?
4 In the control matrix—why is "Letting Go" may be the most important of the four options? And which of the four is the most dangerous?
5 Double-loop learning requires an organization to routinize and share what it has learned. How do organizational silos slow shared learning?

Learn more

• *The Fifth Discipline: The Art and Practice of the Learning Organization*— Peter Senge (1990). Currency Doubleday.

- *We Have Never Been Modern*—Bruno Latour. (1993). Harvard University Press.
- *Emotional Intelligence: Why It Can Matter More Than IQ*—Daniel Goleman (1996). Bloomsbury.
- *The Theory and Practice of Change Management*—John Hayes (2007, 2nd ed.). Palgrave.
- *Switch: How to Change Things When Change is Hard*—Chip Heath & Dan Heath (2010). Broadway Books.
- *Louder Than Words: The New Science of How the Mind Makes Meaning*—Benjamin K. Bergen (2012). Basic Books.
- *Invisibles: The Power of Anonymous Work in an Age of Relentless Self-Promotion*—David Zweig (2014). Portfolio.
- *The Manager's Path: A Guide for Tech Leader Navigating Growth & Change*—Camille Fournier (2017). O'Reilly.

Notes

1 Poole, M. S., & Van de Ven, A. H. (2004). *Handbook of Organizational Change and Innovation*. Oxford University Press.
2 Ohno, T. (2006). *Ask 'Why' Five Times about Every Matter*. Toyota. https://web.archive.org/web/20110213042925/http://www.toyota-global.com/company/toyota_traditions/quality/mar_apr_2006.html
3 Watson, A. (2021). All the Power in the System is Already Allocated, So Any Change that You are Planning is about Re-allocation of Power. *Twitter.* https://twitter.com/Sifter/status/1416025984885739524
4 Steinberg, J. (2011). *Bismarck: A Life*. Oxford University Press.
5 Paton, R., & McCalman, J. (2008). *Change Management: A Guide to Effective Implementation* (3rd ed). SAGE.
6 Mills, D. Q., & Friesen, B. (1992). The Learning Organization. *European Management Journal*, 10(2), 146–156. https://doi.org/10.1016/0263-2373(92)90062-9
7 Senge, P. M. (1990). *The Fifth Discipline: The Art and Practice of the Learning Organization*. Currency Doubleday.
8 Goleman, D. (1996). *Emotional Intelligence: Why It Can Matter More Than IQ* (Paperback ed). Bloomsbury.
9 Ibid.
10 Eurich, T. (2018). Working with People Who Aren't Self-Aware. *Harvard Business Review.* https://hbr.org/2018/10/working-with-people-who-arent-self-aware

Glossary

Acceptance criteria in Agile development, the requirements that must be met for a feature to provide the intended functionality and value.

Actionable information that, when timely, credible, and relevant, is useful in the decision-making process.

Ad exchange software that allows the purchase and sale of digital advertising from multiple networks.

Ad server a service that places individual digital ad units on web pages and other online platforms.

AdTech (Advertising technology) refers to the collection of software and services used to buy, sell, and manage digital advertising campaigns.

Adjacent innovation is a strategy that identifies new markets to serve with current products or audiences to serve with new products.

Agency a personal sense of control over your environment that is important to emotional well-being.

Aggregation theory was developed by consultant Ben Thompson at Stratechery to describe the disruption of the traditional value chain of suppliers, distributors, and consumers in digital markets where the marginal costs of creation and distribution are effectively zero.

Agile a project management philosophy for software development that values flexibility and development team ownership of the process.

Agile Manifesto authored in 2001, a statement of 12 principles defining the Agile software development philosophy.

Archetype a summary of insights describing a specific abstract category of user that is the target of your design and development effort. In contrast to a Persona, it does not include biographical details.

Artificial intelligence a simulation of human intelligence by computer code, but often used misleadingly to refer to advanced machine learning models that understand and respond to patterns in provided data.

Asymmetric harm the intentional or unintentional decision to maximize profit by ignoring negative externalities resulting in the inequitable impact of a product or service on specific populations.

Attention economy as described by economist Herbert Simon, the market dynamic when information moves from scarcity to abundance, exceeding the capacity for consumer awareness or engagement, thereby reducing demand.

Back of House, Front of House as used in the retail industry, the parts of the business operation that occur behind the scenes and those that are customer-facing.

Backlog in Agile Scrum, a list of requested features, tasks, and bug fixes that have not yet been assigned to a development sprint.

Benefit corporation a somewhat recent form of for-profit commercial entity that balances work in society's best interest alongside shareholders' rights.

Black box typically a complex system where the inputs and outputs are visible to the user, but the internal processes are incomprehensible or proprietary. This limits the public's ability to critique or apply regulating policy.

Bold Type I see what you did there. Excellent pedantry.

Boundary crossing in product management, the act of communicating across departmental and organizational silos to gather information and reduce uncertainty in business processes.

Bounded rationality a concept of behavioral economics that describes the decision-making process as constrained by factors unrelated to the perfect optimization of outcomes as expected by traditional economic theory.

Brand management part of a marketing effort to measure and improve the perception of a product or service among consumers.

BRD (Business requirements document) an inventory of every detail of a product needed for it to achieve the stated goals.

Burndown chart a line graph comparing forecasted vs. actual work completed over the life of a development project.

Business administration the formal management of an organization's people, resources, and time.

CAN-SPAM in the U.S., the legal requirement for businesses to allow consumers an easy process to unsubscribe from unwanted email message lists.

Change management a methodology for guiding an organization as it responds and adapts to new business needs and goals.

Churn The rate of subscription cancellations compared to new customer acquisition. It can be measured across various periods, often monthly. An organizational goal is to reduce churn to grow the overall subscription base.

Classical economics a theory of markets that sees them as rational, profit-seeking but self-regulating systems.

Closure in Social Construction of Technology (SCOT) theories, the point at which previously divergent solutions converge on the form of an innovation and alternatives are largely commercially discarded.

Club good is an excludable but non-rivalrous product like a private park or movie theater accessible to many people, but that may be limited to paying customers.

Co-construction in Social Construction of Technology (SCOT) theories, the act of the public, through direct and indirect feedback, market behaviors, policy, and regulatory efforts, participates in the development of new technologies.

Cognitive bias   an idiosyncratic distortion of perception that creates a systemic deviation from a "rational" norm in a decision-making process.

Cognitive effort   the focus, attention, and memory required to complete a task.

Cognitive load   given that working memory has a limited processing capacity, the complexity of the new details and the volume of extraneous information can inhibit learning.

Command-and-control   a hierarchical management style in which direction is passed from leadership to workers with largely top-down communication flows.

Commodity   an economic good that is fungible or generically interchangeable with competitive products from other producers.

Common good   a benefit shared by all.

Confirmation bias   we see patterns in the data that support a favored preexisting hypothesis, but we fail to recognize or accept contradictory facts.

Conservation of complexity   also known as Tesler's Law, it was created by Larry Tesler while at Xerox PARC in the 1980s. Barriers to the use of a software product should be solved in development, not imposed on users.

Continuous learning loop   the ongoing process of testing assumptions and iterating improved ideas and products.

Controlled vocabulary   a defined scope of text and phrases such as in an index or in allowed responses to survey questions.

Conversion rate   in a paywall funnel or ad serving, the percentage of users who visited the site and became subscribers or viewed an ad and clicked.

Core innovation   the improvement or iteration of current products to better serve a current audience. See adjacent innovation.

Cost center   a part of a business that incurs costs but does not directly generate profits. See profit center.

Cost of entry (barrier to entry)   in an economic market, any obstacles faced by new competitors, including initial investments in capital, regulations, or constrained distribution channels.

Critical path method (CPM)   a project management tool that identifies the duration and interdependencies of required tasks in planning the project schedule.

Culture   see organizational culture.

Daily Scrum   in Agile Scrum, a daily meeting of developers to discuss team organization and collaboration.

Data   raw collected facts, often numbers but also text.

Deep insights   an understanding of a root cause or motivation for a behavior or action that supports a useful explanatory theory.

Delegation of authority   the handing down of responsibility typically from manager to employee in a business.

Democratize   making a tool, process, service, or information available to a broader group.

Demographics (demographic segments) the numerical representation of the population into distinct groups for statistical analysis, i.e., by age, race, and gender.

Design thinking a business-focused set of research methods used to align strategy and tactics through an explicit process of listening to and empathizing with reader needs.

Desirability in Design Thinking, the researched and validated identification of a consumer or community need.

Determinism (technological determinism) a belief that technological innovations are the self-perpetuating result of scientific advances and economic benefit, largely outside broader societal influence.

Development team in Agile Scrum, any member of the organization involved in the production of a software product, including developers, designers, marketers, product managers, and project managers.

Devolve to transfer or shift power and decision-making to a lower level of the organization. It often also implies the decentralization of power from a headquarters to regional or local offices.

Diffusion of innovation a theory developed by Everett Rogers describing the spread of new ideas in society.

Diminishing returns in economics, the point at which an increase in investment results in proportionally smaller profits.

DSP (Demand-side platform) a system allowing ad buyers to manage campaigns across multiple advertising networks and exchanges.

Durable good a physical product with an expected working life of more than three years.

Dynamic metering in a subscription model, optimizing the behavior of a paywall based on an individual user's calculated propensity to pay.

Early mover advantage (first mover advantage) benefits that accrue to the first entrants in a new economic market.

Edge case a potentially rare but non-trivial situation or context that should be considered in decision-making and product design to minimize harm.

Emergent the unplanned and often spontaneous appearance of new properties and effects in a complex system.

Entrepreneurial creating economic value, often through managing risk and innovation.

Epic in Agile Scrum, the description of a set of development tasks that together provide business and consumer value.

Epistemology the study of the creation of knowledge.

Ethnocentrism we write questions and interpret responses through the lens of our own cultural knowledge and experiences without understanding how others might understand those questions or responses.

Ethnography a research method from Anthropology, the observational study of a specific culture or community.

Evaluative or explanatory research supports the design and development of a solution to ensure it correctly addresses the need.

Experience good   a product, like news, where the quality and value can only be known after use.

Expert user   in Human-Computer Interface (HCI) research, a person with advanced knowledge and potentially divergent expectations of a system or product compared to a novice.

Explicit bias   is the overt and intentional expression of prejudice.

Eyeballs   an often derogatory reference to the pursuit of commodified digital visitors valuing the resulting page views over the individual needs or interests of specific consumers.

Fail fast   a philosophy in which risk and misadventure in business are welcomed as a path to learning and iterative improvement.

Feasibility   in Design Thinking, an evaluation of an organization's skills and capacity to deliver an identified product or service.

Five whys   part of the Toyota Product System, a process of inquiry that asks a succession of "why" questions in search of the root cause of a problem.

Forcing function   is a commitment or constraint that encourages positive behaviors through product or cognitive design.

Formative metric   a measurement in a process or project that tracks progress toward a goal but not a final evaluation of success. (See summative metric.)

Free rider   someone who takes advantage of the benefits without contributing to the support of a public good.

Freemium   a business model that offers features or benefits at low or no cost and allows the user to pay for more advanced uses.

Front of house   see back of house.

FRD (Functional requirements document)   like a BRD but with detailed technical specifications for the work.

Fungible   an item that is interchangeable and replaceable with competitive products.

Fuzzy front-end   the early informal and unstructured development process of new ideas and innovations.

Gambler's fallacy   the mistaken belief that a pattern or frequency of random events in the past is indicative of future occurrences.

Gantt chart   a bar chart used to track and visualize interdependencies between tasks and to forecast an overall project timeline.

GDPR (General Data Protection Regulation)   a European Union regulation governing consumer online data privacy rights.

Genchi Genbutsu   is translated as "go and see for yourself" and reflects the need to go back to the source of facts to inform decision-making. In the Toyota Production System (TPS), that means the factory floor and line workers.

Generative or exploratory research   is designed to broadly explore reader needs and preferences to guide the identification of solutions.

Goodwill   in economics, a business's value above and beyond the fair market cost of its assets.

Hawkins block   named for the inventor of the Palm Pilot, now generically any low-fidelity prototype used to cheaply and quickly represent the contextual uses of a physical product.

HCD (human-centered design)   a philosophy and collection of research methods that believes business decisions are best made when deeply informed by the voice of the end-user of the product or service being developed.

HCI (human-computer interface)   a study of the design of digital interfaces and user needs and capabilities.

Horizontal integration   a corporate growth strategy involving the acquisition of other companies in the same segment (i.e., two content producers). (See vertical integration.)

Horizontal prototype   a testable version of a product that represents the full scope of the user experience but with minimal depth or functionality. (See **vertical prototype.**)

Hyperbolic discounting   a bias that leads us to accept a smaller but immediate gain over a larger but future reward.

Human-centered design   see HCD.

IDI (In-depth interviews)   typically discussions with research subjects that are partially scripted but allow an opportunity for relevant follow-up questions.

Implicit bias   the brain's habit of identifying and learning generalizable patterns in everyday life and then unconsciously applying those lessons in specific inappropriate and harmful instances. Assuming a woman dressed in hospital scrubs is a nurse instead of a doctor is a stereotype caused by implicit bias.

In-depth interview   see IDI.

Information architecture (IA)   in User Experience (UX) design, the organization of information structures to facilitate navigation and discovery.

Information good   a product or service that can be delivered digitally.

Information   data that has been organized and processed for human interpretation.

Initiatives   in Agile, a collection of Epics aligned against a specific objective.

Innovation   the creation of new social or economic value.

Insights   are the result of analyzing information and developing theories applicable to business activities.

Intrapreneurial   the application of entrepreneurial activities within an existing business.

Invention   the creation of a new concept or product.

Just-in-time (JIT)   in Lean Manufacturing, the delivery of components to the factory and assembly line as needed for construction to minimize inventory in storage.

Kaizen   is the practice of continuous improvement reflected in the setting of standards and the need for gradual improvement and innovation.

Kanban   means "signboard" and is a key project management tool that has been adopted by knowledge workers to track development tasks and progress.

Kano model   a method of feature prioritization based on the predicted level of customer delight.

Key Performance Indicator (KPI)   metrics used to evaluate the success of an individual product, initiative, or strategy.

Knowledge management   the acquisition, processing, and use of information within a business.

Knowledge transfer   sharing information related to business processes and decisions within an organization.

Land grant university   in the U.S., public institutions of higher education created with a mandate to teach, research, and serve the community.

Leading questions   when the wording of a question implies a specific perspective or preferred answer.

Lean   a business philosophy of improving processes and profits by minimizing waste. It was originally developed at Toyota.

Lean Agile   a development method focused on improving efficiency and reducing waste and errors in team processes.

Lean manufacturing   see Lean.

Learning organization   a company that prioritizes continuous improvement through internal knowledge transfer and the growth and development of its employees.

Loss leader   the marketing tactic of selling a product at a loss per unit to attract new customers.

Luxury good   in economics, a product that increases in demand as the consumer's income increases.

Management by Objective (MBO)   a method of aligning strategy and tactics by cascading goals from leadership to employees.

Management by Walking Around (MBWA)   popularized at Hewlett Packard, the act of leading a team by spending time talking to and observing employees performing the work.

Market failure   an inefficiency created when individual consumer purchasing decisions result in a collective loss of supply of a previously valued good.

Marketing   activities related to the promotion and sale of goods and services.

Marketing mix   a framework that includes product, price, placement, and promotion.

MBO   see Management by Objective.

Mental model   a personal conceptualization that helps us understand or explain how things work. See also System model.

Metered sampling   a paywall strategy that allows readers a specified number of page views before payment is requested.

Mission statement   a declaration of an organization's reason for being.

Moderator's guide   in IDI and focus groups, the scripted set of questions used to direct conversation.

Moral good   an ideal or action that provides societal benefits absent any other qualifications or considerations.

MoSCoW a prioritization tool that evaluates features as must, should, could, or won't have.

Multi-divisional form a corporate structure with a centralized headquarters and semi-autonomous units in different product lines or industries.

MVP (Minimum viable product) the most basic version of a product possible that still meets a consumer need.

Negative externalities as a profit-making strategy, the shifting of organizational costs to third parties, including society at large.

New Product Development Process see PDP.

Non-excludable in a public good, the ability for any consumer to have access.

Non-rivalrous the use of a public good does not consume and exhaust the resource for others.

Normative usually refers to a specific culture, the standards, and expectations developed and accepted over time.

North Star a metric the organization sets as a primary focus and measure of success.

OKRs (Objectives and Key Results) a goal-setting methodology that pairs an organizational goal with specific results and measurements of success.

One-sided market (see **two-sided market**) a transaction where buyer and seller agree to a price for a product or service based on value.

Optimize the analytical models of classical economics assume consumers seek the best possible results in their decision-making and have a perfect understanding of the situation and possible outcomes. See **satisficing.**

Organizational culture the implicitly or explicitly shared and understood mission and goals of a company, as well as the accepted norms of social behavior.

Organizational design (organizational structure) the description of how a business manages its activities, including hierarchical lines of authority, division of labor, and communication channels. Also, the act of developing the structure.

Organizational silos barriers to communication and collaboration within a company, often defined by incentive structures, domain knowledge, departmental lines, or geographic separation.

OTT (Over-the-top) video content delivered via internet protocols directly to consumers, bypassing broadcast or cable providers.

PDP (Product development process) the steps needed to take a product from early concept to delivery to consumers. (See phase-gate.)

Persona a deeply researched statistical representation of a specific consumer archetype for your product, supported by biographical information designed to describe a likely actual user.

PERT (Program Evaluation Review Technique) a project planning tool that evaluates the estimated duration of individual tasks and visually charts activities.

PESTEL   a tool used to review the Political, Economic, Social, Technological, Environmental, and Legal opportunities and constraints of a business or product.

Phase-gate   a process of organizing projects into stages of work in a PDP, with an interdicting approval process. The phases follow a pattern of ideation, research, design, development, and launch.

Pivot   the redirection of strategy and tactics to pursue newly-discovered insights into a market opportunity.

Plan-Do-Check-Act (PDCA)   a continuous learning and improvement process, also called Plan-Do-Study-Act.

PRD (Product requirements document)   an inventory specifying the features and capabilities needed, but absent detail of how the needs should be technically implemented.

Pre-roll ads   advertising displayed before a video segment selected by a viewer.

Private good   a product or service that provides value and can be owned or utilized by a single consumer. A house or a pair of sneakers.

Pro-innovation bias   the assumption that new ideas and products are inherently a net positive influence in society.

Probative   providing evidence or proof.

Product owner   a role in Agile Scrum that maintains the development backlog and assists the team in prioritization.

Product-market fit   the alignment between consumer need and a solution provided by a good or service.

Profiles   a statistical sketch of a target audience, often used in survey design, visual design, or as a pre-research placeholder for a developed persona.

Profit center   the segment of a business responsible for generating revenues. See cost center.

Programmatic advertising   the automated purchase, sale, and placement of digital advertising.

Project management   the process and role of organizing team activities to achieve a specified business goal.

Propensity score   a measure and forecast of a reader's likelihood to subscribe.

Prosocial   behavior intended to benefit another person, community, or society.

Psychographics   the statistical segmentation of consumers according to their attitudes, aspirations, and life stage.

Public good   a value made accessible to the general society without a specific expectation of direct payment for use. (See private good.)

Qualified   in research work, a respondent who matches specific criteria for participation. The desired profile might be based on demographics like age or gender or psychographics like attitudes or behaviors.

Qualitative research   is focused on understanding concepts, needs, attitudes, and beliefs using open-ended survey questions, observations, and interviews.

Quantitative research   uses numbers and statistics collected from closed-ended survey questions or available data sets to develop general theories.

Question order bias   respondents are influenced in their understanding or response to questions by prior questions. To minimize this effect, begin surveys or interviews with broad questions and progress to more specific questions.

RACI chart   the documentation of the stakeholders in a project who are responsible, accountable, consulted, or informed of decisions.

Reader's voice   in news product management, developing empathy for the consumer and bringing their needs, attitudes, and words into the development process.

Recognition not recall   a principle popularized in Jakob Nielsen's list of ten web usability heuristics the user's cognitive load should be minimized by making navigation and other critical information visible or easily retrievable at all times.

Red flag   a signal in a prioritization process that would immediately exclude the project from further consideration.

Reinvention   in the theory of Diffusion of Innovation, the process of adaptation of a product or idea as it propagates through populations with divergent needs and expectations.

Retrospective   in Agile Scrum, a formal meeting at the end of a development project held to identify process and quality flaws that can be improved for future projects.

RICE   a prioritization tool using Reach, Impact, Confidence, and Effort to estimate value.

Root cause   the initial factor in a causal chain that resulted in the observed phenomenon.

Routine change   an alteration in tactics, process, strategy, or structure that can be made without challenging the perceived status quo of the governing culture.

RTB (Real-time bidding)   the buying and selling of digital advertising through ongoing and instantaneous auctions.

SAFe   the Scaled Agile Framework developed to adapt Agile processes to large organizations.

Sampling   in a metered paywall or freemium strategy, the tactic of letting readers experience the value of your product to encourage their conversion.

Satisficing   in behavioral economics, the process of optimizing a decision guided not by a desire for the perfect answer but for the best choice possible given a variety of practical considerations, including time available to research and select between multiple options.

Scientific method   forming and testing a hypothesis and iterating on that process to develop an informed theory.

Scrum   a project management framework for Agile software development.

Scrum master   in Agile Scrum, a role facilitating efficient team processes and collaboration.

Servant leadership   a management philosophy that shares power by focusing on the needs of employees.

Shareware　in software, a sampling strategy that provides a time or functionality-limited application at low or no cost until payment is provided.

Shovelware　the habit of news companies to migrate their printed content online with little specific consideration for the strengths and constraints of the digital medium.

Silos　in business-speak, we often use the term to describe teams that work in semi-isolation from each other, either intentionally or unintentionally failing to share information and resources for the greater good.

Social desirability bias　respondents will seek approval by answering questions in a way they think aligns with the researcher's expectations.

Sprint　in Agile development, a predefined set of tasks the team agrees to deliver within a time-limited work period.

Sprint planning　a development team meeting to define the portion of the backlog that can be delivered in the next work period.

Stabilization　in Social Construction of Technology theory, the process of a specific manifestation of an innovation receiving acceptance and slowing the rate of iteration.

Stakeholder　anyone with a formal or informal interest and concern in a business or organization.

Standup　a daily meeting of development team members to share updates or make relevant announcements.

Story points　estimates applied to items in the development backlog to estimate duration and level of complexity.

Strategy　a plan to achieve a specific objective.

Strict paywall　a business strategy that requires a subscription payment for access to any content.

Subject matter expert (SME)　is common business jargon used to describe an individual with a set of specialized skills or knowledge that is relied upon by other members of the team.

Subsidy　financial support for a product or business operation that is not independently self-sufficient.

Summative metric　a measurement in a process or project that provides a final evaluation of success. (See formative metric.)

Survey　a typically online questionnaire designed to elicit narrowly-focused responses used to inform organizational strategy and planning.

Survivor bias　is a form of selection bias, the inclusion or exclusion of participants that inherently skew research results. When seeking to understand customer feedback, it is easy to talk to current users of your product without recognizing that past customers or non-customers are likely to have differing opinions.

Sustainability　the ability of a business or product to provide value over a period.

Sustaining innovation　the development of an improved product that increases value to consumers or reduces costs to the manufacturer.

SWOT a business analysis framework meant to identify the Strengths and Weaknesses of your business, the Opportunities in the market, and the Threats posed by internal or external forces, including competitors and economic conditions.

Synecdoche a rhetorical device in which typically a part is used to represent the whole. For example: "The White House" to refer to the United States government or "a hand" to refer to a worker.

T-shaped skills a schematic description for someone with a deep and specific expertise in one knowledge domain and a broad but thin understanding of adjacent domains. For instance, an experienced software engineer with practical but incomplete skills in user research, design, and business strategy.

T-shirt sizing a project estimation method that assigns small, medium, large, and extra-large sizes to proposed tasks.

Tactics a detailed description of the activities required to achieve a specific strategy.

Themes in Agile Scrum, a strategic initiative composed of multiple Epics, User Stories, and Tasks.

Tightly-coupled the close interdependence of products and services, rules, regulations, and infrastructure in providing value. The automobile and paved road systems would each be less valuable without the other.

Time to market the duration between an initial concept and the delivery of a new product to consumers.

Touchpoint any method readers use to interact with your business, products, or services.

Toyota Production System (TPS) a method of Lean manufacturing developed and practiced by the automobile manufacturer.

Transformative change an alteration in tactics, process, strategy, or structure that requires disruption of the perceived status quo of the governing culture.

Two-sided market (see one-sided market, above) when a company develops a platform that connects the supply and demand needs of two other parties. eBay, for example, makes money by hosting a service that connects buyers and sellers.

Type 1 error a decision that is false positive.

Type 2 error a decision that is a false negative.

Unit costs (COGS – costs of goods sold) the expense incurred to provide one discrete product to a consumer. One banana, one automobile, one digital news story.

Unitary form the organization of a business as a centrally managed structure with shared functional departments, including marketing, finance, and Human Resources.

Usability test (user testing) the task-based evaluation of a product with users recruited to represent the intended target audience.

Use case   description of a specific user context and need that helps define the specifications of a product.

User stories   in Agile Scrum, the smallest unit of description for a software development task. Written in plain language, describing the value the feature is intended to provide.

Utility   in economic terms, the perceived value, usefulness, or satisfaction a good or service provides.

Value vs. complexity   a prioritization tool that estimates the economic and consumer value of a feature and the organizational risks and cost of development.

Value vs. effort   a prioritization tool that estimates the economic and consumer value of a feature and the cost of development.

Vertical integration   a corporate strategy involving the acquisition of other companies in a different value chain segment (i.e., creator and distributor) to gain competitive advantage. (See horizontal integration.)

Vertical prototype   a testable version of a product that represents a narrow scope of user experience but with full functionality. (See horizontal prototype.)

Viability   in Design Thinking, an evaluation of the company's ability to continue to offer a product or service, often based on the likely revenue or profit generated.

Vision   the long-term aspiration for the value a business hopes to deliver to its customers.

Waterfall   a documentation-heavy project management method where tasks move through a strictly sequenced pre-determined development process.

Work breakdown structure (WBS)   a document of project tasks divided into smaller work components for planning and tracking.

Works in progress (WIP)   in Kanban, the specified limit for tasks at a given stage in the development process.

WSJF (Weighted Shortest Job First)   a feature prioritization tool that balances the value of a task and its duration to optimize economic or consumer value.

Zero-sum game   in economic and game theory, the belief that in a contest between two parties, a gain for one side is a loss for the other. This assumes the presence of limited resources and an absence of cooperation between parties.

Index

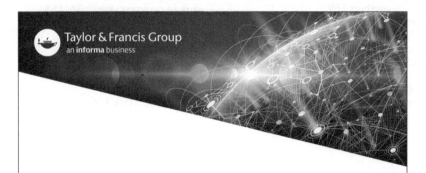

Taylor & Francis eBooks

www.taylorfrancis.com

A single destination for eBooks from Taylor & Francis
with increased functionality and an improved user
experience to meet the needs of our customers.

90,000+ eBooks of award-winning academic content in
Humanities, Social Science, Science, Technology, Engineering,
and Medical written by a global network of editors and authors.

TAYLOR & FRANCIS EBOOKS OFFERS:

A streamlined
experience for
our library
customers

A single point
of discovery
for all of our
eBook content

Improved
search and
discovery of
content at both
book and
chapter level

REQUEST A FREE TRIAL
support@taylorfrancis.com

Routledge
Taylor & Francis Group

CRC Press
Taylor & Francis Group

For Product Safety Concerns and Information please contact our
EU representative GPSR@taylorandfrancis.com Taylor & Francis
Verlag GmbH, Kaufingerstraße 24, 80331 München, Germany